THE LAST TO FALL

Reviews for the first edition of The Last To Fall

"It's a fascinating tale…Wainwright writes about this key historical juncture with lucidity, imagination and insight…cleverly interweaving the essential history of the civil war around Hickman's life."
The Morning Star

"Wainwright's extensive research is evident and his narrative is engaging. This book is a must read and is a worthy addition to Spanish Civil War libraries."
The Volunteer

"Wainwright has used these letters in the context of events in the Spanish Civil War to tell his story, and everyone who reads it will be grateful that he has. He has sensitively woven them into the meticulously researched narrative both of Ivor's life and the story of the British Battalion. This allows the reader a real insight both into the man himself and the realities of the war in Spain."
The International Brigade Memorial Trust

THE LAST TO FALL
THE LIFE AND LETTERS OF
IVOR HICKMAN
AN INTERNATIONAL BRIGADER IN
SPAIN

John L. Wainwright

OPEN EYES PRESS

HAMPSHIRE

First published in Great Britain in 2012 by
Hatchet Green Publishing.

Revised second edition published in 2012 by
Open Eyes Press.

Revised third edition published in 2012 by
Open Eyes Press.

OPEN EYES PRESS
3 Well Cottages
Basingstoke Road
Old Alresford
SO24 9DR
United Kingdom

The moral right of the Author has been asserted.

All rights reserved. Without limiting the rights under copyright reserved above, no part of this publication may be reproduced, stored in a retrieval system or transmitted, in any form or by any means (electronic, mechanical, photocopying, recording or otherwise) without prior written permission of the publisher of this book.

A CIP catalogue record for this book is available from the British Library.

ISBN 978-0-9571923-2-4

Front cover photograph: 'Ivor Hickman' © Harry Randall: Fifteenth International Brigade Photographic Unit. (ALBA).

To Mathilda

*"If a man hasn't discovered something he will die for,
he isn't fit to live."*

Martin Luther King. 1963.

Contents

Introduction to the Third Edition

Introduction

A Very Brief Background Concerning the Spanish Civil War

Prologue

1. A Local Boy in a Photograph
2. Cambridge, Politics & Love
3. A Northern Industrial Town
4. A Noble Cause
5. The Birth of the British Battalion
6. One in Seventy-Five
7. 'Poverty makes better soldiers than poetry'
8. The Calm
9. Baptism & Retreat
10. Chabola Valley
11. Ebro
12. Hill 481
13. The Last Post
14. One of Eighty-Nine
15, Survivors & Premature Anti-Fascists
16. Remembrances & Resurrections
17. Epilogue
18. Ivor & Juliet Hickman – An Afterword

Photographic Appendix to Third Edition
Endnotes
Bibliography
Picture Credits
Acknowledgments

Introduction to the Third Edition

12th November 2011. Wembley Stadium. London.

The day after Armistice Day, the English football team faced the Spanish in an international friendly game. Before the match kicked off the crowd observed the customary two minutes silence for Britain's war dead. The match was being broadcast live on terrestrial television by ITV Sport. The camera panned around the crowd before pausing for several seconds on one single football fan. He was holding a placard that simply read "*We also remember XVth International Brigade British Battalion '36*". The identity of the fan is unknown and it is doubtful as to whether ITV realised the significance of the placard but it did serve as a reminder that the volunteers from Britain who fought for democracy in the Spanish Civil War are not forgotten. The story was highlighted in the national press the following day by the *Daily Mirror* newspaper.

History cannot be forgotten.

September 2011. La Fatarella, Catalonia.

A section of trenches above the village of La Fatarella in Catalonia, were being excavated by a group of archeologists and students from the University of Barcelona and the Associacio Lo Riu. The area had seen heavy fighting during mid November 1938, the final days of the Battle of the Ebro, the last great offensive by the Republican forces. Because an irrigation canal had been cut in years after the battle all that remained of the trenches were a series of preserved zigzags. They began digging into the vertices of the zigzags when they came upon a remarkable find. Preserved in situ where he fell, were the intact remains of a Republican soldier. As the body was exhumed further details emerged.

The soldier had been killed in action; a shell or bullet had severed his right femur, the fragment still embedded deep into the bone. A further nine pieces of shrapnel were found lodged inside his rib age. An explosion had appeared to have ripped his right hand off at the wrist and his left foot was in a near impossible twist under his right leg.

The soldier had fallen onto his backpack. His final moments must have been terrifyingly frantic as many bullet casings from his Mosin Nagent rifle were found close by. Alongside his body, the archeologists discovered three unused Mosin Nagent magazines, two fragmentation grenades and a metal cup, a green bottle capped with a cork along with the soldier's belt, jacket, boots and knapsack. Even more astonishing were the conclusions reached by the archeologists once they had measured the remains. The height of the body along with a curious small piece of plastic discovered in his mouth which suggested a type dental work which was probably not available in Spain at the time, led the team to conclude that the body was that of a foreign fighter, an Internacionale. They named this last soldier of the Ebro, "Charlie". Although all of the International Brigade volunteers had been officially withdrawn from fighting on the 23rd September 1938, some decided to remain behind and continue the fight. The evidence suggests that "Charlie" was one of the few who remained.

History cannot lie buried forever.

3

Introduction

The Spanish Civil War has always held a fascination for me; in particular the Republican cause, and more specifically the International Brigades.

I have always been an avid reader and in my early teens would devour the pseudo-autobiographical pulp novels of Sven Hassel which detailed his experiences in World War Two while serving in the 27th (Penal) Panzer Regiment of the German army. If pushed I will admit that even today when I pride myself on having reasonably sophisticated reading tastes, I still get the occasional nostalgic hankering to lose myself in the company of Hassel and his comrades on the Russian Front. Hassel's books were the staple fare of any twelve year old boy growing up in the 1970s. Although claiming to be autobiographical, the books precariously danced upon the razor's edge between fact and fiction. In fact, upon closer reading of the series of fourteen novels it appeared that the characters often fought in several places, hundreds of kilometres apart, at the same time. This was of no matter to my adolescent mindset; I was too enthralled by the brutal and sometimes bawdy exploits of Hassel and his band of bastard brothers. Wolfgang Creutzfeldt, a giant of a man ironically named Tiny; barracks fixer and shrewd thief Joseph Porta; older sergeant Willie Beier, "Old Un" or "Old Man"; Julius Heide, a Nazi fanatic, the enigmatic Alfred Kalb aka "the Legionnaire"; Gregor Martin, who was a removals man before the war. However, standing shoulder to shoulder with this motley array of characters was my favourite, Peter "Barcelona" Blom. Barcelona was second in command of Hassel's squad and had fought during the Spanish Civil War in the Thaelmann Battalion of the International Brigade. The International Brigade; my imagination swirled with images of an Arthurian column of heroes resolutely defending honour and freedom from the barbaric horde.

The other conscious influence was a grainy black and white photograph; Robert Capa's iconic photograph *"Falling Soldier."* First published in the September 1936 issue of the French magazine *Vu*, the image allegedly depicts the exact instant of death of an unknown Spanish Republican militia man during the Spanish Civil War.[1] Even with no background knowledge of the actual situation; there is no denying the power and emotion held within that frozen moment of monochromatic time.

These crumbs silently matured inside me while my interest simmered as adolescence evolved into teenage and teenage into adulthood. They were always in the back of my mind but for some reason I never investigated further until my mid-thirties when I returned to full-time education and found myself researching and writing seriously for probably the first time. Among the subjects I quickly found myself returning to was the biography of Robert Capa. I have no fixed reason why Capa sprung so quickly to mind but I'm guessing that he'd finally boiled over my subconscious and was now shouting to be heard again. With renewed vigour, I researched; I wrote; and come the time for my final dissertation as an undergraduate, I decided to continue the theme and write a Spanish Civil War based script, this time set amongst the International Brigade. Again I began the necessary research and eventually, with the help of Marlene Sidaway of the International Brigade Memorial Trust, I found myself presented with the immense privilege of interviewing David Marshall and Sam Lesser, two surviving veterans of the British Battalion of the International Brigade. At first glance these two Brigaders were as alike as grape and grain; the enigmatic pony-tailed poet and the left-wing firebrand journalist.

In the 1930s, David Marshall had left his job in a Middlesbrough employment office unable to reconcile his conscience with the barely subsistence level dole payments he administered. After reading a report in *The Times* about the rebel uprising, he journeyed to Spain and was one of the first British volunteers to arrive.

He had no military experience before Spain. In most books written about the International Brigades, there is a photograph of six men and a woman posing around the Tom Mann Centuria banner taken in Barcelona in 1936. The lean bespectacled figure on the far right, holding the banner aloft by his rifle barrel is David. That photograph is now also reproduced on page sixty-five of this book also.

Sam, or Manassah Lesser to give him his birth name, was born in Hackney, a Jew of Polish descent and a veteran of many clashes with anti-Semites and fascists in the East End. He gained a scholarship to the University College of London where he soon joined the College Union and then the Communist Party. In 1936 he was due to go on an archaeological dig in Egypt when he was approached by the National Student Organiser of the Communist Party who persuaded him to abandon his plans and go to Spain to fight for the legally elected Republican government. He arrived in Paris around the beginning of October 1936 and under the *'nomme de guerre'* of Raymondo Cassado entered Spain shortly afterwards, his limited military experience gained in the Officer Training Corps (O.T.C.) at University. Both men took part in the heroic defence of Madrid in the winter of 1936/37 and were wounded and repatriated; David in November/December 1936 and Sam in January 1937. Soon after, Sam returned to Spain as a correspondent with the *Daily Worker* and a broadcaster for the Communist Party. Even in old age, the passion and fire that radiated from both men was tangible and it was easy to imagine the intensity of belief that led them to Spain.

Sadly David passed away a few months after I had interviewed him. Sam Lesser died more recently, in 2010. The oft quoted saying "you shouldn't meet your heroes because you can only ever be disappointed" is not always true. To this day David Marshall remains one of the most memorable and inspirational personalities that I have had the honour of meeting.

The words that follow tell of the journey of a young Hampshire man caught up in a brutal war fought on a truly Brechtian scale. Drawing heavily on letters that he sent home to his wife in England, and on many unpublished accounts provided by others who fought in the British Battalion of the International Brigade, I have endeavoured to tell just one of the many touching and personal stories while meanwhile seeking to contribute an accurate account of the Battalion's history in their fight against fascism.

A Very Brief Background Concerning
The Spanish Civil War

Interest in the Spanish Civil War has increased dramatically in recent years as has the controversy surrounding the complexities of the period. For this reason, at the end of this section, I have suggested further reading for those who are approaching the subject for the first time. Suffice to say that the role of the International Brigades within the conflict in question has, in particular, been subject to endless conjecture and debate. Political bias and misunderstanding; incomplete and absent records and documentation; the inexorable passing of time and the natural effect this has on all mortal men (at the time of writing the British volunteers still with us are few indeed); a tendency to glorify or demonise the participants, assessing their motivation and actions according to a twenty-first century yardstick; any semblance of objectivity has blended into a synthesis of skewed judgements and genuine mistakes. Opinions of the Brigaders range from them being thought of as noble defenders of democracy, to fiendish agents of Stalinist repression. As a human being, I make no grand claims of untainted impartiality. I have my opinions and preconceptions, my heroes and my villains much the same as any other man. We all form our own bar of normality and judge the actions of others by this measure.

The roots of the war can be traced back to the feudal roots of Spanish culture but the immediate causes were cast in the military dictatorship of General Primo de Rivera that followed the economic crisis of the early 1920s. Elections in 1931 followed Rivera's rule and saw a triumph for the political left. In 1931, Spain had a population of 24 million people of which 12 million were illiterate and 8 million poverty-stricken. Entire provinces were owned by one man and two million peasants owned no land at all. The average wage was one to three pesetas a day. To put that into perspective, a loaf of bread would cost one to two pesetas. Against this background it is easy to understand the will of the Spanish people to elect a left-wing party albeit a Republican government with a Socialist majority. King Alfonso XIII abdicated and Spain seemed poised on the verge of casting aside the medievalism that had dominated for so long. A new constitution was drafted for the Second Spanish Republic that declared that Spain was a "democratic Republic of workers of all classes." Nobility would no longer be recognised, both sexes would vote at 23 and unworked land would be redistributed to the peasants. A degree of autonomy was granted to certain regions such as the Basque and Catalan Republics and the power of the church and army was curbed. This was a risky strategy as it was a direct assault on both the Catholic Church and the army.[1]

The government suppressed a military coup led by General Jose Sanjurjo Sacanell in August 1932, but the strikes and violence that followed demonstrated a widespread dissatisfaction with the government. The government resigned and in the elections of 1933, a coalition of right-wing, traditionalists dominated by Fascist and Catholic parties triumphed. The reforms were reversed, estates restored, wages cut and the peasants evicted from their newly gained land. The next two years saw a growth of opposition and insurrection which in many cases were ruthlessly suppressed by the army. Elections were held in February 1936 and a Popular Front comprised of a coalition of the left achieved victory.[2] The new government then went about reversing everything that the right had done and attempted the task of the modernisation of Spain. Some workers and peasants frustrated by, as they saw it, the government's inaction, seized land and burnt churches while fascist gunmen began killing political opponents. This tit for tat behaviour ensured that the violence grew ever more bitter. A conspiracy was hatched amongst monarchist and fascist elements of the officer class of the army and a coup was planned. Spain was plunged into civil war on July 18th 1936, by an uprising in Spanish Morocco with simultaneous uprisings on the mainland. The Popular Front armed the people, organised in their trade unions and militias to counter the uprising.

To put these events into historical context, it must be remembered that Europe was caught on the precipice between fascism and communism. Germany, Italy, Hungary and many other countries had succumbed to the fascists and far right, while Stalin had purged most of his political rivals in Russia and was casting his net across his western borders. In terms of British domestic politics, the East End of London had become the battle ground between Oswald Mosley's anti-Semitic Blackshirts and Jewish, Irish and Socialists groups also (the war in Spain symbolised Europe in a microcosm therefore, but it had a clear relevance to developments in Britain and the British left too). For the Spanish meanwhile, the polarisation between left and right was drawn along the following lines; on one side sat the Monarchists, Fascists, Carlists, Falangists and the Catholic church, and on the other, the Communists, Socialists, Anarchists, liberals, Marxists and trade unionists.

From the outset the Nationalists received material help from both Italy and Germany while the Republicans could only call upon Russia and Mexico for military aid. The rest of Europe including England preferred a policy of non-intervention. The idea for the International Brigade was mooted at a meeting in mid-September 1936, in the NKVD (forerunners of the infamous KGB) headquarters in the Lubianka in Moscow. The idea was to set up a network to get foreign volunteers to Spain to fight in the Spanish Republican Army under the banner of the International Brigade. There had already been a trickle of volunteers[3] from all over the world joining the Popular Front's cause. Recruitment was mostly clandestinely handled through the Communist Parties in various countries. This did not necessarily mean that all of the volunteers were communists; in general terms however, they were collectively anti-fascist.

In Britain, the Communist Party of Great Britain (CPGB) co-ordinated recruitment for what was to become the British Battalion of the 15th International Brigade from their headquarters in Kings Street, London. Volunteers were enlisted and were then sent on a 'day trip' to Paris where they joined other volunteers from across the world to be transported to the French-Spanish border and a perilous crossing of the Pyrenées (Catalan *Pirineus*) on foot. Between 30,000 and 40,000 men and women from over 50 counties were eventually to join the International Brigades. Over 2,300 volunteers came from Britain, Ireland and the Commonwealth of who over 500 were killed. Former Symondian I. R. Hickman was one of these men.

For the modern perspective it can be truly hard to understand how and why a person would volunteer to fight overseas in a foreign country's civil war. Today wars are fought for a number of reasons; for land, over religion, to accrue natural resources and capital (oil, minerals, and of course money) but rarely, if arguably ever, about a purely political ideology. It has often been quoted that the Spanish Civil War was the "last great cause" and in many ways this can be seen as true. However, the quixotic misconception that the bulk of volunteers were made up of an almost Arthurian contingent of artists, writers, romantics and intellectuals holds little truth. Writers and poets such as George Orwell, Esmond Romilly, Stephen Spender and John Cornford all fought, and in the case of Cornford died in Spain.[4] These men, however, were far from the average volunteers. The bulk of the British volunteers came from the collieries of Wales and the cinder-stained manufactories of the North East. Men who had known the hardship of the dole and, in a great many cases, following the stock market crash of 1929 and subsequent depression, a life lived often well below the poverty line; they were often those who had toiled in the factories and mines that formed the backbone of the British Empire, but who were shown scant reward for their labours; those who had fought the Blackshirts and anti-Semites in the metropolitan centres that were the recruiting ground for the opportunistic fascists; and those that foresaw the shadow already being cast by Hitler; not necessarily communists therefore, but all of them distinctly anti-fascist by nature, and not least radical by action.

Further Reading

For those approaching the Spanish Civil War for the first time, there are some excellent texts that offer a good grounding on the background to the war; the manner in which it was fought, where, and by whom; and also its aftermath. It is beyond the scope of this text to offer a detailed account of the war in all its complexity. My intention throughout has been to instead offer the reader sufficient context for understanding the experience of Ivor Hickman and his comrades. While a number of valuable sources are noted in the individual chapters and the bibliography (p.251), the following books each offer a view of the much wider picture and are highly recommended.

Alperte, M., *A New International History of the Spanish Civil War*, Palgrave, 2004.
Buchanan, T., *Britain and the Spanish Civil War*, CUP, 1997.
Darman, P., *Heroic Voices of the Spanish Civil War: Memories from the International Brigades*, New Holland, 2009.
Graham, H., *The Spanish Republic at War 1936-1939*, CUP, 2002.
Lannon, F., *The Spanish Civil War 1936-1939*, Osprey Publishing, 2002.
Preston, P., *A Concise History of the Spanish Civil War*, Fontana, 1996.
Romero Salvado, F. J., *The Spanish Civil War: Origins, Course and Outcomes*, Palgrave, 2005.
Shubert, A & Esenwein, G., *Spain at War: Spanish Civil War in Context, 1931-39*, Longman, 1995.
Stradling, R., *History and Legend: Writing the International Brigades*, UWP, 2002.
Williams, C. *Memorials of the Spanish Civil War: The Official Publication of the International Brigade Association*, Sutton, 1999.

11

The commemorative plaque, presented in memory of Ivor Hickman at Peter Symonds College, Winchester, Hampshire. (Photo: J.W.)

Prologue

Peter Symonds College
Winchester,
Hampshire,
2009

Tucked away by the side door of the Estates Office in the Northbrook Building of Peter Symonds College in Winchester, there is a modest oak bench. It is of a simple design often referred to as a *Cavendish seat* among those who know of such details. Estates staff sit eating their lunch in the sun on it; packages and parcels are unloaded out of multi-drop vans and stacked on it to await distribution around the college; a place for sandwiches and cups of tea, the firm wooden slatted seat ensuring that the occupant doesn't stay sat still for too long. Outwardly nothing remarkable, until one notices the small unassuming memorial plaque (seen left) that is fixed to the slatted backrest. It reads as follows:

Presented in memory of
I. R. Hickman
a boy at this school from 1924 to 1933
he died at Barcelona In 1938
when fighting for the government forces
in the Spanish Civil War.

A six by two inch engraved piece of metal that says so little but hints at so much. I have sat on the bench many times myself, yet it was some while before I noticed the plaque. I. R. Hickman.

1

A Local Boy in a Photograph

Recovering a forgotten past can be likened to trying to piece together a jigsaw puzzle while wearing a blindfold. Some fragments slide conveniently into place but overall the picture lies frustratingly out of sight. Like many a puzzle, there is often a piece missing. Connections in a fragile chain of decaying rusted links. I. R. Hickman is personified in the whispers, echoes and footnotes of obscure memoirs and histories. He is manifest in archives and files; his presence tangible in letters and period documents. However, the definitive man is almost impossible to trace and a certain amount of conjecture and downright guess work is sometimes necessary.

In addition to the memorial bench at Peter Symonds College, I. R. Hickman is physically remembered at two other sites. In the shadow of the Cenotaph in Southampton city centre, a modest plaque is inscribed:

This memorial is dedicated to those men of the
International Brigades from Southampton, who gave their
lives in battle fighting
for democracy in Spain (1936-39)

Raymond Arthur Cox; Boadilla del Monte; December 1936.
Harold Laws: Segura de Los Banos: February 1938.
David Haden Guest: Gandesa: July 1938.
Ivor Rae Hickman; Ebro; September 1938.
"You are history, you are legend."

The memorial was unveiled on October 28th 2006. Alan Lloyd, the organiser and fundraiser for the memorial, introduced the service to an audience of relatives, veterans, trade union branches, local labour parties and supporters. Eulogies were read by relatives and the ceremony finished to the strains of the anthem of the Republican cause *The Internationale*.

I. R. Hickman had become Ivor Rae Hickman.

On the slopes of the Sierra de Pandols overlooking the Ebro valley in the Spain, there is a war memorial which commemorates the men of the XV International Brigade who died there. In all, 89 British and Irish volunteers died in the bloody "last stand" of the International Brigade in Spain, almost twenty per cent of the total of British fatalities in the civil war. The memorial was vandalised by Falangists in August 2007, but a replacement was organised by the Government of Catalonia in conjunction with the International Brigade Memorial Trust, being rededicated in November of the same year. Ivor Rae Hickman is one of the 89 men remembered there too.

Ivor Rae Hickman was born in Southampton on October 8th, 1914 to George Henry Hickman, a collector for a gas company, and Helen Lesser Hickman nee Lawson. His birth certificate shows the family home to be 24a Gordon Avenue, an area of Southampton between the Common and Portswood very close to where I lived during my time at university. It is an unremarkable area of a city that, at the time was a thriving transatlantic port, often referred to as *The Gateway to the Empire*. A mere two years previously, the Titanic had sailed from Southampton docks on her ill-fated maiden voyage and the city was still recovering from the terrible losses. Period photographs show grim faced, black-shrouded relatives gathering around the city's White Star offices awaiting news of the victims. 549 of the city's Sotonians died in the sinking.

The country was at war with Germany. Ivor's infant cries would be competing with the jingoistic optimistic mantra, "home by Christmas." At this stage the mass industrialised scale of the slaughter was unimaginable and Empirical optimism was rife throughout the country. However, by 1918, 2,008 of the 885,000 British service men killed, were from Southampton, later to be remembered on Sir Edwin Lutyen's Cenotaph in the city centre, the basis for his later design in Whitehall. Like many born in this period, Ivor's brief life would be book-ended by conflict in Europe. Research suggests that Ivor's father, George, a 2nd Lieutenant by October 1918, was a 'delayed' casualty of the First World War and committed suicide in 1924.[1] What effect this had on a ten year old Ivor is unknown but in the same year as his father's death he won a scholarship to Peter Symonds School (now Sixth Form College) in Winchester as a boarding pupil. Ivor's mother, Helen, later remarried and moved to Exmoor.

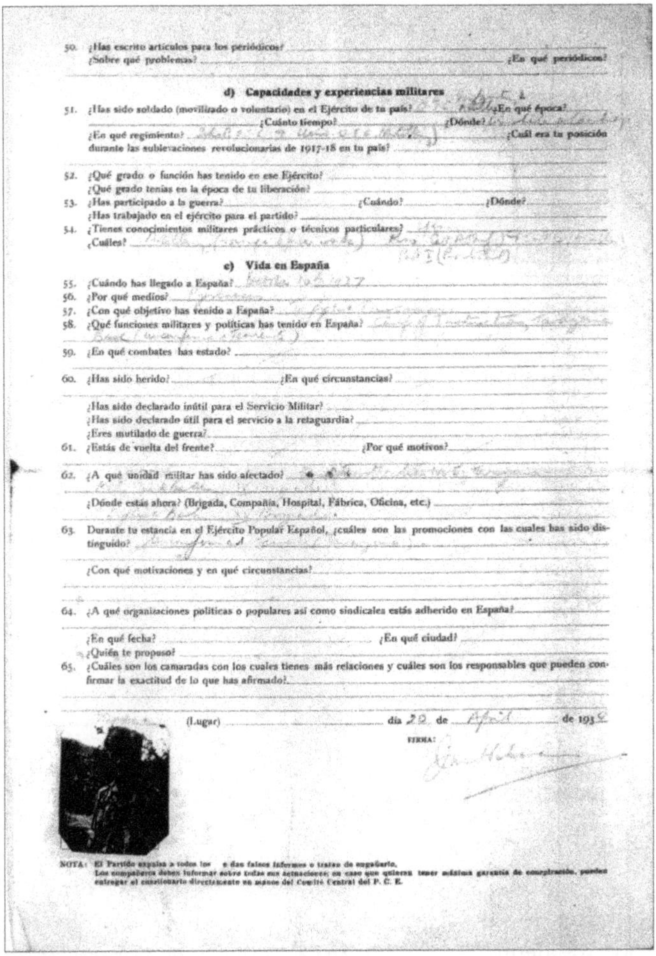

[Spanish military questionnaire form, partially filled in handwriting, with a blacked-out photograph area at bottom left and signature. Key printed sections visible:]

50. ¿Has escrito artículos para los periódicos?
¿Sobre qué problemas? _____ ¿En qué periódicos?

d) Capacidades y experiencias militares

51. ¿Has sido soldado (movilizado o voluntario) en el Ejército de tu país? _____ ¿En qué época?
¿Cuánto tiempo? _____ ¿Dónde? _____
¿En qué regimiento? _____ ¿Cuál era tu posición durante las sublevaciones revolucionarias de 1917-18 en tu país?

52. ¿Qué grado o función has tenido en ese Ejército?
¿Qué grado tenías en la época de tu liberación?
53. ¿Has participado a la guerra? _____ ¿Cuándo? _____ ¿Dónde?
¿Has trabajado en el ejército para el partido?
54. ¿Tienes conocimientos militares prácticos o técnicos particulares?
¿Cuáles?

e) Vida en España

55. ¿Cuándo has llegado a España?
56. ¿Por qué medios?
57. ¿Con qué objetivo has venido a España?
58. ¿Qué funciones militares y políticas has tenido en España?
59. ¿En qué combates has estado?
60. ¿Has sido herido? _____ ¿En qué circunstancias?
¿Has sido declarado inútil para el Servicio Militar?
¿Has sido declarado útil para el servicio a la retaguardia?
¿Eres mutilado de guerra?
61. ¿Estás de vuelta del frente? _____ ¿Por qué motivos?
62. ¿A qué unidad militar has sido afectado?
¿Dónde estás ahora? (Brigada, Compañía, Hospital, Fábrica, Oficina, etc.)
63. Durante tu estancia en el Ejército Popular Español, ¿cuáles son las promociones con las cuales has sido distinguido?
¿Con qué motivaciones y en qué circunstancias?
64. ¿A qué organizaciones políticas o populares así como sindicales estás adherido en España?
¿En qué fecha? _____ ¿En qué ciudad?
¿Quién te propuso?
65. ¿Cuáles son los camaradas con los cuales tienes más relaciones y cuáles son los responsables que pueden confirmar la exactitud de lo que has afirmado?

(Lugar) _____ día ___ de _____ de 193_
FIRMA:

NOTA: El Partido expulsa a todos los que dan falsos informes o tratan de engañarlo. Los compañeros deben informar sobre todas sus actuaciones; en caso que quieran tener máxima garantía de comprensión, pueden entregar el cuestionario directamente en manos del Comité Central del P.C.E.

In the beginning I only had one photograph of Ivor. It was a small passport sized photograph attached to the second page of his Spanish military file. I have a poor copy of a copy that offers little more than the merest nuance of identity. Not much more than a black smudge, it is a vague silhouette of a man concealed. Flicking through various photographs of unidentified volunteers of the International Brigades, I tried to mentally transpose Ivor's outline onto theirs. A Battalion meeting just before the Ebro offensive; Battalion officers on Hill 481 during the Ebro; At times I almost convinced myself that faces matched. I had painted in all the numbers and the picture was complete. In truth, though I often wanted it to be him, my need for a physical identity was irrational. Slowly that necessity receded – it no longer mattered what he looked like, it was what he *did* that mattered. (Source: MA)

To a boy from a relatively unprivileged background, the lower middle class of a provincial town, Peter Symonds must have seemed somewhat overwhelming to a 10 year old Ivor. The origins of the school are steeped in history and can be traced back to the 16th and 17th centuries. William Symonds was three times mayor of Winchester in 1575, 1585 and 1596. The slab over his tomb can be found in the north aisle of Winchester Cathedral. Peter (1528-1586), his brother, was a successful businessman and a member of the Mercers' Company. Broadly speaking the trade of 'mercery', derived from the Latin *merx, mercis* meaning wares, can be used to describe all forms of merchandise although in London the term had evolved to mean trade in luxury goods such as silk, linen and also hemp. The records of the Mercers' Company date back to 1348 although the Company is far older.

Peter, inspired by Christ's Hospital's foundation for needy London boys, decided to give Winchester a similar foundation, and thus in his will of 1586, he provided for an almshouse, Christies Hospital, to benefit the people of Winchester. The foundation was confirmed by Letters Patent July 15th 1605, and provided for the maintenance forever of six poor old and unmarried men, four poor young children, and for two poor scholars, one in Oxford and one in Cambridge, that should study to preach God's word. By the end of the 19th century, enough money had been earned from the sale of land to increase the educational side of the foundation and Peter Symonds' School was opened in May 1897, in Southgate Street. In December 1899, the school moved to Owens Road where there were by then eighty-seven boys on the register. Although there have only been six headmasters in the school's one hundred and two year history, Ivor would have known two of them, Reverend Telford Varley (1897-1926) and Dr "Doc" Freeman (1926-1956).

Reverend Telford Varley was described as a "formidable" headmaster, held in awe by the boys. He was capable of fearsome outbursts of temper and the more unusual forms of punishment that he meted out to offending boys. On one frequently referred to occasion he caught a boy climbing through a classroom window and invited him to climb in and out 50 times after school while he sat in the room marking. Slouching around with hands in pockets resulted in boys being paraded in Northbrook Hall at 4 o'clock and being invited to "assume an attitude of hobbledehoy." Shambling around the hall the boys were then told to assume "the attitude of a gentleman." During any pauses in these exercises, trains could be heard arriving and departing from the nearby station and this added to many of the boys discomfort as they heard their train home leaving without them. "This is called the old game of keeping the headmaster in," Varley gloated. "That was the 4 o'clock to Eastleigh. There will be another at 5 o'clock…" The first inspection in 1898 reported "Here you have proof of three things: 1st, the energy and organising skills of the Headmaster; 2nd, the loyal co-operation of the staff; 3rd, the hearty obedience of the boys." When Varley retired in 1926, he was succeeded by Dr Freeman, a graduate in mathematics. He began an expansion of the buildings and facilities with the aim of making Peter Symonds a public school. His energy and enthusiasm for all aspects of school life was boundless.

Ivor blossomed. As well as being highly academic, he also became a Company Sergeant Major in the Cadet Force. His promotion from Sergeant to C.S.M. is recorded in the Lent term edition of the Peter Symonds' School Magazine of 1932. In an article entitled "Musketry Report" Ivor writes,

> Generally speaking, the chief fault lies in lack of concentration – a fundamental error in rifle firing. More technical faults include trigger bearing, casualties with sight-setting, and a tendency to tilt the rifle right or left. Also the spotting in application is put to little use.

He then quotes the advice given by the European Miniature Rifle Champion of 1929.

> Squeeze the trigger as if the whole hand were holding a sponge or by applying as much pressure with the thumb or trigger finger. Breathe deeply, and just before final aim exhale naturally. Do not shoot with lungs full or forcibly empty. Concentrate on every shot.

In five short years, Ivor would be following his own advice on Spanish soil. The Summer term edition of 1932 displays Ivor's early awareness of military tactics. The Company were to be issued with 8 Lewis guns, 2 per platoon, and Ivor asks for volunteers to model mock-ups in wood during the holidays so that the Cadets would be well versed in the tactical use of the weapons by the time they arrived.

> The differentiation between Lewis Gun Sections and Rifle Sections is of the greatest importance from a tactical point of view, and the Lewis Guns, it must be remembered, are not specialised weapons (as are Vickers heavy machine-guns), but regulation weapons used by infantry in normal circumstances.

Ivor's academic achievements did not go unreported either. In the Lent term school magazine of 1933, the examination results record that he passed his High School Certificate, University of Bristol and his Somerset County Senior Scholarship in July of the previous year.

Life was not all academia and military training for Ivor. In February 1933, he produced and starred in the school production of R. C. Sherriff's play, *Journey's End*. The classic anti-war play was first performed in 1929 and was based on the author's own experiences in the trenches in World War I. It tells the story of Lieutenant Raleigh who has joined the army straight from school and finds himself posted to the Company of Captain Stanhope, barely three years Raleigh's senior and his idol from school. Stanhope, promoted beyond his experience and years, has changed and faces the inevitabilities of the frontline. Ivor's performance was described in the Lent term edition of the school magazine thus:

> The part of Stanhope, the nerve-racked infantry Captain, obsessed by the fear of succumbing to cowardice, was played with power and realism by I. R. Hickman, who succeeded in conveying the intense mental agony imposed by the unending strain of trench warfare.

The article goes on to praise Ivor's production skills also:

> As the producer, I. R. Hickman's work was as splendid in his inspiration of the play as a whole, as in his personal performance; to his unflagging enthusiasm and resource the success of the production may be largely attributed.

In July 1933, Ivor passed his Oxford Higher School Certificates in Mathematics, Advanced Mathematics and Physics and won an Open Scholarship in Natural Sciences at Christ's College, Cambridge. He was also awarded a Lord Kitchener Memorial Scholarship. Ivor Rae Hickman, it seemed, was destined for great things.[2]

While Ivor was immersed in academia, events in Europe were beginning to darken the peaceful horizon. On January 30th 1933, Hitler was made Chancellor of Germany by President Hindenburg and within a month had passed the Reichstag Fire Decree in response to Reichstag fire, nullifying many German civil liberties. By March the Enabling Act was passed declaring Hitler dictator of Germany. A few weeks later, a one day boycott of all Jewish-owned businesses was declared by Nazi party Gauleiter Julius Streicher as a prelude to other anti-Jewish measures relating to commerce. What followed could be seen as a grisly dress-rehearsal for later events as Jews and other social and political groups were systematically removed from Germany's social, cultural and political life. Trade unions were banned, books were burnt, and laws legalising eugenic sterilisation were introduced. Ominously in May 1933, the Gestapo was founded. By June all non-Nazi parties were banned and by October, Germany had declared its intentions of leaving the League of Nations – permanently.

In Italy meanwhile, Benito Mussolini was flexing his military muscles and propaganda events such as General Italo Balbo's mass transatlantic flight by the Italian Air Force barely concealed his ambitions. In Austria Chancellor Engelbert Dollfuss kept members of the National Council from convening, starting the Austrofascist dictatorship that culminated in the fascists eventually turning its artillery on workers' municipal housing blocks that were naturally a focus for Social Democrat activity. Dollfuss narrowly survived an assassination attempt in October, only to be killed by Nazi agents the following year. In 1933, members of the Iron Guard, an ultra-nationalist anti-Semitic, fascist organisation killed the Liberal prime minister of Romania, Ion Gheorghe Duca also. The same year, the German author Theodore Lessing who had fled to Czechoslovakia was shot in the back in broad daylight by Nazi Sudetens, so-called German exiles. In Spain Alejandro Lerroux Garcia, leader of the Radical Republican Party was elected Prime Minister during the Second Spanish Republic. With both Britain and America still emerging from the economic depression however, both nations appeared generally detached from events on mainland Europe.

2

Cambridge, Politics and Love

By this stage Ivor's story had become a "work in progress" that was not really progressing for me. I was no closer to really knowing him. I had a set of dates and events, shadows of third party meetings and tributes but in essence he was still just a blurred silhouette on a poorly photocopied form. I'd begun to question the whole project. Summer turned to winter and my productivity remained pitifully low. I hadn't given up but I felt that I was treading water, waiting for some exterior force to inspire me to continue. In early February 2009 the impetus arrived in my email inbox,

> ...I can now confirm that the eldest daughter (from her second marriage) of Juliet Hickman does indeed have a bundle of letters written by Ivor from Spain. She dug them out of the attic after my first call, never having looked at them previously, but has not read them having found it all a bit upsetting.
>
> Apparently some of them are difficult to read, largely due to the passage of time and the fact they were all written in pencil on odd bits of paper.
>
> Alan Lloyd.

Attached to the email was a photograph. Dressed in 'Oxford Bags' and a dark jumper, a tall fair haired man leans casually against a wall, head tilted slightly on one side, deep set eyes looking thoughtfully into the lens. The caption read "Believed to have been taken on his honeymoon." So this was Ivor Rae Hickman. Maybe I'd lied to myself; maybe it did matter what he looked like.

Alan Lloyd had managed to trace Juliet's daughters from her second marriage, Sarah Rhodes and Janie Shepherd. They had been unaware of any details of Juliet's marriage to Ivor and the realisation of their relationship carried much emotional impact for both sisters. They had discovered a series of letters written by Ivor to Juliet from Spain, from his arrival until shortly before his death. Janie later discovered a further collection dating from their first meeting through to their marriage in December 1936. I cannot describe my excitement at this news and my gratitude for the opportunity to read this, at times intimate, correspondence.

Alan and his partner Beth laboriously transcribed the Spanish letters and a few weeks later I collected what had become known as the 'courtship letters' from my village post office. My excitement was immeasurable at the prospect of reading the words that Ivor had written over seventy years before. The scent of age and history oozed from every neat handwritten word. Line by line revealed more and more about the name on the memorial bench; each phrase illuminated the man himself; every youthful insecurity recorded imparted upon him a humanity once forgotten and lost in the passing of time. The immortality that is memory had resurrected Ivor and I was honoured to meet him.

As I was to learn from his own hand (his own words now form the much of what follows) Ivor entered Christ's College Cambridge at a time when radical elements were beginning to establish themselves within the country's universities. Often the centre of controversial debate, the Oxford Union had passed the motion "This House will under no circumstances fight for King and Country" on February 9th, 1933. The motion was passed by 275 votes to 153. The result was denounced by Winston Churchill as "that abject, squalid, shameless avowal...this ever shameful motion." R. B. McCallum, a Fellow of Pembroke College, Oxford, said of the motion in 1944,

> The sensation created when this resolution was passed was tremendous. It received world-wide publicity...Throughout England people, especially the elderly people, were thoroughly shocked. Englishmen who were in India at the time have told me of the dismay they felt when they heard of it..."What is wrong with the younger generation?" was the general query. (177-80)

The Daily Express described the motion as the work of "woozy-minded Communists, the practical jokers, and the sexual indeterminates." Two hundred and seventy-five white feathers, one for each vote of the resolution, were anonymously sent to the Union. However, shortly after passing, the Oxford Pledge, as the resolution became known as, was adopted by both the University of Manchester and the University of Glasgow. Indeed across the country a strong peace movement was growing. As Sam Lesser recalled,

> With all due respect to the current generation but they think that they discovered 'Peace'. I was what they called a 'war baby'. I was born in 1915 but grew up with World War I hanging over me. There were such massacres at the front. So many households where father, brother, son, all had gone and didn't come back. So this anti-war feeling grew and grew. And more came out on the left, not only to the horrors of the Great War but that war was itself in general unnecessary. The Peace Movement developed a great deal at that time and this Oxford University resolution was part of it.

Britain was as ideologically divided as the rest of Europe with all the extremes of the political spectrum being represented.

The physicist and novelist C. P. Snow became Ivor's tutor. Later Snow would describe Ivor affectionately,

> He was a man of singular charm, good nature and human warmth. He was liked by most people at first sight; he enjoyed life so much that one found it difficult not to do the same in his company, even if at one period in his undergraduate career the sight of his shock of fair hair coming round the door meant an interminable discussion on the meaning of meaning. In those days he was exuberantly fond of abstract thought, and he had an endearing way of assuming that all his friends shared an identical passion. But he was also interested in most things: physics, the world of affairs, his friends, himself. (1939: 47)

By December 1935, Ivor had joined the Cambridge Communist Party, Christ's College Group after being nominated by Party members Comrades Early and Golter. However as C. P. Snow continued,

> Anyone who knew him will remember that his political devotion only took up a fraction of his life. His liberal views were part of his nature... but he was too much of a whole man not to put them in their place among the entire variegated mixture of living. (47)

In his book titled *The Year of Hope: Cambridge, Colonial Administration in the South Seas and Cricket*, C. P. Snow's brother, Philip, recalls Ivor as "a dashing friend [...] his blond hair flying in waves after the style of Rupert Brooke." (10)

One of Ivor's lecturers at Cambridge was Ludwig Wittgenstein, the Austrian philosopher and mathematician who is regarded as one of the

Ivor Hickman *(circa.* mid-1930s) apparently fitting the description that would later be given by C. P. Snow's brother Philip;"A dashing friend, his blond hair flying in waves after the style of Rupert Brooke:'(Courtesy: Sarah Rhodes & Janie Shepherd)

twentieth century's most celebrated contributors to the fields of the philosophy logic, mathematics, mind, and language. Wittgenstein's ground-breaking work in these interconnected fields must have appealed to Ivor's insatiable quest for knowledge and the two men became friends and corresponded after Ivor had left Cambridge. In one of his letters to Wittgenstein (dated October 25th, 1936) the bond is apparent as Ivor bemoans his dull life as an apprentice in Manchester,

> I miss my friends, I miss – if I may be allowed to say it without incurring your almost inevitable anger on this point – your lectures and the type of mental activity I associate with you.

Wittgenstein was a member of the Cambridge Conversazione Society better known by the nickname The Apostles. This secret society, founded in 1820, was initially developed to provide a forum for discussing modern ideas, which at the time were ignored by the University and eventually its influence had helped to broaden the curriculum at Cambridge. The scope of discussion ranged from liberalism to homo-eroticism and represented a brotherhood of tolerance, open mindedness, critical thinking and self-examination. Since its conception, members of the society became involved in numerous world events such as the failed insurrection of exiled liberals against King Ferdinand VII in Spain in 1830-31, and several became involved in the Irish struggle for independence. Prominent Victorians such as Tennyson, Balfour and Darwin's brother Erasmus, were known to be members. By the twentieth century notables such as Bertrand Russell, E. M. Forster, Rupert Brooke, Victor Rothschild and John Maynard Keynes had become members and the society's influence could be located in most areas of British culture. Several members are now known to have fought for the Republicans in the Spanish Civil War. It may be a leap too far to suggest that Ivor was a member of the Apostles but Wittgenstein's obvious influence may have been enough for Ivor to have later decided to go to Spain.

In 1935, during his time at Christ's Church College, Ivor also met Juliet MacArthur. Juliet was born on September 9th, 1914 in Sabathu, India, the daughter of Major Donald Hector MacArthur a MD in the Royal Army Medical Corps and Mary Florence Lusty, a dispenser. At the time of meeting Ivor, Juliet was at Newnham College studying psychology. Coincidently her mother, by now a widow, lived in Foxcote, a cottage in the grounds of Bedales School in Steep, near Petersfield, Hampshire where she worked, just some 20 miles from Ivor's hometown of Southampton.

The first tentative steps of their relationship can be seen in a series of charmingly innocent letters from Ivor to Juliet.

Juliet MacArthur: Born on September 9, 1914, Sabathu, India, the daughter of Major Donald Hector MacArthur and Mary Florence Lusty, a dispenser. At the time of meeting Ivor, Juliet was at Newnham College studying psychology. (Courtesy: Sarah Rhodes & Janie Shepherd)

Christ's College,
Cambridge.
Friday

Dear Miss MacArthur,
Thanks for calling on me in Dunster, and apologies for being away.
Somebody or other who saw you said you were attractive in a racehorse, shy sort of way, so that I think I know you superficially without being introduced. I am afraid I don't like racehorse, shy attractiveness but there must really be more to you than that. Anyway may I come and see you next Sunday, say at 4 and have some tea on you. I hope this will be alright.

I. R. Hickman
P. S. if I may come, don't bother to answer.
Also – I'm damned if I like chaperones

Christ's College,
Cambridge.
Monday

Dear Juliet,
I like you. Come and have dinner with me in my room (A7) at say 7 on Thursday. I hope this won't clash with any of your arrangements.
Cheerio
Hickman
I suppose I ought to have included a "please."

Christ's College,
Cambridge.
Sunday

My darling little Juliet,
I want you so much. This last 24 hours before seeing you again irritates me and I wish to God it were gone.
Even now I do not know when you will arrive in Cambridge, so if you realise when you receive this that I will not know (or perhaps you have written over the weekend) then send a wire from town telling me what train to meet and I will come along if I can.
I stopped for two days in London but London depressed me so much that I had to push off back to Cambridge.

I am looking forward feverishly to seeing you again – because I want you – every little bit of you. Still only 24 hours – hell.

Love – Ivor
I am like a little schoolboy in my excitement at the thought of seeing you again. If by any chance I miss you at the station, come and have tea or something with me – as quickly as you can.

Christ's College,
Cambridge.

Darling,

Christ I feel dead and would to God that bloody little bell hadn't tolled away. But no doubt after a week or so of rowing I shall feel better; and after a week or so of you much better.
Tomorrow is full up, which is perhaps all to the good, but I will try to see you on Thursday for supper, after I have had two hours of Wittgenstein. Anyway I will write and let you know definitely.
God your body's marvellous. I realize that, but my body is at the moment so weak that it is an insult to yours.

Thank God now that I sent that postcard.

Yours
Ivor

These early letters show a fledgling love of uncommon intensity; Ivor, five foot ten and half with his shock of long blond hair and Juliet, olive skinned, her face framed with raven black hair; quite the spectacular couple with the world at their feet. Juliet's sister, Jean recalls Ivor visiting Steep; "I was at school when Ivor first came to stay in Steep, Hampshire," she said in my research correspondence with her. "I liked him very much and he took me quite seriously and we had interesting talks, not only about politics."

By this time Ivor's mother was living in Dunster, a medieval village amidst the sweeping beauty of Exmoor where she ran the Forester's Arms Hotel. From here during the Christmas holidays of 1935, Ivor wrote a succession of letters to his beloved "Chamois." Far from being just frivolous love letters, his words show both the maturity of their relationship and his developing political beliefs. He talks of living and working in Russia as a naturalised Soviet citizen, his disillusionment with England strongly apparent.

Dunster

Darling,
I am very sorry that you had such a hell of a day and that you can't go down to Gerald and Elaine's.
But don't be depressed little one. Please write to Rosalinde and ask her for the name and address, etc. of the agents for the owner of 4 Portugal Place. I am going to take it soon as I get a reply – and of course you are going to live with me in it.
I shall be able to find the money somewhere – I will have about £20 over at least by next Tues and that should last for 2 months or so. By then everything will be ok. Please write away by return.

My love to you little one and cheer up –
Ivor

The Foresters Arms Hotel,
Dunster,
Minehead,
Somerset,

Thursday night

My little one, you've made me conceited. And since I have come home I have been suffering for that weakness. Perhaps you remember my "lovely yellow hair"; well, to mother, it's "that bloody mop of yours", without beauty, without attractiveness, like Maxton, and much more.[1] There am I feeling so marvellously natural after being with you, suddenly called a freak, an eccentric and ugly ass.
All this is difficult to bear particularly as I have developed a cold of moderate unpleasantness. I suppose you also have the same cold, because we have been sharing everything for the last few days and perhaps a cold might be thrown into the bargain. However this usual phase of bitterness the old woman shows to me whenever I come home will wear off and become more mellow. It has happened so before. I find that I have mislaid a hairbrush, so that possibly it is among your stuff, but it does not matter.
Today I wrote to the Russian Consulate asking for particulars of jobs in the U.S.S.R. and also of naturalisation. Since my contact of one day duration with this part of the Great British Public my feelings of hopelessness and disgust are reinforced. Everywhere I go it is the same and at last it seems that the environment at Cambridge is the most congenial. At least one doesn't have to remain at ordinary basic principles whenever we have a conversation – down here it is always a hellish attempt to refute suggestions of the type "there can't be a classless society – you're silly" and such formative ideas. The most progressive idea comes to be that there is less individuality in a Communist Society than in ours.

This might suggest that it is a spur for me to write my paper. On! On! Get – it done!! Hell, it doesn't take me that way, it makes me a little more depressed but even so I did two hours' work on it this afternoon. Also I find that the tendency of this paper is to become more relative to everyday matters than to philosophy as I first started off. I feel the ideas are so ordinary – unconventional but even so, ordinary. Perhaps this is not right. Naturally I do not expect to express an idea as great as Marxism or as Wittgenstein's philosophy; I am even not trying to in this context. Still I think I must go on with it even if its only value is a record of how I thought in December '35. – But you must remember that I have a cold and it might make a difference.

Juliet I have missed you a hell of a lot since I left you at Waterloo. Last night it was a bit of a strain having no surprise waiting for me when I got into bed.

Last night when I arrived home I went upstairs to see Pat who had gone on to bed. She was asleep and while I watched her the similarity between you two struck me. She has dark brown skin and that particular greasiness of the face that you characteristically have after you have been in bed for a little while. In some strange way my stomach responded to that impression by tightening up for a moment.

I hope that now you have gone away from me you still love me. But I never know, particularly after the attack I had today on the cue of freakishness.

Well, goodbye darling and my love – write to me when you feel like it or when you have something to say.

Love

Ivor

Dunster
Thursday 19th December '35.

My little sweetheart,
Many thanks for your letter – I need not say that I metaphysically nearly kissed the postman, need I? But I did.

You will receive from me a record of Prokofiev's Love for Three Oranges, "March and Scherzo and Waltz Scherzo." The march you will like I hope quite a lot, but the "Waltz Scherzo" is more difficult. Anyhow it is different if nothing else. Personally I think it is much more than different. Will you please accept this for Christmas from me. If you have decided to choose your present in town I would have given you much more but I find myself with very little cash and a host of obligations.

I have just been listening to the news and it turned out to be the most interesting news I have ever heard on the wireless – there is no doubt that what with the international situation and the potential coal strike (and potential General Strike? I wonder) the Government would never have been returned if it had played decently and acted constitutionally and waited until its 5 years of office was up.

I have heaps of letters to write sweetheart and so I must make this one short. But just long enough to tell you that I miss you a hell of a lot and that my passion makes

me strive to come back to you. But I can't because of this physical distance – and no other reasons.
Juliet I love you – I don't know why. Does it matter why?

Ivor
Write to me again soon – and don't send me a present because we know how we feel towards each other and so – oh well, don't.
Love

It is easy to pour scorn on Ivor's idealised view of Russia but it must be remembered that the Communist revolution was less than two decades old. Since coming to power in 1924, Stalin had wasted no time with his creation of the cult of both Lenin and himself. To both the privileged and the working class, the attraction of the apparent Communist utopia was great. These decades saw the birth of propaganda and media manipulation on a previously unseen scale. To the educated radical idealist such as Ivor, Stalin's Russia provided the answer to the discontentment felt by many in Britain. Russian women under Stalin were the first generation of women able to give birth in the safety of a hospital, with access to pre- and post-natal care. The generation born during Stalin's rule was the first near-universally literate generation. Millions benefitted from mass literacy campaigns in the 1930s, and from workers training schemes. Engineers were sent abroad to learn industrial technology, and hundreds of foreign engineers were brought to Russia on contract. Transport links were improved and many new railways built. Workers who exceeded their quotas received many incentives for their work; they could afford to buy the goods that were mass-produced by the rapidly expanding Soviet economy. Compared with Britain, a country with her antiquated Victorian values of class and place within society, a country still slowly recovering from the great depression and clinging stubbornly to a soon to be lost empire, the lure of the East was understandable. In times of economic crisis, political life often becomes polarized and it is then that extremism, both to the left and to the right, has best chance of gaining a foothold.

Ivor had seen with his own eyes the situation in Europe. In July and August 1935, he travelled through Germany and Hungary where he would have witnessed first-hand the inexorable rise of fascism strangling the last breath of freedom from the peoples' throats. The fear that Mosley and his Blackshirts would gain power and ally Britain with these regimes was as real to Ivor's generation as the perceived threat of global terrorism is today. Ivor toured Munich, Dresden, Hamburg, and Budapest, cities of rich history and culture now under the rule of the ignorant and ruthless fascist dictators.

Politics aside, by 1936 Ivor and Juliet were simply two people in love however. The series of letters that follow chart Ivor's often convoluted arrangements for meeting up with Juliet in London shortly after Christmas. As is evident, his feelings for Juliet, juggled with his youthful insecurities, are juxtaposed with his practical and more pragmatic nature. The more risqué elements of his words echo with a timeless innocence that cannot fail to charm. These are the words of a man in love for the first time in his life; the words of a man of science and mathematics and all things practical who has found himself in uncharted and unpredictable waters. At times he is insecure, at times he appears playful, at times he seeks reassurance but throughout his determination is wholly apparent.

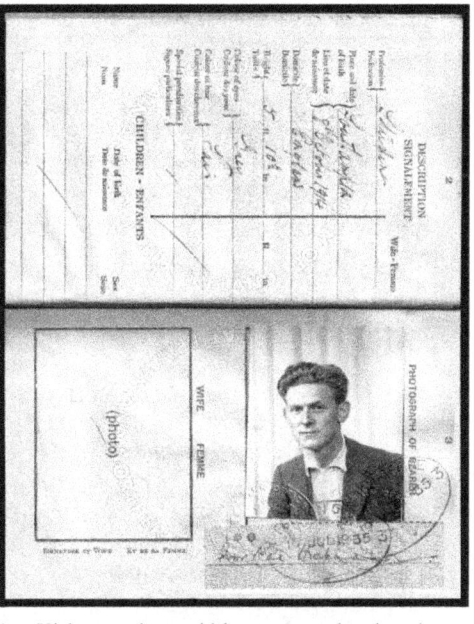

Ivor Hickman as he would have appeared to those he met on his travels throughout Europe during 1935. (Courtesy: Sarah Rhodes & Janie Shepherd)

Dunster
New Years Day

My little Juliet,
Many thanks for your letters and for "Poets' Pub"; [a paperback novel by Eric Linklater] *...which I have not yet read because other books sent to me on condition that they are returned quickly have occupied me. But later.*
This is not going to be an interesting letter but merely one of arrangement. You go to town on Jan 6th. I shall come up with Mother on Jan 11th and we shall probably stay with Tex Austin a man who went down last July and who – quietly – has a crush on Mother (I say "crush" because it is not a passion, he is too frightened).[2]
We are now very hard up indeed so that we shall spend practically nothing while we are in town. Mother usually goes up with me in January so she can smell around the sales. I vaguely hoped you would have a flat as before but perhaps that is too much to hope for. The disadvantage then is that if I don't sleep at Tex's then Mother won't either – she will only go there on the condition that I come too – and she will have to sleep in a hotel; which is rather unpleasant.

But I want to introduce Mother to you and to Hugh – I am sure she won't be a drag, but if for some strange psychological reason you don't want to meet her then say so and you won't. But I see no normal reason against your seeing her. By the way I have told her that I spent the long weekend at the end of term with you – properly I mean. She didn't object. She only observed that you must have a real passion for me – I ratified this – but she wondered how you tolerated me, my conversation, my ideas. But then she corrected herself and said "Of course she must have passion for the other side of you and so will tolerate anything." (She meant any intellectual sideline, etc).

I showed her what you wrote about The Artist, etc to which she replied that you don't like me because of that, but you want me (I suppose she means here by "me", my affection body respect and god knows what more) and this you know is one way of keeping me. This was not said nastily – I could naturally enough have said it for her, except of course you must have had those interests before ever you met me – even so, the crux is true. I am glad.

After all this do you feel like meeting her? I hope so.

Hugh wrote an interesting letter to me and mentioned your reference to our stay in town and sympathised with the shortness of the time. I want to introduce Mother to him; I believe she would like him.

Sweetheart, I wish you an excellent New Year and I am looking forward to kiss your brown thighs. I had better remind you to put on another browning polish for Jan 11th, because I shall be really disappointed if your thighs are white.

My love darling – I am looking forward like hell to having you again and I hope I don't arrive in town and wake up to find you in love with someone else.

Goodbye for only a few days – Ivor

P. S. My paper seems to have gone to hell.

Dunster,
3rd Jan. '36.

Sweetheart,
Thanks for your letter and apologies for not writing to you before I did. Also I am sorry that I was unable to interpret Mother's remarks as they were really meant and so made you lose your appetite for tea – but I will talk to you about that letter when I see you on the 11th if you will keep it till then.

Mother and I will definitely be in town on the 11th and we will be going to a private dance on that evening, being invited by Tex with whom we are staying. And we all invite you to come with us then. I hope this will be alright. I cannot dance at all well but you must forgive that – as naturally I hope to dance with you more often than with anyone else.

I arrive in town from Beaulieu near Southampton and pick up Mother who arrives from Dunster and then I go to Tex's for lunch. So that I will come to your rooms at 4 o'clock on that day. You must let us know where you will be – Any other arrangements we can make then.
Also I am booking seats at the Little for "Lady Precious Stream" for Monday 13th and hope you will come with us.
Even if you have a flat of your own and cannot see the way clear for my stopping with you – because Mother says she won't stop at Tex's place unless I am there as well. But perhaps that objection can be overridden. Also sweetheart get in touch with Hugh, whom I want Mother to meet.
I will send you another gramophone record but I have not yet made up my mind which one.
Many thanks for your letter – my God Sweetheart I am looking for to seeing your brown thighs once (!) again.

Love to you darling,
Ivor

P. S. Why are you so strangely touchy? Why are you so super – sensitive about our love? I don't complain. I say it is magnificent to love and be loved by such a sensitive creature as you. Yes, this is to be our year.
P. P. S. I could spend the night Jan 10th to 11th with you if you had a flat somewhere by coming up from Beaulieu a day earlier quite easy.

Dunster,
7th January 1936.

Darling,
Your last letter made my blood boil – because I realise the situation perfectly. There was the theoretic possibility that you could somehow have a flat lent to you – it was not very probable but it was pleasant even as a possibility. So therefore my mind dwelt on it.
As you are not fixed up for the 11th, the day when I arrive, would you prefer to meet my train at Waterloo at about 11.30. I will let you know the accurate time later.
Then we could go on and meet Mother at Paddington at 1.15 and also discuss what you are going to do. I will willingly help you out with the 15/- for your bed and breakfast – 15/- for 3 isn't very much, is it? At the moment I am very hard up for hard cash but no doubt Mother will lend me some until I get my allowance in Cambridge.
I would like you to go to the Prom concert at Queen's Hall on Thursday – it is a Russian concert and in it is included Stravinsky's Fireworks, Mossolov's Machines and Prokofiev's March and Scherzo from Love for Three Oranges. The last piece being the one I wanted to give you. If you cannot find time or money enough to go, then listen over the wireless. (I will give you the price for a seat with full warmth of heart).

If you can find Hugh please tell him that we should like to meet him on Sunday after lunch and if the idea is a good one go to the Chinese Exhibition [the Royal Academy's International Exhibition of Chinese Art] *with him.*
I have been out shooting today and have climbed up improbable valleys and sunk down into more, even more unreal.
But I don't feel very pleased tonight because I have to pack in preparation for tomorrow when I go up on a motorbike to Beaulieu until Saturday morning.
If you wish to write to me for any thing, my address will be

C/o
G. W. Hartley,
Hatchett Mill,
East Boldre,
Hants.

My love to you Sweetheart – Saturday morning if you wish –

Ivor

Hatchett Mill,
East Boldre,
Hants,

Thursday

My little one,
The time when I shall see you again seems tantalisingly long even yet but it will soon be over and I will be with you again. I desire you strongly and the physical distance between us angers me. Damn me if it doesn't.
I shall arrive at Waterloo at 11.44 on Saturday and I would like you to meet me – but if that is inconvenient and you don't want to, then I will come round at 4 as arranged before. If I do not hear from you I shall expect you at Waterloo but if you are not there I will go on my way and call for you at 4. Also Tex asks you to dinner at 7 or 7.30 on Saturday with us at Hampstead.
I apologise for the many bad constructions of grammar, of sense and of God knows what else that I have used in my letters to you – I am conscious that there are bad constructions which is something.
The last letter you wrote me was completely devoid of any trace of your love for me. I am not asking for soft – soap love because I don't like it and it is so easy to affect and to receive – I have no need of it. But the absence of any love in your letter pricked my pride, that is one way of interpreting it; another is that your love seemed so elusive to me that I despaired of it. Damn this physical distance, it would all be so easy if it were not for that; then we could love and not be worried by tones of letters, by dreams and phantasies and such hellish things.

I find that whenever there arises some difficulty which offends my sensibility – and there are many difficulties – not of coarseness but of hopelessness – then I miss you particularly strongly. It was so last night when I was talking to Hartley; brother, a sculptor and a reactionary – who describes Lawrence as a nasty degenerate little consumptive. Nasty and degenerate are the two inevitable adjectives for Lawrence. But I think in the end Lawrence wins this destructive fight of telling the Star man he is worthless. Primarily because Lawrence is not worthless and most of the bourgeoisie are. Anyhow I missed you then.

If you have fallen out of love with me – your last letter suggested it but I don't think you meant it – then you have. I shall admit it and fight for it. If I fail, then I fail. But I won't. See?

My God I want your lovely brown body
Ivor

Friday morning.

My little Juliet,

Thanks for your exceedingly attractive letter written on unattractive paper.
I am sorry you missed the Prom because you missed Prokofiev's piece Scherzo and March from the Love for Three Oranges – and I was thinking last night as I listened to it that that piece alone is enough to justify the existence of the modern technique of music. I do not say that it is a masterpiece which will remain to the end of time but a piece which illustrated modern techniques and justifies it. It may be a masterpiece, I don't know – but I feel inclined to think it isn't.
The train arrives at 4.44 from Southampton – we could have an hour together before we go our separate ways to separate lunches (what a thought!) but should you wish to wait until 4 before you see me then don't meet me. Naturally I would prefer to meet you at 11.44. Of course you can change at Tex's place – you can borrow my room if you like.
Do I "by any chance" still love you? Hell I do. Last night I was wild and wanted you like hell – and I couldn't go to sleep because the night was so mild and the wind so deafening and irritating. But eventually I dropped off to sleep.
There is very little time now before I see you again. Marvellous.

You know I love you; I couldn't write this if I didn't –

Ivor

*19 Tufnell Park Road,
London, N7.
Thursday*

*My darling little one,
I have arrived in London as you see and so write to me at the above address rather than at 46 and tell me your arrangements, etc. This place is alright; the bed is a bit short for me – and of course it is not half as good as the flat because I haven't got you. Still a few days will fill that want –*

*My love to you –
Ivor*

*What will you do if I have changed beyond recognition?
My kind regards (unlike me) to Joyce. Love – I am looking forward to you.*

Frustratingly there is no further correspondence recording the outcome of their meeting but one can assume that it went as planned. Maybe some matters are best left private and lost to time.

3

A Northern Industrial Town

After graduating from Christ's College in June 1936, Ivor moved to Manchester to begin an apprenticeship as a Mathematical Engineer for the Metropolitan Vickers Electrical Company.[1] The summer before he departed was spent in Zennor, near St. Ives in Cornwall. As he wrote to Juliet,

C/o Bennetts' Farm
Trewey,
Zennor.

Aug 27th 1936.

My little love,
I have been neglecting to write to you, in fact I have only written you once in these last three weeks. But that does not mean to say that I have not missed you, it only means that very seldom have I felt like writing – what with harvesting and fishing my time seems full.
I went out long lining again for 2 days, this time in "Our Katie" an older boat than the "Madeline." The sun shone all the time and my face smarted fiercely in consequence. But "Our Katie" had a smell about her and anywhere I went the smell was ours to go. The sun brought it out and as there was no sea the water went down into the bilge to relieve the smell. The smell was a matured mixture of 19 years of paraffin, fish, oil and acetylene. I was not sick but the smell got into my clothes and my stomach with the result that I only ate toast for 36 hours. Still even so I enjoyed it. Now there is a wonderful breeze blowing and yet I'm not out in it. I am thinking of going out tonight trawling in Mount's Bay. Also I am going to spend a week out on a Brixham trawler.
Then what am I going to do? I am not going to Scotland because it is too expensive – £5.14/-9 fare to the Hebrides, so I will try to come back to my little Juliet. I should prefer to go to Rye but if that is impossible I will come to you at Steep. (What does it matter if your sister is away?)

Now why in one letter do you say you want a job in Manchester and in the next try to get one somewhere else? I am glad things look promising for you but I am sorry to hear that you won't be near me. I suppose that eventually you will drift away from me.

Bennetts'
Zennor.
1st of September 1936.

My little darling Juliet,
Many thanks for your postcard with your address.
As you know – I hope – from my wire I intend to leave here tomorrow and then leave Dunster for Paddington on Friday. I do not yet know what time I shall arrive but I will let you know as soon as I decide definitely.
If you can manage it, ask Mrs. Hopkins if she will let me stop with you – preferably really with you, otherwise in another room. Otherwise will you please find me a bedroom somewhere near you – What a damned farce the latter would be!
I am going on to Manchester on the Monday and I will presume return to London again on Thursday or Friday. Anyhow I will be with you my little love very soon now. If you don't like the idea of a bedroom away from you we might go out to the country and stop together for Friday and Saturday nights. Or even stop at a hotel in the centre of town – in a way I'd rather like that – although it couldn't be like the flat. Write to me from now on at home. There remains very little time now down here for me and I must think about packing and God knows what else.
I am looking forward to seeing you and I am very glad you got such a decent job. £4.10/- a week is too much to begin with. £2 more than me! And I hope you have enjoyed your first 2 days work and my God – I hope you won't be too tired out on Friday.
Gerald has found your ring; I will bring it along with me. It has a crack at the back – was it like that before?
Your body is as beautiful as it ever was – still, isn't it? I want it to be and I want it and I want you. Oh hell – Friday won't be long now.

Love
Ivor – I am going to kiss you all over.

Once in Manchester, Ivor took up lodgings at 71 School Road, Stretford, renting a room from a local family. Metropolitan Vickers had been set up in 1899 by George Westinghouse on a site at Trafford Park and by 1936 had around 17,000 employees. The company produced industrial electrical equipment such as generators, steam turbines, switchgear, transformers, electronics and railway traction equipment. It had been rocked by scandal in 1933 when six employees (Allan Monkhouse, L. C. Thornton, W. L.

Macdonald, J. Cushny, C. H. de Nordwall, and A. W. Gregory) working in Russia were arrested and found guilty of espionage and sabotage. The trials took place in Moscow and although Gregory was acquitted, the other men were found guilty. However, shortly after the trial the men were released and allowed to return to Britain. By 1935, the company was working on producing the largest steam turbogenerator in Europe for use in Battersea power station.

Ivor worked in the factory as an ordinary apprentice-workman. He would start work at 7.30am, break for lunch at 12.15 for an hour, then finish the day at 5.00pm. As an apprentice his duties were fairly mundane and consisted of tightening up bolts, painting castings and assembling transformer parts. In the evenings he took night classes in German and Russian. This together with works lectures and Technical College lectures meant that he had little spare time. In addition to work and studying, Ivor joined the Stretford branch of the Communist Party of Great Britain. In his letters to Wittgenstein, Ivor hints at the dissatisfaction that he was beginning to feel with his life in Manchester. He had little in common with his fellow apprentices, finding them clever but dull and conservative with little emotional understanding. He preferred the company of the workmen who he describes as having "something mystically attractive about their completeness of make-up." At first he ate in the staff canteen but soon found the hurried way the staff ate rather disgusting, comparing their manner with that of the machines in the factory. His dissatisfaction was not just confined to the factory but to Manchester itself.

> Manchester is an attractive city because it is a real city and unpretentious; but so lowbrow. By that I mean so commercial, so bourgeois. I've never seen anyone wearing peculiar and striking clothes, anybody with a beard. So often when I am in the streets I feel myself to be so much madder than my sane drab fellow workers.

However, he felt that the work was immensely beneficial to his understanding of electricity as the practical aspect he was experiencing in the works supplemented his theoretical knowledge studied at Cambridge. "Compare the mystery about Time (the clock is the answer) to my mystery of Electricity (the works is the answer)."

Outside of his working life Ivor was becoming increasingly dissatisfied with lodgings in School Road. In one of his letters to Wittgenstein he tells of his irritation at his landlady's wireless radio that would sound through the wall of his room. He began to feel uneasy at the sound of footsteps outside his door and once caught the 'old man' listening in on him. He would, he planned, begin saving to try to afford the rent on a small house or flat of his own, a place his 'wandering friends' could come and stay. Soon he was making plans for the future with Juliet too. The following letters show a sense of increased confidence and self-assurance on Ivor's part. His playfulness was maturing from the coy into an intimate frankness not seen in earlier letters. However, by the end, his practical nature is still apparent as he discusses marriage and his plans for his living arrangements.

71 School Road,
Stretford,
Manchester.
Saturday afternoon.

My darling little love,
Many many thanks for your three lovely letters. And you shouldn't make love to my crocus like you do! – Yes you should if you want to – I do love you.
And I was so glad and happy when you wrote me and told me about your sketching your lovely cunt for me. You are a brave beautiful girl and I do wish you were here with me.
And your last letter, your EGO letter, was very marvellous to read; and I wished you were here with me and in my bed.
I am so sorry I didn't know what to say when I was talking to you over the phone. Your voice was so beautifully musical.
You have got I hope the information William Deacon's Bank. I rang up the Borough Estates Manager and found out. I believe Wednesday will be alright; in fact it will have to be, but as you know these damned borough people are so slow. Still once there is in Stretford the guarantee about £40 p.a. it will be ok. Will you send it my love? I don't really like the idea of using your name as a guarantor but after all it is better (is it not?) than a personal friend. The blasted Estates manager hasn't sent the key so that I cannot get the measurements for the curtains but perhaps Manchester will do as well, because after all it is the centre of the cloth trade. And also you will be able to see the wallpaper and then decide which curtains and also which wallpaper you want removed.
But unless you arrive on Monday I will make measurements and so on and send them to you. You see, the key if in my hands allows me to get into the house more quickly and so disturb the Estate manager – and being a borough official doesn't like it I suppose.
We are collecting quite a wonderful lot of presents, aren't you? Despite our secrecy. Although it is very nice to get them from the people that we like.
I do wish you were here; I would kiss you all over. Your lips and your cheeks, your hair, your breasts and belly, your cunt and love you so much.
To return to soberness. I got a letter from Mother today. She hadn't told you but she suggested to me that we wait in rooms until we can find a flat. She didn't mention it to you because it would worry you.

I bear in mind all you say about your difficulties darling and I can assure you that I will defend you against anybody's attack, your Mother or anybody's. Once we are married I will do that for you for ever.
So I am writing back to your Mother a veiled attack. No, we have thought it out and I have decided otherwise and I think Juliet agrees. Why would your letter telling Juliet worry her when we've discussed it together both verbally and in innumerable letters? "She doesn't want to interfere but..."
Her letter was very unhelpful because everything in it we've said before and decided as now. So that will be one of my efforts and I suppose not the last. But she presents no difficulties to me, because I have no childhood associations with her and I will free you from your unconscious fear my love. Be assured of that.
But still she is kind and I won't hurt her unless a difficult issue is forced.
Bad news – I have been to the dentist today and he tells me that my stoppings want overhauling. After all stoppings don't last for ever. £4.5.6 for a first class job. So I have paid a deposit of £1.5.6 and will settle up the rest with him in two weekly instalments of 30/- (if they can be found). This figure is terribly high but my teeth are teeth requiring much care and I will not let them go under any circumstances.
It is snowing outside now. I hope we have a white Christmas. Our first Christmas together!
Darling I do hope you will be happy with me here in Stretford. And I do hope you won't be disappointed with the house. Come up on Wednesday of if you like on Monday. If you could manage and L.S.D. [Pounds, Shillings & Pence] *allows come on Monday. But not to return to London, only York. I have just looked on a map to find that York is North of Manchester and quite near. So come up on Monday if you can, and go on to York later. You could help make the arrangements with the Estate manager and hurry him up. Also you would see me; and you would have an idea of the size, etc of the house.*
So my love, if you can manage it
Manchester Monday
York Tuesday
Manchester Wednesday, et seq...
Oh, hell, I forgot. You have to see Dr Graff, that excellent woman again. So I cannot make any arrangements for you. Except perhaps you could go back to London to see her on Monday week. But you know.
Still I'd love to see my love and love my love. Thinking of you makes my crocus feel very strong because he wants you.
I don't give him a Capital C.

All my love to you my sweetheart darling.
See you soon and we'll be married!
Love
Ivor

You had better bring the Birth Certificate, just in case.
So it's £600!

The extra 9/- a week will help us immensely my love.
It looks as if I shall be indebted to you financially as well as emotionally.

71 School Road,
Stretford,
Manchester.
Sunday night.

My darling little love,
I'm sorry I haven't written to you before. And many many thanks for your letters to me. I am glad you are moving nearer in and I hope you will like your room and grow to love it.
Just now I feel difficult. For this reason; my landlady who is a nice person has on my mantelpiece two photographs of her beloved daughter Phyllis. This daughter is extremely attractive and is on stage and married although she is only my age. Naturally she thinks very highly of her. But to have two photographs of a highly attractive woman before you, and you don't know her and she means nothing is so unpleasant. As you know I believe in living in my rooms and making rooms a reflection of myself. I have brought my Pisanello [probably a reference to a reproduction of a work by the renowned artist of the Italian Renaissance] and my books and altogether I am just beginning to feel it to be my own. So that I suggest with difficulty to her that she should put Phyllis' photograph somewhere else. This hurt her a lot. "So you don't like my girl" is her instinctive feeling. "And it has always stood there since it first came into the house."
So she moved one to another place. "And I will think about it tomorrow."
What the hell ought I to do?
In other parts of the room it is not so bad, but on the mantelpiece, the very centre heart of the room!
So I have just gone along to a new friend of mine, a most fascinating man although he is an engineer apprentice and asked his advice. He suggested that I should go along into her room and face her and point it out. So taking his expert advice, which sounded so obvious as he told it, I went in and was met with "It will stay."
Now, let me tell you about myself. Tomorrow I go to Moiseiwitsch [Benno Moiseiwitsch, the Ukrainian-born British classical pianist] to forget myself. The work here is magnificent. I feel a strong feeling of loyalty to my fellow workers and to our unity. The activity efficiency and drive of our works astounds me. I work under a man, Tommy, an excellent man who has been with the firm for twenty years and who has about him a finesse and completeness which is beautiful. He is a socialist and so we are not at loggerheads on that point.
And this man Hallowes who has fascinated me all day is a magnificent chap – he loves and craves after music, is religious and capable of feeling, which is more than almost anybody in that staff canteen. He is pleased – so he says – to have found me and I pleased – my God yes – to have found him. Here's to a long and fruitful friendship.
And I have met a rather attractive woman, a Christian Scientist. I picked her up on the

spur of the moment one day and she hasn't got over that. Her convictions are strong and rather dreadful. I'm afraid I miss you very very much my love and I'm looking forward to seeing you again. And yet in a way I don't want you to come up because it will be an anticlimax I'm afraid after Cornwall and Cambridge and London and Rye. You see I'm surrounded everywhere here by stinking conventionality; that's partly why I wanted to get rid of the photographs on the mantelpiece.

Oh, darling, Thomas (from Christs') has probably got a job in Manchester on the Daily Mirror! How splendid to have Thom with me here! Perhaps we could share a flat, Thom and I?

Then you could come and feel nothing of the stinking conventionality.

I've just written a frenzied letter to Thom and asked him to share a flat with me – let's hope he'll do it. Then I'll be alone and yet be with Thom whom I can understand. Whereas here there is the sense of the other person under the same roof.

Well, goodbye, my love. You come up to our flat. Wish it were ours don't you? I'm upset as I was when I read of Henry Trembath's death.

I have seen Joyce, she's well –

Love to you my sweetheart

Love – Ivor

71 School Road,
Stretford,
Manchester.
Sunday night Oct 15th 1936.

Well my little love,
It's time I wrote to you. This change of environment has stimulated me immensely because I am kicking against it harshly. It is making me return to a previous state of mind when I wanted my hair to come down over my face – when in fact I wanted to be mad. Yet I like my work and am glad to be working. But Manchester is so appallingly lowbrow in every respect, I must kick against it and say and feel and enjoy highbrow things. (I think this word 'lowbrow' is exactly suited to Manchester). I have hundreds of things to say and feelings to realise – to achieve – and yet I don't tell you because you know them already. Some might surprise you, but even so that would be only superficial, because you know me so well. I stand before you like a naked child; I'm like a fool before you, but not so before anyone else. This makes me introspective and impulsive. Introspective because I am forced back into myself and into my own thoughts; impulsive because it means I care less for the outside world. And it is surprising how "successful" my impulsiveness is. I think the people come in contact with like me for it. Yet they don't know the real me, do they?

I should like to talk to you about physical proximity, but this subject is so near to the two of us – just think of Cornwall – that even by talking I could not get over *the real difficulty which does exist and which neither you nor I can fathom. So I won't say anything.*

I shall fairly soon – perhaps in 4 or 6 weeks time – be moving I expect. Maybe my mood will change but much as I like my landlady – she has removed the pictures from the mantelpiece – I hate this physical proximity side of digs. So I am going to a flat, perhaps to live with Tom, probably alone. I have no furniture but what does that matter? In fact I am even glad, so that I can help myself get away from the bloody bourgeois rut I am forced into. But my money is very short.

Now I shall move I expect before Christmas. What I want you to do is to spend your 2 or 3 weeks (let's hope it's even more) Christmas holiday in Manchester with me. I shall have about 8 days extra leave (not on pay I'm afraid) when I would be with you all day but the rest of the time could you stop at home and wait for me after work? Or would it be too slow for you my little love? Then you might find a job in Manchester and settle with me.

I can't see how I can get into my new place – I haven't fixed on one yet – before Oct 29th. If I don't move before then, what are we to do? Will you come up and stop in digs near me and shall we go away for the Saturday night somewhere? Or will you keep your money until you can come up and stay properly with me? I would love to see you again bit I am frightened at the thought of the bloody bloody sense of disappointment we will find until things go differently from what I expect.

The real answer is to get out before that date. I will try my love to do that but it may not be easy, because I must find a place near my work. I have one in view. A garret flat, separate entrance, only 10 minutes by bike from the works and looking out onto the country! But the workmen are still in it and I don't know when it would be ready. Then I have to get my bed, etc sent on from home. They'd do that alright though. Nor do I know how much L.S.D. [Pounds, Shillings & Pence] *But if I share with Tom it may work out better. Even so I'd rather be alone with you.*

I spoke to Joyce about this problem of where you might stay and how horrid it would be if you couldn't stay with me. She didn't understand and in fact was veiledly contemptuous – meaning "do you two just want to fuck and nothing else?" But she doesn't understand. How can she when she isn't you and not even me?

Do you remember your Common dinner when you were naked in front of me and her? I often remember your body and that wonderful lack of symmetry about your lips which makes your face so beautiful. But I am not often aggregately lustful after you. Because you see I work too hard and rush here and chase there and am tired. But even so I desire you often. Yet I am not irritated. But I know that sooner or later that must come and what am I to do stuck in this rut of stinking bourgeois death and sterility? Drink? No that will be chalked up against me. Have you? Damn, physical circumstances of geography – the fact that I am in digs – makes that so difficult. I want to make something with you and that could never happen in this room here – of that I'm quite sure.

I suppose you feel now steadfastly installed in your room. Let's hope it is good. I'm sure you could make it attractive and warm for me. Hell, but I can't come to you. The thought of your body makes me feel strong in the loins. And your hearts.

Hell – Goodbye for a little while my love. I would that you could be with me tonight

Perhaps later. My love to you my dearest sweetheart –
Ivor

I have told you nothing about my works. But all in due time. That is too big a thing, too complex a feeling and to be able to describe it a few words. And I come to you for something different. I love you Juliet.

Stretford,
Manchester.
Tuesday.

My darling little love,
I have with some difficulties and arguments sent off the marriage article of registration. It's so awfully kind of the civil authorities to marry us. That's their attitude.
Many many thanks for your lovely letter. I hastened through it at 7.10 this morning and then read it in the Department behind a good barricade of tin-boxes.
It is so generous of your mother to give us £50. £50!! 4 months work for me, the equivalent. Surely it is too much. I understand exactly how you feel about your independence. I understand your objections to your mother and anybody else taking as it were a 'part-share' in our marriage.
This £50 brings home to me the social gap between our families. We will get perhaps a few presents from my side but nothing immense like £50. You say you decide to take it. I leave it to you entirely as it is your Mother – I have my own to deal with. We can do without it and we can do well with it. But it is terrifically generous of her. I went over a flat yesterday night in the rain – 18/6 a week: 30 mins from my work, 5-10 mins from Piccadilly: big, would be decorated out at our requirements if we promised 2 years; quite on its own. Biggish rooms with much light, etc and a garden. But I wish you were here to help me choose.
Going on about the social side, you must remember that my father committed suicide – beyond doubt – not that that has any real reflection on me. Socially we are a complete hot-pot. Tell me something about the social side of your family. What rank was your father? Of course now I think of it he was a captain in the R. A. M. C. Mine was a ranked 2nd Lieut. by Oct, 1918.
I come from a family of lawyers, bankers and marine engineers on my mother's side, on my father's side also marine engineers and a mixture of manual labourer in the country and in the town. I have one very distant trace of mental deficiency and that's all; and that is only slight. That man is intelligent enough to be a good coal merchant!
Both sides of my family contain sparks of brilliance scattered very far and wide around. My father was a man of great sensibility, my uncle Phil is as clever as he is unambitious, my grandfather Hickman is a man of immense religious force and bigotry – he refused promotion on the grounds of "It is more difficult for a rich

man to enter the kingdom of heaven than a camel..." and is a prig and a hypocrite. Yet not a sneaking hypocrite. Mother has her own brilliance – my Grandfather Lawson has immense activity and experience – he is 70 but he works like hell even now. Uncle Jack (Lawson) is a prosperous man. He owns works in Antwerp (600 men) doing central heating fitting and marine boiler cleaning, ship painting, etc. He married a Belgian.

The Raes are Scotch, clever and wealthy. John Rae, a cousin of mothers was chairman of the Westminster Bank. [Rae had been appointed to the Committee of Finance & Industry to investigate the underlying causes of the 1929 stock market crash just a few years previously]

The Adams although they are only step relations count quite a lot. You know Mrs Adams and Helena and you can use your judgement.

I thought I would tell you all this because Mother raised this social question and pointed out that you were different from me to a certain extent. Also she was genuinely interested in your family.

You seem to be a family of doctors. Your father was a doctor wasn't he? There are no doctors at all in ours.

Still I'm marrying you and not your family. And when we sail away – it will be very pleasant to come back. I ought to do my Russia now.

So my little love, 3 weeks on Thursday and we will be married! Without trumpets and fanfares.

But we will make up for that. Do we need conventional cement to stick us together? I do hope the registration form, etc is filled in correctly. Such a damned farce. As if it matters whether we are 22, at least a month, Barton Lancaster, Petersfield, Southampton, birth certificates. I suggested at one point in momentary anger "Does it matter?" The Registrar was aghast. "Of course it matters!"

Tra-la-la-la-boom-dee-ay!

All my love to you my little love.
Ivor

71 School Road,
Stretford.

My love,
I have been over the house in Edge Lane near Langford Park and I think it is just what we want.
There is;
1 sitting room. Large
1 kitchen, with hot water, oven and store.
1 large scully with fine deep sink and gas store, cupboards, etc.
3 bedrooms.
1 good large and clean bathroom
(about 12'x 9' with bath, washbasin and lav)

Many cupboards and wardrobes.
The house is very clean. (Not detached) The wallpaper is quite good taste and clean. A front garden with path leading up to house with trees. Set very well back from road. Outside back door coal shed, etc, little yard and a good garden! with lawn. Next door to the Park and about 5 mins from Railway for City.
£40 p.a. rent = 15/4d per week.
Cheap!
I will make enquiries about rates but they won't be huge and I could ride to work (10 mins bike. 20 mins walk). Although you'd hardly realise you were in Stretford. The fogs are very very bad and cold.
Now do you want to come up to see it? It would save a £1 railway fare if you came up, as it were, for good. Will you trust to my judgement? The home is such that we should not use two or three rooms, so don't be frightened at 3 bedrooms.
Really darling I think you will like it. It is quiet and surrounded by trees. There is a drainpipe up the front – wish that weren't there.
I don't want to lose this like I did the flat so shall I take it you trust my judgement? I do hope this reaches you.
All my love to you. We will live in that house darling. Let me know by return whether you will come up or not.
The bathroom is so big.
You will look beautiful in that bath.

All my love
Ivor

My darling little love, are you sure you have on your marriage certificate the same information as I have on mine? Otherwise marriage impossible till they are standardised. Make sure about this love.

On December 10th 1936, Ivor Hickman and Juliet MacArthur were married in the district of Barton-on-Irwell, then in the Borough of Eccles, but today subsumed into the City of Salford, Greater Manchester.

Ivor Hickman: A photograph believed by Juliet daughters to have been taken after their mother's marriage to Ivor in 1936,and possibly during their honeymoon. The location of the photograph is unidentified however.(Courtesy: Sarah Rhodes & Janie Shepherd)

Juliet Hickman: According to her daughters, a photograph of Juliet taken after her marriage to Ivor. The architecture resembles that of Edge Lane, Stretford, adjacent to Longford Park that is mentioned in Ivor's letter. (Courtesy: Sarah Rhodes & Janie Shepherd)

4

A Noble Cause

The Spanish Civil War began on July 17th, 1936, and by the beginning of November the first of the foreign volunteers had marched into Madrid to help shore up the city's defences against Franco's advancing Nationalists.

In the first few months of the war volunteers had a relatively simple journey into Spain. In my interview with him, the late Sam Lesser recalled,

> It must have been the end of September or the beginning of October [1936] when I arrived in Paris. I went to the French Communist Party and they told me where to go to get a hotel. Later we were told to go to the Gare de Lyon to get the train. We were told strictly that it was all hush-hush "You mustn't tell anyone." When I got to the Gare de Lyon there were large numbers of people there and you'd have to be deaf, dumb, blind and silly not to realise that these were people planning on going to Spain. As we pulled out, I'll always remember this, you had people working along the line there, railway workers, who put up a clenched fist and shouted "Des avion pour Espagne"; Planes for Spain. So we went down to Perpignan and were taken to a place which was a sort of hospital where we were put up. After a few days we were told, "You are going to be loaded up into buses and coaches to take you across." Again it was all very hush-hush. We were told that if the police stopped the buses and asked where we going, we were to answer that we were Spanish workers working in France and that we were going home on holiday. Nobody stopped us but it was it was to the extent of each of us being given a Spanish name. Mine was Raymondo Cassado. So all in all I had quite an easy passage sitting in a bus. We were put up in this castle in Figueras and then moved to Albacete and

the headquarters of the International Brigade.

At this time, the British government had declared itself neutral; although certain factions felt that Britain's best interests would be served by a Franco victory. The Foreign Secretary, Anthony Eden (Later to be Prime Minister 1955-1957) publicly toed the government line of neutrality but privately expressed his preference for a Nationalist victory. The Anglo-French arms embargo left the Republicans with only two sources of weapons, Russia and Mexico while the Nationalists received war materials from Germany and Italy. Britain did supply food and medicine to the Republicans but actively discouraged its citizens from being involved. The Non-Intervention Committee was set up with the principle of preventing personnel and materials from reaching Spain. The agreement had been proposed by the British and French governments in a joint diplomatic initiative in 1936 and was aimed to prevent a proxy war. The Committee first met in London on September 9th, 1936. Representatives of all European countries except Switzerland attended. As Sam Lesser stated,

> At the time it was an open secret that Hitler and Mussolini were already sending large quantities of people and arms to Spain. The French closed the frontier and the only way to get to Spain was across the Pyrenées with the aid of smugglers' paths and local guides.

Just how much of an open secret it was, Sam discovered upon entering France and an encounter with French customs officials,

> There were already rumours going round, or actual reports, that the Fascists were already using gas. And so these mates of mine, old Bill Gale, clubbed together to get me a good gas mask. They decided no messing about, and went to the Army and Navy store in Victoria Street and bought an officer's gas mask. I had a rucksack and put it in. Now I thought, there are going to be some difficulties with the French customs on the way in, Newhaven–Dieppe I think it was. Well like today, they didn't check every bag that went across. You went through the customs and opened your rucksack and there was my gas mask. Deliberately as I didn't want them to start looking underneath so I put the gas mask on top clear to see. They said, "What's that?" "Gas mask," I shrugged, "I'm going to Spain." "Why do you need that?" "Well," I said, "They might sort of start using gas." So this fellow, he calls over his chief. I spoke quite a bit of French then. And this fellow looked at it, turned to his mate who'd discovered the thing and said, "Les Anglaise…fou!"

That's French for crackers. Well, it wasn't long I discovered that this
mask was a bit of trouble. It was very useful to put sandwiches in.

Despite the apparent lack of secrecy, for later volunteers like Ivor the journey into Spain would clearly involve more than a simple bus ride. Londoner George Wheeler left for Spain in the spring of 1938, a few months later than Ivor but his experiences of the crossing of the Pyrenées must have been similar. In his book *To Make the People Smile Again* (2003), George describes his journey. Along with a coach load of other volunteers from all over Europe, he arrived in Perpignan as night was beginning to fall and was led to a farmhouse. Upon arrival George was surprised to discover more than fifty volunteers were there already. A speech was delivered by one of the organisers of the trip and after eating they were informed that they would be led across the Pyrenées into Spain by local guides. The volunteers were each given a pair of *alpargatas*, traditional Spanish rope soled sandals which were especially useful in the precarious mountains. They then left to begin the long trek across the frontier. Keeping low to avoid frontier guards and in total silence, they made their way through the back ways and along railway tracks. Arriving at the foot of the mountains the volunteers put on their *alpargatas* and began the climb.

> And so we began the long and hazardous climb over the Pyrenées; hazardous because in order to evade the non-intervention patrols, we were unable to use the regular paths. Indeed at times we formed a human chain to negotiate particular rough passages. But it was a marvellous night and, being young and fit, I really enjoyed the climb. (Wheeler: 42)

Eventually, with the scent of the pine trees in the dawn air, the volunteers reached the summit. The views were spectacular as mountain mists formed around the rocky crags. However, of the fifty men who had started the climb, four were now in a state of exhaustion and had to be carried. The descent was far easier and brisk progress was made. Finally they arrived at a Republican army outpost and were given a warm welcome by the soldiers. An officer informed them that transport had been arranged to take them to Figueras and the International Brigades. George describes his feelings upon arrival. "With my back against an olive tree and the Pyrenées in the near distance, I am not ashamed to say I felt just a little homesick." (Wheeler: 45)

There are no records as to what if any trigger prompted Ivor to undertake the journey to Spain but his intense political belief, apparent in many of his letters, obviously fuelled his desire to join what he saw as the universal fight against fascism. He was leaving his new wife and a promising future in England for idealism and uncertainty in Spain. Together with Juliet, he journeyed to Paris in October and, after saying his farewells to his beloved wife, travelled to Spain by boat arriving on October 10th 1937. Fred Thomas, later of the Anti-Tank Battery, undertook what must have been a similar journey to Ivor in mid-May 1937. He describes the voyage thus,

> …we made our way to the harbour and were guided to an alarmingly small fishing boat. As our feet hit the deck we were at once whisked below to an evil smelling hold. When our dozen or so were on board the hatch went down and there we were, in complete darkness and ordered to speak only in whispers. (1996: 12)

For Ivor, a sea journey of noxious smells must have brought back memories of his time aboard Our Katie in August 1936, while staying at Bennetts' Farm in Zennor. Fred Thomas continues the description of his voyage to Spain.

> And so began what for some of us was nineteen hours of misery and all for all of us a journey into a new world. The sea was choppy, the boat small and built to carry fish, not people. The hold stank and was airless. But as soon as it was considered safe we were allowed on deck [...] Several were ill for much of the time we were on board, but I was lucky, only occasionally feeling a bit squeamish.
>
> They gave us plenty of strong black coffee with hard, coarse bread and much harder dried fish. We saw few other craft though once we were sent scuttling below when it was thought a warship of one of the Non-intervention nations was sighted. All such boats had the power, self-awarded, to stop, search, and arrest such as we. To general relief it was a false alarm. At length, land ahead! Spain was in sight and a green and pleasant land it looked to us. (13)

Within days of arriving in Spain Ivor was writing to Juliet;

My Dearest Love,
I think the day is Thursday, about 0830 I'm not quite sure. The day will not matter for the next six months so that I am not bothering. Anyway, I will not tell you my address because we are not yet at our final training ground, so that it would be useless as well as liable to censorship. At least I am in Spain. A very nice hotel, good meals in France and a good sleep. Then a longish journey to the sea – the

blue Mediterranean and it was blue too. I saw for the first time the boats used in that sea that have lateen rigs, so: and the rowing boats – dory's – as we have seen in Van Gogh's painting, remember? Drawings of boats.

But I'm sorry that I have not wished that your journey back was interesting and not too sad and that you are settling down at the Basque Camp or somewhere and not missed me too much. As you can well guess my bed is terribly empty and I do miss you terribly, not only at night but also like hell to talk to and do things with. I wish you were with us – of course impossible – because you would have enjoyed the walks immensely and the dawns and the climate. But to continue – no I won't – not yet – before I remind you that I love you immensely and that I feel a bit miserable even when I think of my loss of you. Still, wait until I return to you!

A comrade has just come up to me and told me that the above will be censored – that is, not the bit to you. At any rate if they use ink and don't destroy the whole sheet it won't matter. Except that it has rather put me out of my stride. Of course politics wouldn't be censored but you don't want to hear too much of that, do you? You can get most of that in The Worker – more general politics I suppose, than I shall know. I am writing this in a reading room. There are a few newspapers on a blackboard but otherwise nothing to read, except what's on the walls. Of course I can only read a little of that because of the many tongues it is written in. At the head, the Soviet Five Pointed Star and of course 'Proletarios de Todas Paises! Unios!'. Then paintings of Marx, Engels, Lenin and Stalin so weiter. And paintings of Spanish leading men, an immense military map, showing the front. Then "Camarades François le Battalion Andree Marthy – " then Polish, then "Guarda't dels marls ventris com les bades!" or in German "Juelet euch vot Geschlechtktahnk – heiten wie vor scharfen schuessan." And in English, French and Italian. Then a map of Europe showing the political state of affairs and finally four military diagrams – c'est bon – c'est mal, tables and a light. The hammer and sickle is everywhere. What is fine to see is the Comrade Commandant wearing a hammer and sickle on his lapels!

The climate and the scenery is beautiful. I lay today in the hot sun – and I'm in the north of Spain still. As hot as an English summer sun and the sky the richest blue and no cloud. Of course you remember the Menai Straits – the colours seem always as rich as they were that day we spent together there.

The beautiful stone the building I'm in is made of and the richness of the whole scene. This morning at about six o'clock went out into the middle of the ground to the pump, stripped and had a beautiful cold shower in the sun, there were no women, nor Spanish soldiers, only a friend of mine, it was marvellous a shower in the sun! I only wish you were there to have a shower with me in that sun.

Monday night 18th Oct 1937
Well, at last we have arrived at our final training camp in a beautiful village – and I am officially allowed to write to you.
Let me warn you my dearest love that the post office is at the moment in a process of re-organisation and so you may not receive letters regularly from me. I will – as well as I can – try to let you have letters regularly.

My address is;
S.R.I. NO. 270
Plaza De Altazone
Albacete
España

The people here will know my movements etc. I do hope mother has taken the news not too badly and that the house is let – or nearly – and you've a job and are happy. Do write to me immediately you get this letter. A letter will take I suppose three weeks to get to me, but oh boy! Won't I devour it when it arrives.
Now I will close and will write to you tomorrow or next day. All my love to you my sweetheart – and may you be very happy at home. Don't send me anything in parcel form darling – only in letters. I'm sorry about this letter but we must be in by 9 and it is 8.50 now and I must post this, all my love to you as ever

Ivor.
I will write a better letter later – Love.

By the time that Ivor arrived in Spain, British volunteers had already been involved in most of the major actions since November 1936, and had suffered many significant losses before the official formation of the British Battalion in early 1937. From the barricades of Madrid to the chaos of Jarama, the Brigade had become the 'shock' troops of the Republic: the first ones on the battlefield and the last to leave.

5

The Birth of the British Battalion

British volunteers had been involved in the war for nearly twelve months when Ivor finally arrived. One of the first to arrive in Spain had been the sculptor and artist, Felicia Browne. Born at Weston Green, Thames Ditton in Surrey on February 18th, 1904, to a well off London family with 'progressive views', Browne studied at both St John's Wood School of Art and Slade School of Art. An active member of the Communist party and a member of the Artists' International Association (AIA), in essence a left of centre political association which embraced all styles of both modernist and traditional art. By the mid-1930s the AIA was becoming a significant force in left-wing politics. The AIA held a series of group exhibitions on political and social themes including, in 1935, an exhibition entitled *Artists Against Fascism and War* in Soho Square. However, there is little record of Browne's personal role in the exhibition. During the summer of 1936, Brown was on a driving holiday to France and Spain with her friend the left wing photographer, Edith Bone. Originally the intention of the trip had been to attend the People's Olympiad to be held in Barcelona. However, their arrival coincided with the violence that engulfed the city in the aftermath of the military uprising against the Republic. Browne immediately joined a communist militia group on August 3rd. On or around August 25th, she was part of a band of ten raiders that attempted to dynamite a Fascist munitions train near Tardienta in Aragon. Browne and two others were left as lookouts while the rest of the patrol set the explosives and waited for the train to pass. On their return, the group passed the dead body of a Republican airman, and soon afterwards they spotted a dog nearby. One of the group was sent to investigate and soon spotted a group of thirty-five to forty Nationalist troops around fifteen metres away. The Fascists opened fire hitting an Italian member of the militia in the foot. While attempting to bring first aid to the wounded comrade Browne was shot several times in the chest and back and instantly sank dead to the ground. She was the first British volunteer to be killed in Spain.

John Cornford arrived in Spain with his friend and fellow Trinity College student, Richard Bennett shortly before Britain's arms embargo to Spain. He briefly fought with the POUM militia units (POUM being the *Partido Obrero de Unificación Marxista* or, in English, The Workers' Party of Marxist Unification) on the Aragon front before returning to Britain to help raise more volunteers. Other volunteers to arrive were almost immediately called into action. Nat Cohen, Sam Masters, Richard Kisch, Tony Willis and Paul Boyle participated in a failed raid on Mallorca in which Kisch was badly wounded. The surviving group, led by Cohen, returned to Barcelona and became the Tom Mann Centuria. A short while later the Centuria was joined by David Marshall and Keith Scott Watson (later of *The Daily Express*). Further volunteers included Tom Wintringham (later commander of the British Battalion) and Phil Gillan. Towards the end of October, the Centuria became attached to the mainly German Thaelmann Battalion and were transferred to the base of the International Brigades in Albacete. By November, the British group were involved in a number of small skirmishes to the south of Madrid. During one attack on Cerro de los Angeles, a hill to the south of Madrid, David Marshall was badly wounded. A short while later he was repatriated back to Britain.

In the weeks before Christmas, the group were transferred to the village of Boadilla del Monte to the west of Madrid. In the chaos and confusion of the Republican retreat, the group became separated from their Spanish comrades and came under intense machine gun fire from a ridge that had, moments before, been occupied by the Republican forces. Attempting to retreat, they were caught in a fierce crossfire from both the enemy forces and troops of their own side. Seven of the British volunteers were killed.[1]

British members of the French Commune de Paris Battalion including Jock Cunningham and H. Fred Jones had also been suffering heavy losses as part of the XI International Brigade. During early November, the British volunteers were involved in the defence of the Madrid in the Casa de Campo – a former royal hunting ground to the west – and in the nearby university.

In interview, not long before his death, Sam Lesser, a British volunteer who was then in the Commune de Paris Battalion, recalled the intense fighting that took place in Madrid,

> We were out in the open between the Philosophy and Letters Faculty and the Hospital Clinical. At one stage the Moors had

Members of the British Tom Mann Unit (September 1936). L to R: Sid Avner, Nat Cohen, Ramona Cohen, Tom Wintringham, George Tioli, Jack Barry and David Marshall. (IBMT)

got into the hospital and then we had to withdraw back into the building into the Philosophy Faculty. The University City was in course of completion; there was quite a range of new buildings there. There was one notable Spanish millionaire, supporter of Franco of course, who had given enormous sums of money for this university. Right down to the toilets, it was like a posh hotel, including bidets. This was a problem of its own as most of our chaps hadn't seen a bidet before and started shitting in them. There were some Cambridge students who hadn't seen a bidet before. I had. Not that I'm particularly cultured or anything. It started and you were allocated to certain places. Then one of the first things we had to do, in order to get any sighting was to knock holes in the walls of these brand new buildings. Our first experience there was done in a little crowded sort of place in the Philosophy and Letters Faculty. Some chaps went looking around and came across the library. The books were very useful, the bigger ones, volume wise; when you make a hole in the wall and you find one of the hole's a bit too big so you get something to block it out. The books came in useful there. We were all set up when I found some posters. I always remember those posters; there were two, touristy sort of posters. There was one, a thing with a bull on it. I remember the slogan, *Spain. The comfort of the East with the charm of the West*. And the other one was with a bull, *The sun is waiting for you in Spain*.

We were in this lecture room and on the sort of lectern were stuck up these two posters. The others were disposing of their books that they'd collected. There were some they were going to read. One bloke came across an old collection of *Everyman* books in English, a great find. Suddenly there was a boom. A bloody enormous explosion. We couldn't see. Shit falling on you from the ceiling. I looked around and when the dust settled I could see John Cornford with blood pouring out of his head. I think there was always an argument as to whether it was of the enemy artillery or, as others said, one of our own anti-aircraft shells that had fallen short. What's called nowadays 'friendly fire'. So John is taken away. "Poor old John, that's the last we'll see of him." So we all clear up the mess and sort of settle down again and after a bit John turns up, head bandaged up all over looking most Byronesque and heroic. Apparently he was lucky; it was just a bit of shrapnel. Scalp wounds bleed a lot you know, especially if it just skims your head. There's a lot of blood up there. So anyhow he wasn't going to go away. Somebody said "No you must be taken to hospital." No he wouldn't so we carried on. Anyhow we were in and out those buildings, up and down the bloody stairs. My O.T.C. experience did not include fighting in buildings. It was out in the open. We were in and out those buildings and moving around trying to hold that sector. (Lesser: 2005)

During their desperate defence many of the British group were killed including the leader, H. Fred Jones.

Sam Lesser poignantly recalled Jones' death also,

One night we were ordered to move. We were to be moved to another sector. It was dark and we were told "No smoking. No talking. Be as quiet as you can." We were going along a road and Freddie Jones was the chap who was in front walking along when suddenly someone said "There's something behind us." I looked back and it seemed to be a lorry or truck coming along. We were told no lights or anything but this thing was flashing its lights. The first thing we did was to separate on either side of the road. Suddenly this bloody thing accelerated and drove straight through us. There was a great deal of confusion. We pulled ourselves together and looked around. "Where's Freddie?" Freddie had vanished. Anyhow we continued on and arrived at our rendezvous point and by which time its dawn and coffee had been produced.

I, along with two others, was sent back to find where Freddie was. I came across Freddie. What had happened was that near the front there was a lot of telephone wires around, all lying around. This lorry when it accelerated picked up a lot of these wires on the front mudguard such that they were fully extended and then snapped. The wire had flown and curled around and got Freddie round the neck and actually tore his head off. I saw his body lying there and a few yards along there was his head. Well, we had a lot of losses there one way or another. By the December the order came and we were moved back to Albacete for reorganisation. Of that thirty-three or so only six of us were left. (2005)

By November 23rd the Nationalists realised that, although they had captured approximately two thirds of the area of University City, the Republican forces were now well established and rather more organised than they had expected. The direct frontal attack on Madrid had failed. Reluctantly General Mola called off the attack.

By the end of the battle for Madrid, volunteers from Britain were arriving in such numbers that it was now a realistic possibility to establish a British Battalion. The first steps came in December with the creation of the English speaking company within the XIV International Brigade. 145 British volunteers comprised the No. 1 Company of the French XIV (La Marseillaise) Battalion. On Christmas Eve they were involved in an attempt to capture the town of Lopera in the south. Although the company had among it veterans of previous engagements, many were inexperienced and the company was beaten back by the better armed and better trained Nationalist forces. Again Sam Lesser tells of the carnage,

It was during that battle at Lopera, that we had a hell of a business. Maybe we advanced; at least we thought we were advancing as we were told to advance. We soon became aware that we were under fire from our own side. By that time the Number One English Company was not just an ordinary rifle company. The Machine-Gun Company in that Battalion was a completely French one, and we realised, at least I realised, that we were coming under fire from our own French Machine-Gun Company. Well there was nothing we could do about that. That was one of the other problems, communication. We started getting field telephones but it was very difficult so you had to rely on runners and runners tend to get killed. So we then had to retreat and I was wounded then. John Cornford, who was not more than a hundred yards from me, was killed. Ralph Fox was killed in that same battle. Jock Cunningham realised that I was missing. He came over. I was by then in no-man's land and if he hadn't dragged me out I would have been dead.

One of things that we discovered was the Fascists, particularly the Moors, were killing the wounded. There was no proper medical service and I, with Jock's help, was crawling on my hands and knees until I collapsed. He couldn't find a stretcher anywhere. The first words I heard in the night, laying there, were French. After dragging me, Jock was pretty much exhausted physically by then. What with me and Madrid, he'd had a rough time, as had we all. He finally got me a stretcher and I was taken away. Inevitably there were quite a number of walking wounded but I had a thing in my leg and also one across my back. I didn't realise how close it was. I think it must have been a sort of farewell gift from the French Machine-Gun Company. There were some dung carts with mules and we were put in there until we finally got to a point were we were transferred. There were still no ambulances, but open trucks. (2005)

After the failure to capture Lopera in January 1937, the survivors of No.1 Company were transferred back to Madrid where they attempted to recapture the Madrid-La Corunna road at Las Rozas. For the poorly trained and badly armed volunteers, it was an impossible task and as the casualties mounted, they were withdrawn and sent to Madrigueras, near Albacete. Here they joined up with the recent influx of volunteers from Britain and Ireland. By this time the number of volunteers had risen to around 450, Battalion strength. However, many of the Irish volunteers, many with IRA backgrounds, were unhappy at the prospect of taking orders from ex-members of the British army. As a result many elected to fight alongside the American volunteers. The remaining Brigaders were formed into the British Battalion briefly to be commanded by Wilf McCartney.[2] McCartney was replaced in February by Tom Wintringham with George Aitken as Battalion commissar.

The British Battalion was transferred on February 9th to Chinchon, twenty-four kilometres to the south of Madrid. Here the 500 Brigaders would face Franco's crack troops, the Moorish *Regulares* in an attempt to prevent the Nationalists from cutting off the crucial road between Madrid and Valencia. On the morning of February 12th, alongside other members of the XV Brigade, the British Battalion were moved up to the heights overlooking the Jarama River at Arganda. Once again the lack of training and equipment were soon apparent and the casualties rose at an alarming rate. The Machine-Gun Company had been issued with the wrong type of ammunition for their Maxim machine guns. The lorry carrying the correct ammunition belts was overturned and wrecked while on its way up to the company by a drunken British Battalion driver. The ammunition boxes were recovered and finally carried up to the position where the guns were emplaced but further delays were encountered as instead of using the customary machines to load the belts, the ammunition had to be loaded by hand. The beleaguered volunteers had little choice but to pull back to the Battalion headquarters on the plateau behind them. Once the Machine-Gun Company had finally managed to load its Maxims, the Nationalist onslaught was repelled. The cost to the Battalion was heavy. Less than half the men who left Madrigueras were left standing. In his memoir *Crusade in Spain*, Jason Gurney talks of the horrors of the first day of Jarama,

> The absolute crescendo of violence, fear and excitement as our three infantry companies had been pounded to pieces on the Casa Blanca and its attendant hill. But I had finally grown up into the reality of war only when I stood amongst that ghastly collection of dead and irretrievably mutilated men left behind in the retreat. This was the reality, not fear or excitement or drama, just pure horror and the knowledge that I was utterly powerless to do anything about it. Finally I slept the sleep of pure exhaustion. (116)

The morning of the 13th, would prove no easier. Desperate to hold onto their flank, the commander of No.4 Company pulled his soldiers back leaving the Machine-Gun Company sited on a knoll to the Battalion's right, which became isolated and was surrounded. Despite several lives being lost in an ill-judged attempt to rescue them, the company commander, Harold Fry and adjutant Ted Dickenson were captured alongside over thirty men. Miraculously, the remaining men in the Battalion held on until nightfall. Jason Gurney would later describe the 13th February 1937, as "the worst day of my life." (1976: 124) Day three began with a sustained attack from hugely superior Nationalist forces supported by artillery and tanks. Finally the line broke and the disorganised and exhausted troops drifted back to the cookhouse. Here they were addressed by Lieutenant-Colonel Gal, the commander of the XV Brigade. He explained that they were now the only troops between the Nationalists and the Valencia Road. Rallied by George Aitken and Frank Ryan, the one hundred and forty mentally and physically exhausted volunteers marched back to try to recapture their lost positions. The Nationalists were fooled. They believed the Brigaders to be fresh reinforcements and retreated back to their earlier positions. Over the following two nights, Republican units were brought up and the gap in the line was plugged. With defensive fortifications dug, a stalemate which neither side could break ensued and the line remained static for the rest of the war.

The next major challenge for the British Battalion began in July 1937. Now led by Fred Copeman, they were thrown into battle as part of a major Republican offensive designed to relieve the pressure on the northern front and break through the Nationalists at their weakest point to the west of Madrid. The British Battalion moved towards the heavily defended village of Villanueva de la Canada on July 6th. Short of water, they were pinned down by well-directed machine gun fire and forced to take cover in temperatures of over 40 degrees centigrade and await nightfall. Finally at midnight, the village was captured. Again the Brigaders paid a high cost as a number of volunteers were killed when Nationalist soldiers attempted to escape by using civilians as human shields. The Battalion's major objective, the heights overlooking the Guadarrama River, and the village of Boadilla del Monte, were reached the following morning almost a day behind schedule. The British members of the Thaelmann and Commune de Paris Battalions had fought on this ground six months earlier. Again thirst and fatigue alongside the constant bombardment from the air took their toll and the Battalion was unable to advance rapidly to capture the unoccupied heights before the Nationalists quickly took advantage and moved into the position themselves. At the beginning of Boadilla, the Battalion could boast three hundred and thirty one volunteers. At the end only forty two remained.

In an attempt aimed at capturing Saragossa, and diverting Franco's attention from the northern front, as part of the 35th Division, the British Battalion was transferred to the Aragon front. Guernica had been bombed on April 26th and Bilbao had fallen and Santander was increasingly under threat from the Nationalists. On August 24th the Battalion helped capture the town of Quinto but in doing so suffered significant losses including the death of its commander, Peter Daley, and the wounding of Tom Wintringham, the veteran of Jarama. Wintringham was later repatriated to England. The fighting continued at Belchite and Mediana but despite the Battalion's progress, Saragossa stubbornly remained in Nationalist hands. In a frequently repeated pattern, the Republican offensive ground to a halt.

The next stage of the campaign was the over-ambitious plan to capture the Fuentes de Ebro, a town within sight of Saragossa. It was here on October 13th that the Battalion lost another commander, Harry Fry who was temporarily replacing Paddy O'Daire while he was away on officer training. After failed attempts to carry troops on tanks, the depleted Battalion was withdrawn for two months rest. However, on December 31st 1937, the International Brigade was rushed to the front to help the Republican forces defending against a counter attack by the Nationalists at the recently captured Teruel. Struggling through the bitter snow and despite a Nationalist artillery bombardment, the British Battalion moved into a frontline position on January 17th 1938. Holding their ground, they successfully brought a halt to the counter-attack. Although the Battalion and its commander, Bill Alexander and political commissar, Walter Tapsell were commended, the cost was high. Twenty-one British volunteers had been killed in this one action. Once more the depleted Battalion was withdrawn for a short-lived rest and recuperation before being recalled to the line as the Nationalist counter-attack gained ground. On February 16th, sixty-four kilometres north of Teruel, the Battalion advanced on Segura de los Banos, their aim a diversionary attack to draw the Nationalist's attention away from the city. Although initially successful, the Nationalist's superior numbers began to tell and the Battalion was forced back. Bill Alexander injured his shoulder and was replaced by Sam Wild. Teruel fell to the Nationalists soon after.

On March 9th, Franco launched an attack on the Republican forces in Aragon. This massive and well-planned attack began swiftly and the weary Republicans, their lines virtually collapsed, were forced to retreat. The British Battalion were forced into making a fighting retreat through Belchite, Lecera, Vinaceite and Caspe, the latter surrendering on March 17th. Finally the Battalion reached Batea. By this time Republican reinforcements had been brought up and the Nationalists were halted due to lack of supplies. The Nationalists launched a second offensive on March 30th however, towards the Mediterranean coast. Disaster befell the Battalion as they were marching from Corbera towards Calaceite. Mistaking Italian tanks for friendly forces, the Battalion was ambushed and the Attlee Company was forced to surrender. To compound this loss, the Battalion commissar, Walter Tapsell was shot and killed as he tried to approach an Italian tank to convince the driver that they were on the same side. Temporary commander George Fletcher was badly injured and the eighty volunteers left of the Battalion retreated to Gandesa. At the beginning of April and after delaying the Nationalists as best they could, the survivors of the Battalion retreated back over the River Ebro at

Cherta. The Nationalist advance was finally stemmed when the bridges across the river were blown. Tragically many Republican soldiers were trapped on the 'wrong side' and many were either captured or drowned trying to swim the fast-flowing and wide river.

The flow of volunteers from Britain had begun in July and August 1936, with the arrival of Felicia Brown, John Cornford and their comrades, but the highest influx came in December 1936 and January 1937 when just under four hundred volunteers arrived in Spain. Approximately four hundred more arrived in the following eight months between February and September 1937. In October 1937, around seventy-five British volunteers arrived. Ivor Hickman was one of them. (Baxell, 2007: 20)

6

One in Seventy-Five

Albacete is a city in south-eastern Spain, 258 km south east of Madrid in the autonomous community of Castilla-La Mancha. In the Spanish Civil War it became the headquarters and training base of the International Brigades. In command of the base was the controversial figure of André Marty. Born in Perpignan, France, on November 6th, 1886, into a left-leaning family, Marty had tried to win a place in open competition for the prestigious École Navale but failed and instead took an apprenticeship as a boiler maker. Later he joined the French navy and served on the battleship Jean Bart as a mechanical engineering officer. In April 1919, the Jean Bart with Marty on board was sent to aid the White Russians in the Russian Civil War. However, the crew's sympathies lay with the Reds and not with the Whites and on April 19th; the crew mutinied; their main grievances being the slow rate of demobilisation following the end of the Great War, and the atrocious quality and small quantity of the rations. Although the French government acceded to their demands, the ringleaders were pursued and arrested. Although Marty's role in the mutiny is unclear, he was arrested, tried and sentenced to twenty years of hard labour. This notoriety elevated Marty's reputation with the left and he was symbolically elected to the Soviet of Moscow by the workers of the Dynamo factory. In 1923, he was pardoned and released from prison. He immediately joined the Communist Party. His alleged role in the Black Sea Mutiny enhanced his reputation in France also, and in 1924 he was elected to the French National Assembly for the constituency of Seine-et-Oise. In 1931, he became active in the Comintern and by 1936 had been elected to both its Praesidium (executive council) and Secretariat (administration).

At the outbreak of the Spanish Civil War, André Marty had been sent to Spain to represent Comintern interests and by October, he was appointed Political Commissar of the newly formed International Brigades at Albacete.

Always courting controversy, Marty was a strict disciplinarian. He was not adverse to executing men who he felt had lost resolve or lacked ideological soundness. In addition, he was an individual who appeared to suffer from a form of chronic paranoia, seeing traitors and spies everywhere. In *Crusade in Spain*, Jason Gurney describes Marty.

> He may have been a great chap in his day, but in Spain he was both a sinister and a ludicrous figure. He was a large, fat man with a bushy moustache and always wore a huge, black beret – looking like a caricature of an old-fashioned French petty bourgeois. There is no doubt he was quite literally mad at this time. He always spoke in a hysterical roar, he suspected everyone of treason, or worse, listened to advice from nobody, ordered executions on little or no pretext – in short he was a real menace. (54)

These qualities earned Marty the nickname of the "Butcher of Albacete." In *For Whom the Bell Tolls*, Ernest Hemingway's novel set amidst the mayhem of the Spanish Civil War, the author has Marty make a brief appearance in Chapter 42. Ultimately Hemingway depicts Marty as a vicious and paranoid intriguer whose obsessions interfered with the Republican objectives in the war and the record shows that this was thought to be true, at least to the extent that in a report in November 1937, fellow Comintern member and head of the Italian Communist Party, Palmiro Togliatti, insisted that Marty radically change his work methods and to stop his interfering in the military and technical matters affecting the Brigades. While mostly in agreement with these assessments of Marty, former volunteer Bill Alexander writes in his book *British Volunteers for Liberty*,

> Marty is remembered for his drive, determination and single-mindedness as one of a leading group – which included Luigi Longo ('Gallo'), Hans Kahle, Karol Swierczewski ('Walter') – who were required to turn a collection of individuals into a military unit, or units, within days. British volunteers who worked with Marty at the base found him irascible, suspicious, unpredictable and a little nationalistic, but paid tribute to his drive and determination. The British who met him at the front at Gandesa and Mora, organising the retreat from Catalonia, were greatly impressed by his courage. (27)

It was at Albacete, under the increasingly paranoid rule of Marty, that the volunteers from all over the world would be processed and divided up into nationalities. The English-speaking volunteers were then transferred to their base at Tarazona de la Mancha to begin their training.

The majority of the British volunteers had little, if any, military experience however, and the training they were about to receive was fairly rudimentary to say the least. Indeed, the apparent lack of military experience and training was the first of a great many many problems faced by the Battalion. In interview, Sam Lesser described the situation thus,

> From the beginning, an extra problem with the British in Spain was that unlike people from other nationalities, there was no compulsory military service in Britain. You were called up at the age of eighteen in Germany, France, Italy, yet in England there was no conscription. I was one of the few out there with any military knowledge. There were quite a number who had been regular soldiers. Large parts of the recruitment into the British Army, at that time, were people who were unemployed. We had three or four people who had been in Scottish regiments, Jock Cunningham, who became a great friend of mine. He saved my life later on in a big battle. He'd been in the Argyll and Sutherland Highlanders. There was Nobby Clarke who was in the Argyll and Sutherland Highlanders as well. Then there was a chap Freddie Jones who had been in the Coldstream Guards. There were various people, Joe Hinks; he was another one who had been in one of the Guards. So there were quite a number of other people who had military experience or military knowledge.

As he went on to state,

> We started training and very soon discovered there was a lack of weapons too. When the rifles finally did turn up they were vintage Austrian rifles from the 1870's. There were cases, wood cases, with rifles in that were covered in grease like any machine to stop it rusting. You had to start cleaning them up with lots of boiling water. We finally got them cleaned up but then the next problem was the ammunition. As they'd been lying around for all those years, the copper had sort of started going *verdigre*. The result was the actual point of the bullet and the cartridge case was loose. What would happen was you'd put the thing in, cock the rifle and fire. The charge was sufficient to send it up the barrel but it would jam there or even worse as sometimes the bloody thing would explode in the barrel, which was a nasty thing. So it meant you had to go through every cartridge. What it was going to

be like in action, Christ knows!

According to Lesser, even after the Battalion was finally equipped with better and more modern weaponry, the problems still persisted.

> We were issued with these Russian machine guns, which were the Maxims [7.62mm Pulemyot Maxima]. The basic thing was the same except that the Russian gun was water-cooled and was mounted on a two-wheeled gadget thing. I had seen them on Soviet films and they looked a great thing. However, it was very heavy [72kg]. On an old Vickers machine gun you had two cocking handles, which meant you could rapidly dismount the gun from the tripod. One man would take the gun; the other the tripod on his shoulder. But with the Russian gun, the thing sort of slid onto this two-wheeled thing. Now, when it slid on, you had two grooved things and when you are trying to get the two grooves together you had to get it sort of lined up to slide it on, which when you're sort of shitting yourself because you're under fire isn't easy. Then if you think "I'll do it the way it's done on the films" then you don't dismount it and just pull it along. Well then you come to the first bump and you realise that if you're not careful you'll knock the bloody sights on the ground you see, because it'll tip over. You'd pull up one end to pull the thing along and the barrel starts knocking on the ground and bang! You have to take it apart. We had three on a machine gun team. We had a man firing, a man who was lying by the belt feeding the belt out of a sort of tin can, and another one there on the other side to sort of deal with this and that. Very soon we realised that when the thing got overheated, just pissing on it doesn't really make a lot of difference. It just makes an awful stink.

A typical day's training for the volunteers is illustrated in the Battalion orders that were issued on the January 20th, 1937. The day began at 8 o'clock with a Battalion parade before each section was assigned a duty. Section 4 was to carry out special instructions with Comrade Dickinson; Section 5 were under the command of Comrade Freedman and designated for fatigue duty; Section 6 were placed on guard duty while No.3 Company were placed on tactical operations consisting of a series of repeated manoeuvres. Finally the Machine-Gun Company was to undertake a route march. At 2 o'clock there was another parade followed by further drill for the Machine-Gun Company and a route march to Tarazona (misspelt as Tarragona) for Numbers 2 and 3 Company. Company Commanders were to report every evening at 8 o'clock to Headquarters. Practice manoeuvres often simply consisted of learning to advance over open country. The very idea of practicing any other would have been thought of as negative by the political commissars. Ideas such as the training in building fortifications and beating an organised retreat were ignored. In the event these would have been far more valuable skills for the volunteers and the decision brought disastrous results on the Battalion's first day of battle at Jarama. For Jason Gurney the whole experience was reminiscent of the O.T.C. of his youth with "rattles to simulate machine gun fire" . In many cases there were no firearms of any sort to practice with.

Some historians view the apparent lack of training as intrinsic to the International Brigades fighting methods. Many of the volunteers were veterans of street fights against fascist elements within their country and viewed the battlefield as an extension of this fight. One English volunteer baulked at the idea of military training stating that he had come to Spain to fight fascists and not to be made into a soldier. There was a commonly held assertion that the best training available was on the actual battlefield. The idea that battling strike-busting police or fascist demonstrators could be adequate preparation for what would confront a volunteer on the battlefield may seem a little odd, but it must be remembered that this was a volunteer army formed of idealism and political conviction. There was a feeling that the volunteers would lead by example and inspire others to follow in their footsteps in the fight against fascism. It could be seen that untrained troops led by a strong moral conviction would blindly and unquestioningly follow orders that trained experienced troops would question. In his book *Fallen Sparrows*, author Michael Jackson argues,

> In general, the men of the International Brigades knew as little about making war as they did about conjugating Spanish verbs. Ignorance made them as incandescent and extraordinary as a shooting star, possessed of neither origin nor destination. They were men literally prepared to stand up to machine gun fire, once...the International Brigaders did things no trained soldiers would have done. (1994: 102)

However, once on the battlefield the reality of the situation struck home as the Nationalist troops did not die easily. Esmond Romilly later reflected on his first day in battle, "I never took aim. I never looked up to see what I was firing at. I never heard the order to open fire. I never saw the enemy." (1937: 102) The level of training did vary from Battalion to Battalion but in essence this made little difference, for to the trained soldier having untrained comrades guarding your flanks was potentially lethal to both units.

In one of his first letters to Juliet from Spain, Ivor describes his daily life while training.

My dearest love,

Today is I believe Thursday October 21st or so. So that we have been doing 3 or 4 days training in all. I have very mixed feelings indeed about this training base and the instructions given here. But let me first outline my life here – about 12 Englishmen and 8 Spaniards sleep in the same large loft as I do. We sleep on the ground on palliases and are quite comfortable, except that it's damn cold sleeping alone at this time of year.

We are woken at 6, work in the yard behind the house, breakfast – coffee and bread – in the mess with the other companies. Then parade at 7.30 until 11.30, with a Spanish lesson in between. Then dinner – generally soup, and some odd sort of stew and bread and occasionally coarse Spanish red wine. Parade at two until 5.30. Supper at 5.30 – stew and perhaps some rice. Then free time until 9.0 when the outside doors are locked and we generally go to bed.

Oddly enough I am beginning to get involved in political rather than military work. Naturally the ground here is very ripe for political work. But I will tell you more of that when I am deeper in it.

As you would expect, the military aspect fascinates me. Naturally I am afraid of the idea of going to the front, but when I look round and see many of my comrades I am damned glad I've had the military experience and interest that I have had.

It is more or less impossible to foretell how individuals are going to shape, except that the more intelligence a man shows here the more intelligent he will be at the front and the more able to face it – (in general).

You could divide us into three categories; – the goods, those who are light hearted here in training and turn out OK at the front and the rats.

The casualties are going to lie chiefly in the middle group.

My mood fluctuates terribly. I really am very pessimistic about the military training and the military job we have to face. I can see nearly all of us being rather undisciplined here and neglecting to learn fundamental points of military technique. They simply won't face the fact that they will be dead if they don't learn here. I am sure that the mass of the men don't realise what they are in for. They believe that political morale is enough – is it hell! You never yet heard of political morale turning aside a bullet. Living here under these conditions and seeing the old Spain still going on around me, makes me realise the immense task the Soviet Union had to face and the terrific success they made of it. Living in England doesn't drive that home. But here I am slowly growing to understand the backwardness of nations and growing to appreciate the work of the U.S.S.R..

This Spain is really very inefficient, from an English standpoint. The Spanish conscripts who are training with us are fine fellows, but so damned inefficient. Some of them are extremely handsome in a good sense and they sing vigorously. But I'm damned if I would like to go into action with them, maybe they'll change before they go up – maybe not.

I am not looking forward at all to two months training here – I would sooner move up to the front very soon – but I don't suppose I will. I sent into the Base Commandant a note of my qualifications and he may transfer me to artillery or some damned thing. I hope he does from one point of view because as you know the infantry bear the brunt of this war and I have no desire to be killed. Things are better now than they have been, but even so Germany and Italy can't afford to lose and must win. Also I feel I ought to stop in the infantry – excuse the smugness – because my batch are as far as I can see none too sure of themselves and I may be able to help keep things up. But for all I know I may be a rat. What then?

Saturday

I am sorry I am neglecting you so badly with my letters but last night I met a young comrade training at an officers training school (he knew Winnick but did not like him!) and we talked of military tactics and so on. He said the standard of the Brigade was improving in leaps and bounds both politically and militarily – others say different.
Toddy I don't care either way. At any rate they are here. He tells me Cornford was killed in a genuine military action. He was ordering a retreat of three machine guns on the Cordova front and he stood up instead of lying down and directing from the ground. It seems a waste that he should have forgotten himself like that.
There are very many things I would like to tell you – and will tell you when I come home – about the Brigade. One odd fact that is interesting and perhaps unsuspected. Naturally everybody swears a lot but in general the interest is not sexual (in the sense male – female)

In the letter, Ivor makes mention of "Winnick." Wilfred Winnick was a comrade from Ivor's time in Manchester. Born on December 10th, 1907, in Stockport, Wilfred Winnick was a Jew, a member of the Communist Party of Great Britain and, as a tailor, a member of the National Union of Tailors and Garment Workers. He was also to subsequently become a member of the Spanish Communist Party too. In England, he had lived with his wife and two children at 8 Eastham Avenue, Fallowfield in Manchester. He arrived in Spain on May 13th, 1937 and joined the British Battalion. He fought at Quinto in August and at Belchite in September and was then posted to the XV Brigade Sanidad. His father appears to have been a man of reasonable influence as permission was granted for Winnick to return to England and attend a Jewish religious ceremony on one occasion. Although he was granted one month leave, Winnick declined to go however, and along with fellow Manchester volunteer, George Westfield, was assigned to the Brigades post office in January 1938. In March of the same year, while fighting with the Battalion at Caspe, Winnick was wounded though. After recovering from his wounds he returned to the front line and months later was again wounded during the Ebro campaign in August 1938. He returned to England in the December.

Training Base 31st October 1937

My dearest little love,

*"And we will Franco's ranks diminish,
The great Miaja leads us on,
Upon our rifles depend our freedom,
No Passaran! No Passaran!"* –

I am writing to you from the library and this portion of a song came up to me from the street below.
My "friend" John Smith from Iraq, Baghdad, is also writing a letter. He tells me today that I am his friend from now on, more than his comrade. "And 'my friend'," he says, "means that you must ask me for anything I have and I will give it to you – and you must ask without shyness." He is the most cultured man I know out here and he is always bemoaning the lack of culture among the comrades. He believes in Communism but also realises that it means a broadening and inferior culture, leading on later, to a cultural renaissance.
There seems no doubt that this life here is in very bad conditions and under circumstances of mental conflict there is the worst of a man to anybody who can see it. Yet it also develops many and improves them. We must expect difficulties when so many people from such varying social and economic backgrounds are joined together, each having slightly different conceptions of what they are, want to be, did want to do in Spain.
You'll be interested to know that I have been promoted to the rank of Sargeanto (Sergeant in English, although my duties are very different from an English Sergeant). Under me I have three Cabos (Corporals) and 12 comrades, that is 15 men. Now among these 15 men in my platoon (Peloton) are 4 ex-servicemen and 5 Spaniards. The Spaniards are difficult because of their language and also because of their lack of discipline. I realise why anarchism is so strong in Spain.
But the real difficulty with regard to my platoon is the ex-servicemen. One is a nuisance, and loudmouth; but not of sufficient character to trouble me. Another is an ex foreign legionnaire and a drunkard. The next is a tall ex-Sergeant of the Irish Guards and the fourth an ex-Sergeant of the Royal Artillery. This latter is of coarse material throughout, two faced, loud mouthed and without culture. Still ultimately, there is some hope for him, at any rate as an efficient anti-fascist soldier.
Now these men object to my being made Sergeant over them, none of them are politically conscious and ultimately they are only suitable for the imperial armies where they are kicked from one order to another. Fundamentally they still only understand the boot. At present one is in the jail for attempted desertion – or rather slipping off from parade without authority – the other for being drunk and breaking a C.B. order.
The third, the artillery man had a showdown with me in which he as good as told me I was useless and that he had "forgotten more than I would ever know." I then answered him back and told him exactly what he was – an unintelligent lout,

jealous – who came out here thinking the authorities would put the flags up for him and so on. He hit out at me and I answered, only to be separated by the Comrades around us, who I am glad to say have sympathy with me. He wishes now to settle the affair by a fight this afternoon, which offer I declined, wondering what it would prove. I feel better about it now because the air is cleared and when the air has been cleared once again in a few weeks time, we shall be able to settle down to some very useful work.

I don't think for the moment that this rank is to be held at the front, although I have no information to the contrary.

Nowadays I attend a special course of instructions given by the Base Commandant and his staff. They are very very useful and I am glad to be able to attend. I learn much every time.

My immediate Commander is one Sergeant Joe, a fisherman by trade and with absolutely no military conception whatsoever. On Friday on manoeuvres my hair nearly went grey. I had to obey his commands which in actuality would have meant complete disaster.

Still we lurch along. Actually I think we might riot before accepting him as our immediate commander in the line.

As one of my Comrades who sleeps next to me – a carter – from Miles Platting says "You don't realise how much your wife means to you until you come out here." Partially that's true. Except that enjoying you I appreciate you more than I ever could do from a distance.

I had a strange dream last night – I had a rod and I attacked a man. He had a strange small face. I hit him once and knocked him down. Then I threatened him again and as he lay on the ground his clothes opened and showed me your breasts. I recognised them immediately and then woke up. Of course I know your interpretation of that dream. Do you know that I can picture in my mind every part of you? Your hair, your breasts, navel, triangle, legs – only your face I can't do justice to. I can remember exactly your eyes, your chin, the point of hair on your forehead, your unsymmetrical mouth, and everything but I can't quite picture your face as a totality. I should hate to be killed without seeing you again. I will try very hard not to. If a shell has my number on it there is nothing for it, but I will try so to increase my military efficiency that only the chance of war will kill me, not my own stupidity.

Yesterday we had a demonstration advance by the Officers Training School and they use live rounds. The crack and zip of the bullets made me jump like hell. I'm afraid I shall be a nervy soldier. Still no doubt I have enough will power to overcome that. And I should be ashamed of myself all my life if I ran away.

Still I will able to write about that later. Then possibly I won't feel inclined to.

Darling excuse all this military stuff. But naturally I have entered into it wholeheartedly now and it would be very unreal not to write about it.

And I am looking forward to hearing from you again. I want to know your state – you remember we weren't sure of that when we parted in Paris – and what you are doing – have you seen Allan again, and Mona and Arnold [surname unknown – they were present at Ivor and Juliet's wedding]. *I feel I ought to write them and let them hear from me. As I say, I am itching to hear from you I have written you two letters before this. I hope they have arrived by now and another is on the way from you to me. My address is: –*

*Soccorro Rojo International
Nr 270, Plaza de Altazona
Albercete, Spain.*

Or just S.R.I. – international red aid.

Conditions here are not what they might be – in fact they are the worst I have ever lived under. But it doesn't upset me. This is war and we can't pick and choose them. I have not had a bath for a fortnight and I smell. I have not shaved for 3 weeks and I have the semblance of a beard, I definitely like the feel of it on my face. Dark at about 6 and after that time the only light is – blast it – candles.
There is electric light but when it is switched on the bulbs glow just the slightest and emit no light. So we can't read properly or do anything properly. All we can do is drink. Otherwise we can only buy bread, maybe sweets. And otherwise nothing. There is a library – that is something – despite the candles and there are intelligent friends – that's a lot. Still, the great benefit is that we have plenty of food regularly. By the way, tonight I think I will have a special meal out – 2.50 pesetas! There is some mention of fried potatoes – But I mustn't say, because as you know, there is a censor and why the hell should he know?
When you read my letters you must always remember that there is a censor and although he is a long way away from here and he must be used to the job, never the less he is there. In the same way I wouldn't kiss you too publicly in the street. I think I will close now – this is a quite a respectably long letter, isn't it?
All my love to you, my little beauty. Don't forget my love will you, that you are the most beautiful woman in my world – for "I love you" the Spanish say "Yr te quiero" – "I want you" –

*So "Yr te quiero"
Hasta la vista,
Ivor*

*Oh, if you hear anything particular about Spain, tell me won't you? There are Workers and bulletins etc. here but even so you may find something I miss.
I am reading "Romeo and Juliet"*

Ivor's "friend", John Smith was a less than typical volunteer. Although known in the Battalion as John Smith, his real name was Gopal Mohan Huddar. Born in Baghdad of Indian parents in October 1908 (sources vary regarding his date of birth placing it between 1908 and 1910), University educated Huddar worked as an etcher and journalist and lived with his wife in Swiss Cottage in London. He arrived in Spain days after Ivor on October

17th, 1937 and joined the British Battalion. He was later captured during the fighting at Calaceite on March 31st, 1938 and imprisoned in San Pedro de Cardenas until his release and repatriation in late October 1938.

"Sergeant Joe" was former trawlerman Joseph Henry Latus. Born on the March 4th, 1912, in Grosvenor Avenue, Hull, Latus served with the Tank Corp as a driver/machine-gunner from 1928-30. He arrived in Spain around the same time as Ivor and took part in the fighting at Belchite, Caspe and Calaceite during the Aragon Retreats in March and April 1938. He was wounded in the leg and head slightly by shrapnel on the August 21st, 1938, in the Sierra Pandols. Latus was a long-standing and active member of the Communist Party of Great Britain. A heavily-built man, he became a lieutenant machine gunner and observer. An amusing encounter between Latus and Battalion commander Sam Wild is described in the unpublished memoirs of fellow Brigader William ('Billy') Griffith (1997),

> One evening, while larking about, Joe Latus started to wrestle with one of his mates, an electrician from Liverpool. Joe was a big chap – not tall – about 5' 10." His opponent was well over 6' and well muscled. It was a good scrap. While it was on, Sam Wild came along. He watched for a while and when it was over he challenged the winner. I think it was Latus. Sam was not very big – about 5' 7", wiry muscle and bone. They rolled about stripped to the waist, over stones and pebbles and rough ground until both were exhausted. It finished in a friendly atmosphere. I relate this incident to indicate what sort of a man Wild was, perhaps one most fitted for the job he had to do.

Latus was repatriated to England in December 1938. It is believed that he was an amateur boxer or maybe a weight-lifter which illustrates perfectly the tenacity of Sam Wild during their "scrap." Later in life Latus became a director of Hull FC and for many years ran a left-wing bookshop on the site of what is now the tourist information centre under Hull City Hall. His name is present on the plaque dedicated to volunteers from Hull in the city's Guildhall.

The 'carter' mentioned in this letter refers to Joseph Canniffe, from Steele Street, Miles Platting, Manchester. Older than the average volunteer at 39 and a member of the Communist Party of Great Britain, he had two addresses in Manchester, one of which was his wife's. He was with the British Battalion at Calaceite and captured on March 31st, 1938. Imprisoned at San Pedro de Cardenas, he was repatriated on the February 5th, 1939. His service record lists him as "a Good Comrade."

Besides basic training and lectures on both political and military matters delivered by the Battalion commissar, the volunteers had a certain amount of free time. One of the most common ways of utilising these valuable moments of calm was through competitive sports. Football matches between different units proved popular but as George Wheeler discovered, sometimes even these games had their complications. Catalonia, where Wheeler was based at the time, has a long history of anarchism. A football match had been arranged between two mixed sides from the Brigade. All went well in the first half and at half time the teams left the field for a brief rest. As the teams returned another two sides also took up position on the field. Wheeler continues,

> We protested that our game had not yet finished, expecting the newcomers to be reasonable and to wait until our game was over. But gesticulating wildly, they refused to move and even began playing. There were forty-four players on that field – some kicking the ball, others arguing, the rest looking completely nonplussed. After a while we gracefully retired, leaving the pitch to the anarchists. (50-51).

Another popular distraction from Battalion training routines was the wall newspaper. The practice of displaying a wall newspaper dates back to the time of ancient Rome. Newspapers featured press cuttings and contributions from various people who were writing up their own reminiscences and observations. It was an ideal medium in which to display propaganda and political items. The wall newspaper was always a popular rendezvous point for volunteers to meet and discuss the great many topics of interest. Often the compiling of the stories for the wall newspapers was a task assigned to the Battalion's commissar; however, one of the most popular exponents of the wall newspaper project was the ex-music teacher, Miles Tomalin. Tomalin was a graduate of Cambridge who later achieved fame as a Communist poet. He had worked as a music teacher at Bedales School from 1925 until 1931 and was known to Ivor through Juliet as is confirmed in a letter to Juliet dated March 26th, 1938.

Tomalin was in charge of the cultural activities of the Battalion. Bob Cooney referred to Tomalin as, "the genius behind the wall-newspapers [...] who, in addition to the soul of a poet, possessed a flair for organisation not usually associated with devotees of the muse." (Hopkins, 1998: 248) Another Brigader described Tomalin as "a grand chap…an intellectual, but with his two feet firmly on the ground." (Ibid.) At Ambite Mill Tomalin took over a ground floor room in a one-up one-down house and produced a series of wall-newspapers under the name "*Assault and Battery News.*" Jim Brewer recalls writing on the wall newspaper with Tomalin,

> We commandeered the mill and we got a table going and chairs and a bottle of wine and we set out to write the wall newspaper. I always had a column in it because Miles came to the conclusion that there were a hell of a lot of things I didn't like and I wasn't averse to showing it, so my first contribution was, *'Things I Don't Like'*. We used to put this paper up with various articles from the lads and they used to come from far and near to see this. (IWM a)

As later letters confirm, Ivor also had the responsibility of compiling the contents of the wall-newspapers or as he refers to them in a letter dated Christmas Day, 1937, "technical boards." Ivor's apparent satisfaction at the training and social aspects of life in the Battalion contrasts dramatically with Jason Gurney's experiences. He writes,

> At no time was any attempt made to consider the welfare of the men. Owing to the absence of washing facilities for either person or clothing, the entire Battalion became infested with body-lice. No reading matter except propaganda was provided at any time, leading eventually to boredom and cynicism. And nothing was done to try and improve the deadly monotony and dirt of the food, which produced frequent attacks of diarrhoea [Ivor's letters reveal that he suffered from a series of ailments, confirming Gurney's appraisal]. It is fantastic that no one in the hierarchy seemed to realise that dirt and boredom are the two most totally destructive forces in any body of men. (1976: 85)

Nevertheless, Ivor's military training had begun, and as it turned out he was destined for a different role within the Battalion than he had envisaged.

7

"Poverty makes better soldiers than poetry"

By the time that Ivor joined, the British Battalion had been through a period of change following the costly failure of the Brunette campaign. Indeed, in Chapter Five, above, I already outlined both the achievements of the Battalion, as well as the many costs it paid as it began to take shape but, in what follows, it is worth revisiting some of those achievements (and more controversially some downright failures of judgement) in much greater detail, this time in the context of Ivor Hickman's own experience.

On Ivor's arrival, morale among the volunteers was low and questions were being asked of the brigade's Spanish members in particular. Stalin himself had ordered Marty to report on the situation and to suggest proposals to deal with the crisis. Disputes amongst the Battalion's command which had been simmering for months finally came to a head. Battalion commissar, Walter Tapsell was one of the most vocal in his criticism of both the commander of the 15th Brigade, Gal, accusing him of gross incompetence and of the overall strategy of the Republican forces. The losses the Battalion had suffered at Mosquito Ridge prompted Tapsell to rashly state, "Only stupidity or a deliberate disregard for life would keep men in such an exposed position. Gal isn't fit to command a troop of Brownies, let alone a People's Army" (*Reynold's News*, July 23rd, 1961, cited in Baxell, 2007: 93). Tapsell was nearly shot for insubordination for his outburst but Battalion commander Fred Copeman, backed up by Joe Hinks' Machine-Gun Company, persuaded Gal to withdraw from his threat. However, the arguments continued, splitting the Battalion command in two. On one side was Walter Tapsell and on the other George Aitken and Jock Cunningham. Tapsell believed that Aitken and Cunningham were isolated from the Battalion from their position on the brigade staff. There were plans to amalgamate the British Battalion into the American Battalion which Tapsell referred to as 'the annihilation of the

British Battalion'. The arguments also took on a personal perspective with Tapsell claiming that Aitken's ambition had made him distrusted and disliked throughout the Battalion. Cunningham fared no better in Tapsell's mind; he accused him of both hysterical outbursts of passion and laziness. Both men, according to Tapsell, were more interested in personal gain rather than the interests of the Battalion. The assistant brigade commissar, Dave Springhall, claimed that the Battalion leadership was at the point of disintegration. Many senior members were 'at the end of their tether' and morale was at an all time low. He accused Tapsell of being panic-stricken and wrong in his criticisms of the command of the brigade. It was subsequently obvious that Tapsell and Copeman were suffering from nervous breakdowns following the Brigade's recent action at Brunette.

Unable to resolve the situation in Spain, Harry Pollitt, General Secretary of the Communist Party of Great Britain, called Jock Cunningham, Bert Williams, George Aitken, Walter Tapsell and Fred Copeman back to Britain in August. The accusations and arguments continued until Pollitt ordered Tapsell and Copeman to return to Spain while the other three were to stay in Britain to start to build up political support for the dependants of the volunteers. Aitken would later call Pollitt's decision "monstrous and dangerous" and a "grave mistake." (cited in Baxell: 95)

By this time the volunteers were required to remain in Spain for the duration of the war. The Republican government passed a decree in September 1937, which brought the reformed International Brigades under the auspices of the Republican Army. The 15th International Brigade became part of the 35th Division under the command of General 'Walter'. The Battalions would now count a quota of Spanish troops amongst their ranks as well as international volunteers. Internal reorganisation was implemented with Hugh Slater replacing Malcolm Dunbar in charge of the Anti-Tank Battery. Dunbar became chief of operations for the brigade. Tom Wintringham had by now recovered from his wounds and joined Dunbar on the brigade staff. By August 1937, the British Battalion numbered just over 400 men, of which just under half were British.

From mid-August 1937, the 35th Division was transferred to the Aragon front. Tom Wintringham was wounded once again during the street-fighting in Quinto and Peter Daley, commander of the British Battalion, was killed along with two other volunteers during the attack to secure Purburrel Hill. The new commander, Paddy O'Daire, withdrew the Battalion until artillery support could be provided. The hill finally fell to the Battalion on August 26th, thanks to the accuracy of the Anti-Tank Battery and the thirst-induced weakness of the Nationalist defenders.

The British Battalion had a compliment of just over 100 men when they were moved on to the nearby town of Belchite. After the losses of the previous week's fighting, morale was so low that it reached the point that when the Battalion was ordered to move to Mediana to hold off approaching Nationalist reinforcements, some volunteers refused to obey. The situation was resolved when O'Daire called a meeting of all Communist Party members in the Battalion asking them to obey the order and persuade the others to do likewise. Reluctantly the Battalion marched on Mediana. After some of the bitterest fighting seen so far in the war, Belchite was finally captured on September 6th. The Battalion was then withdrawn from the front line for a much deserved rest and recuperation.

The short period of rest ended on October 11th, when the Battalion was called into action once again. As outlined briefly in Chapter Five, the next stage of the campaign was to be what I previously termed the over-ambitious plan to capture Fuentes de Ebro; it was there that Harry Fry had been killed having barely recovered from wounds inflicted at Jarama. Looking at it in more detail, the tragic death of Fry was only part of the story however. With the 15th Brigade attacking Fuentes de Ebro, and the 24th Spanish Battalion going forward on tanks, the British Battalion along with Lincoln-Washington and Mackenzie-Papineau, had been ordered to attack the Nationalist lines and then advance on Saragossa. As we have seen, the plan was a disaster however, with the Anti-Tank Battery being forbidden to open fire leaving only one bombing raid for support. The terrain was unsuitable for the tanks and they left the infantry behind to suffer the heavy casualties previously referred to. Though his was one loss among many, the loss of Fry who had commanded the Machine-Gun Company at Jarama, was felt greatly by the Battalion and, though they remained in the line for a further ten days, eventually it was felt as a great relief to return to Mondejar and Ambite for further rest and recuperation.

Although Ivor had only been with the Battalion a few weeks, his letters to Juliet from this period reflect a fairly accurate insight into the Battalion's morale and the overall strategies of the Republican forces.

Monday Nov. 8th 1937
S.R.I... 270, Plaza le Altazona,
Albacete, Spain

My dearest love,
It is a long time since I wrote to you. About 8 days I believe. Since that time much has happened. But still I have not heard from you. Of course I can hardly expect to yet because it was only a month ago that we were together on my birthday.
You will be interested to know that last week the Base Commandant asked me to join the Officer's Training School (henceforth O.T.S.). Previously I had made

arrangements to be transferred from the infantry to the Anti-Tank Battery attached to our brigade. So that when the Commandant shot the query at me I decided against joining the school. My immediate reaction was of course an emotional one, because naturally enough I'd want this period here in the training base to be as short as possible so that I can "find myself" at the front and so be confident or otherwise that I can stand the racket of fighting.

But when I spoke to my friends and to my company commander and others I decided that my decisions had been short-sighted. This war seems doomed to linger on for a long time. Perhaps you do not realise the immense store of human energy and training that is involved in any military advance. And the Republican Army is just entering into a period in which persistent offensive is the tactic. Only when this tactic has been maintained for many months will the end come in sight.

I may well be unable to stand up to war conditions so that I might well be no use at the front. But even so a man may have 2 months training and may be killed before he reaches the line. That doesn't mean to say you should not train men as soldiers if they have the potentiality. Similarly under the circumstances the people here think I have the potentialities and so give me an O.T.S training.

To me it will mean 3 things. Firstly it means another 9 – 10 weeks here – I shall spend Christmas here – secondly when I do go up I will be a fairly highly trained man and so stand considerably more chance of surviving and be less likely to make elementary mistakes. Thirdly I will be with better quality men on the whole and should be able to get along with them with less conscious effort than with my present comrades.

You will be pleased to hear that the company seems to have "turned the corner" we had a change of Company Commander and after a few days there came a change much for the better. Now my confidence in the Company has returned – the political morale and the training has improved considerably.

Nov 10th 1937 – c. 6.45pm.
I am sorry my little love that I have neglected you again for two days but we have been extremely busy with the Battalion manoeuvres. On Tuesday were up at 3.15 and away on the defensive. We arrived back at about 2 in the afternoon. Then was rest and a Battalion reunion and discussion. Then bed and up at 4.30, away at 6 after coffee and bread and back by 11 o'clock (a.m.) and finally Battalion reunion again. Now I am free to write to you. – These manoeuvres are the climax in the Battalion training and we all expect a large batch to be sent up soon. These batches are sent up every 6 weeks or so. Of course I shall not be in that batch but shall be studying at the O.T.S.

During these manoeuvres I was a peloton leader (Sargeanto) again – so that I had 15 men and 1 infantry light machine gun under my direction On the whole we did moderately well. It made us realise the seriousness and extreme difficulty of the job we are undertaking. And of course we learnt many many lessons.

Still I have received no letter from you although I expect by now you have received some of mine. At least I do hope so. And I am looking forward like hell to news of you. I think of you very often every day – when I am training or on manoeuvres I think of nothing but the immediate matter but when I am on rest or am talking to my comrades or when I am on guard or I see the dawn – then I think of you and want you with my self.

This life is changing my outlook considerably. I am learning to look at my fellow men objectively. Conditions out here are so unusual, and life if so cheap that I am learning to look on things differently. As I have told you, this life shows the inner nature of man to those who wish to see. So that I am consciously striving to preserve my decencies. Tonight I had my second bath here – the first was on my arrival and I was pleased to get it too. I felt the animal in me for a moment as I was under a hot shower. I have not known that feeling since I left you – and it was refreshing to have that feeling again.

And a comrade has just been lancing a boil (!) that I had on my cheek. I have only had one very small boil before in my life.

I'm afraid my little love that you must think I am depressed and fed up and perhaps wish I had not come. Well sometimes I am happy, sometimes depressed, sometimes very depressed. But on the whole I am nullified – this applies to my sex urges to myself. Now I am striving as hard as I possibly can to become a highly efficient and intelligent soldier. I doubt whether I ever will. And if I had the chance to return home (unless the war was over!) I would not for a moment hesitate and would say "NO." Not that I don't want to see you again now – I do. But despite the awful lack of you and your love I do not regret it.

There is something heroic about some of us ever coming out of here but there is nothing romantic about it. So that to us ourselves the heroism being unromantic is nothing and does not help us.

Oh, you'll be interested to know that I'm letting my beard grow. I haven't shaved since I left you in Paris so it is beginning to shape itself. Nobody takes much notice of it out here. It is not important at all and I am glad to say that it attracts very little attention and merely satisfies me.

There is no doubt that being one of the chosen I am receiving some very fine lectures in military technique. Lectures from the base commandant, from a terrifyingly shrewd German machine gunner (he lectures us on how to place our heavy machine guns and mow down the enemy from all angles) and from a very fine instructor from the most efficient army in the world, (he speaks neither English or Spanish) but I can understand him the slightest bit. (Of course he is interpreted).

It has just struck 9 – we have to be in by this time but I was just thinking that it might sound like a harsh restriction but really it is nothing and we are on average in bed by this time. We are up by 5.15 and in the open air most of the day so naturally we feel ready for the bed. Unfortunately I miss my bed at Stretford and I miss you most of all. Well I must get into bed now as I am tired after today's manoeuvres (I have had two hours sleep in the afternoon).

The Anti-Tank Battery of the British Battalion mentioned in the above letter was formed in May of 1937 with forty men, then in training at Madrigueras, and would go on to fight on every front from Jarama to Belchite.[1] The battery had three Soviet-made 45mm calibre guns mounted on a light rubber-tired carriage, which was considered to be the most advanced weapon of its type available to either side at the time. Two types of shell, both of high velocity, could be used; armour piercing and high explosive. In his book *To Tilt at Windmills*, Anti-Tanker Fred Thomas recalls his feelings on seeing the guns for the first time,

> It was impossible not to feel a tingle of excitement as we looked at them. They were Russian, and quite new. Now they were ours. We crowded round and positively fondled them, our hands sliding along the polished steel of the long barrel, squinting down the rifled muzzle, kicking the big heavy-tired wheels. Like school boys we took turns crouching behind the thick protective shield, pulling the breech open to insert an imaginary shell, a sharp upward pull to close it, then yelling "Fire!" as another pushed the red-painted firing mechanism. Removed carefully from its own wooden box, the telescopic lens was fixed in position and again we all lined up to look at the mystifying crisscrossing lines until we got the hang of it…This was great fun. We were playing at soldiers in the pleasantest way possible, with no enemy to answer back. (22-23)

However once it came to moving the guns, Thomas' enthusiasm was somewhat dampened.

> …trucks would transport them and us on journeys of any length (though we frequently found later that trucks were by no means always available) but basically they had to be manhandled. In the firing position the long and solid legs were splayed wide; on the order "Prepare to move," these were lifted by two men apiece, run together and clamped fast with an alarming clash of metal. Then with all eight of the gun crew placed at different positions, "Lift!", and the bods at the tail-end heaved up; "Move!" and as they pulled the rest pushed until, with much heaving and staggering and losing balance, the thing was moving. On a good smooth, macadamed road it was relatively easy. Over rough fields with hillocks and deep ruts everywhere it was emphatically not. Hard enough when the "Heave," to get over some mound, lacked sufficient power so the damned thing (already?) rolled back causing the pushers to forsake all and scramble sideways with the barrel dipping to the ground and the two tail-men either jumping clear or being carried several feet in the air if they hung on. Worse still, though, when one wheel went down into a deep cleft in the ground, then the tail would be flung sharply to one side and woe betide any gunner who got caught

by several hundredweight of solid steel! (23)

Despite the casualty rate being as high as the rest of the Battalion's, the Anti-Tank Battery evolved into a cohesive unit with high morale. As the crew and their guns were, theoretically, towed everywhere by lorry, there was space left for the gun-crew to stow away not just ammunition but also *luxury* items such as books and writing paper. From their first action in early June 1937, at Jarama where, using high velocity shells, they knocked out the troublesome Nationalist machine-gun nests, to their final engagement as a battery at Belchite in March 1938 where, under the command of Arthur Nichol, they fired continuously all day at tanks and other vehicles as well as groups of infantry, the Anti-Tank Battery served with great efficiency and effect. During the withdrawal from Belchite the Battery was forced to abandon one of its three guns and another was destroyed by Nationalist planes while under tow shortly afterwards. Unable to obtain more guns, the Anti-Tank Battery personnel were incorporated into either the ranks of the British Battalion or into the Brigade Machine-Gun Company.

Thursday
November 11th 1937
1 o'clock

I have just got 10 minutes to scribble a note to you before I go to a special lecture and when I asked the date I realised that in England it is Armistice Day today. And then my mind jumped to my father and his death on October 12th 1919. Odd that on the anniversary of his death I never remember anything of it. It is strange how humans can live vividly and die and then be forgotten so completely in such a short time. Actually I have often thought of him lately because I realise that I am passing through some of the stages through which he passed. But I shall come out differently. My friend from Iraq says that a man cannot be happy unless he be surrounded by men of his own mental standard.
– In general, true. Here particularly it is true. He thinks we would be better divided into units according to our intellectual level then that would make things much more tolerable. Out of the question of course. And when I get to the O.T.S. then it will as Wolf says be better in this respect.
By the way the my friend from "Iraq" has been in prison for five years on a faked charge – Of course he does not come from Iraq but elsewhere. And yet we in England say "it can't happen here." And people refer to fascism as a foreign product when they need only to go to British India to realise how close to us in England it is.

This letter reveals Ivor's realistic expectations of his own abilities. It must be remembered that unlike many of the volunteers, Ivor was raised in a fairly privileged world. Until his arrival in Spain, his struggle against fascism was confined to the debating chamber and to academic theory rather than to the street barricades familiar to the majority of working-class recruits. He has doubts as to his own contribution but is pragmatic and realistic in his self-appraisal. His willingness to sacrifice the self for the good of the whole is apparent throughout and remains unwavering throughout his correspondences from Spain.

November 12th – 8.30am.

My dearest love.

I am growing ashamed of myself about this letter. I have started it at odd times but have been interrupted. Now I have 20 minutes to scribble off something more to you. Now I am interrupted by somebody shouting for the sick– damn him.
Yesterday and today we have seen our Brigade Commander and a Company Commander from the English Battalion. The Brigade Commander has been trained in the best army in the world and the Company Commander is a fine man – working class of course and quiet, direct and obviously a good leader. I liked him myself. It is good to meet these men because it makes one more confident. The fact that in Spain the men at the top are good is obvious from the course of the war and of course you know where they have in general been trained.
The loss of the Asturias is taken quietly here.[2] Few comrades refer to it but of course it is a (sic) *in the sense that, it liberates thousands of Franco's troops for concentration on a major front here. We of course have our ideas about which front this will be (if he does decide to make an offensive) but at any rate our Brigade being one of the best trained Brigades in the army is one of the Brigades promised the job of stopping him.*
Our military policy at the moment seems to be – according to our Base Commandant in a lecture – defence is the best form of attack. In military actions against the desperate tactics persistently used by Franco there comes an "ebb" in the state of affairs and our Brigade looks forward to the time when we can help to drive a hard blow home against Franco when he is in such an ebb.
I personally am quite unable to judge the end of this war. I believe time is on our side and I believe we will win. I can only judge from the few things I see. At any rate there is a widespread feeling among the responsible people I know of confidence that the war trend will gradually turn with us – it is doing so already and they believe it will slowly and surely continue to do so.
But surely you my love will be tired of all this military gossip. But it is difficult to avoid writing so as it absorbs all my energy. The political side is not as efficient as it might be. I very much want to know of the evolution of the army, the position of the peasants and so on. But I do not get my political food to the extent I should like. But under war conditions advance is difficult.

8.15pm.
I often wonder how you are getting on, whether you are in Manchester, London or even Spain. Whether you are busy or looking for a job, whether the house is OK – or not? – hell, I hope it is. And I hope all goes well with you and also mother is not too upset.
I read in the Worker that friends and relatives of members of the I.B. should send parcels for Christmas not later than Nov 16th!!!
Time I wrote my Christmas cards, etc? Actually it is time I wrote to Mona and Arnold and Ray and Frank and Tex and Joyce and the Cambridge C.P. and to mother again and to Marsden and to Sherrin. (Oh god I'd forgotten that) and so on – and of course Allen. I want to know where he is.
I am sorry to let the weight of telling people where I am fall on you my love but somehow I don't seem able to settle down to writing lots of letters. And then after all this military business I like to talk to my friends here about many odd topics.
There is one danger here for me at this time – that of becoming a prig. After all my job is "research physicist" and I left a job to come here and I am on the whole more cultured in both a communist and bourgeois sense than some and so on.
So being derived from the sources that I am derived from, I have a mixed scale of values. This experience here is of course helping to purify them, but even so there is in the process a tendency to become priggish. So I must combat it.
There are here some men who are more truly communist than I have ever met. They have sacrificed any personal ambition for efficiency, that is the first step. After that you can build up a truer man, more nearly a communist.
There are some very complex and intelligent working class fighters here; and I emphasis very complex. But by living and working with them, seeing them on parade, at mess, and lit up, I am beginning to fathom them.

Saturday 7.20am.
Now this letter is getting on apace, because I have left the company now. The O.T.S. starts on Monday and since Friday I have been engaged on navvying – re building an extremely insanitary latrine so that when we settle in, our sanitary system may not be too insanitary. I like dropping military work for a few days and doing a little dirty navvying. Also it gives me more time. I start work at 7.30 instead of 6.35, so that I can wash etc in great comfort, clean my boots (a sign of an emotional change in me) and get off a few lines to you. – I have been mixing cement for the first time in my life. I quite like it for a change.

7.30pm
Well I have spread this letter out. I am so sorry my love I haven't written to you for such a long time. I would not have finished it tonight as we had arranged night operations but the rain came on quite hard and as we have no change of clothes they were abandoned.
Well my love because I have not written to you for a whole fortnight you must not think that I have forgotten you. On the contrary I remember you always and am very proud of you. Only yesterday I was putting forward your arguments about the

bringing up of children. And of course I miss you, your beauty and your intelligence immensely. Still later on I shall be back with you and ready to appreciate you again. You know the Worker always talks of the lack of milk in Spain it is only too true the children have almost no milk – we have none ourselves and damned little sugar. So don't forget to canvass for tins of milk for the Spanish children, my god they need it – I am thinking of sending Arnold an old copy of the Bulletin which we receive each day. I am sure he would be interested.
Remember me to your mother, to Frances and to Mary and Jean and assure them that I shan't be near a fascist bullet for another two months at least.
– Unless of course Franco makes a desperate breakthrough. But I don't think so. Let him try!

All my love to you my beauty. Time flies by, doesn't it? So I'll be seeing you again in not too long a time, eh?

Love Ivor.

S.R.I. No. 270,
Plaza de Altazona,
Albecete, Spain

Sunday
Nov 21st 1937

My dearest little love,
I have received my first letter!
I received a letter from Mother and Pat on Thursday – I had of course expected my first letter to have been from you, but for some odd coincidence it turned out to be a very nice letter from Mother and an equally good letter from Pat. Pat seemed to show just a trifle of cynicism – "I don't expect you like it now you know what it's like in Spain." And "Can't you come home even if you want to? Won't they let you?"
It was a most moving thing to receive my first letter. And I got it on the very day my batch moved up towards the front and left me and a few others behind here in the base. And as you can imagine I was very upset seeing my friends even though of only 4 ½ week's making, lining up to get their rations and then clambering in the rain onto open lorries, shaking hands and giving the Red Front salute and smiling. So that when my first letter arrived I felt torn to shreds.
Seeing one's friends off for the front leaves that same feeling as death leaves when it removes someone connected with you. It was not the fact that men were moving off but that my friends were going. It will be 2 to 3 months before I see them again and many things may happen here in that time.
Pat tells me that you have been cooking at the Basque Children's camp. And also that some of them have sent a letter to me. I have not received it yet. I am glad you

are (or have been) working there and I hope you like it. But I want to know more and I wait impatiently for my first letter from you.
I was very glad when I heard from Mother that you had received 2 letters from me. Now that we have established contact I am glad. You had to wait only about 4 weeks, so I figure it, so that it was not to impossibly long.
I do hope that you enjoyed those letters and they were (partially) what you wanted. I feel I am never demonstrative enough in my letters to you. Please excuse me for that my love, but if you came to me here I would show you sure enough that I was still in love with you – in fact more so than ever if that is possible.
But I find I am very responsive to any emotional appeal out here. Anyone giving us speeches and encouragement disturbs my equilibrium so easily and gives me a feeling of a swollen throat. In fact I do not care at all for any stirring speeches because they excite me too easily. And seeing my friends off and getting my first letter from Mother – all in one day – was much too much for me and I could hardly stand it. We are all supposed to be men and tough and so on, but I am damned if I am. Of course the English particularly are undemonstrative; which is foolish of them and hard on those of them who are by nature more demonstrative.
I have had a week at school now, but only 2 days lectures. Before that we painted and built latrines and god knows what else. We made our own home, in other words. (Very unlike an O.T.S. in a bourgeois army). Most of the men here are good, very good. As Arne Winnick said, the standard of intelligence etc, is much greater here than in the ranks and this has its reflection throughout the school. We are a mixed bunch. There are about 60 of us – a few English, Americans, American Finns, American-Russians/Chinese, 3 negroes from the States, Irish, one Greek, one American-German and of course many good Spanish Comrades. I think I am the only man who is a graduate of a university. (I wish really that I wasn't so noticeably "University"/Comrade Hickman BA!) (No, nobody says that). And I'm told the English and Canadian Battalions particularly are in need of trained officers. So that it looks as it something might come my way pretty quickly provided I prove myself worth it. With regard to academic intelligence I suppose I have the highest in the whole school. Which is something but not much. Ability to control men in this army is more, much more important. And also of course courage (not madness) on the field. Then again quickness of decision is as necessary as hell for an officer and I am particularly lacking in that. Also self control, in which I am conspicuously lacking. I am glad now that I took this opportunity and went to the school. Because firstly I have confidence in myself that at any rate my time here won't be wasted from the point of view of the Brigade and secondly for our personal sake's that is, I shall be a trained soldier if I behave sensibly at this school and even if I prove myself quite hopeless as an officer I shall be better equipped to remain alive and return to you and get on with my work at home. And as you know a man doesn't leave a beautiful wife at home without always remembering her and without always wanting to return to her. I didn't come here to give my life, but to give my services and by Christ, I am going to try every means (without dishonour) of accomplishing that. And, my love, when I do return home to you, won't there be a reunion.
Last Sunday I wrote a longish letter to Arnold and Mona, but I not yet posted it. If

you are in Manchester, you might read it as I write quite different things to them from what I wrote to you; so that you would be interested.

We have just had a cigarette issue. 20 Raleigh's, American cigarettes. Oh, but the way, Mother said she was making a Xmas Cake for me. Fine!

All I hope is that it reaches me.

Remember this, my love. Always send my letters with nothing else in them. If cigarettes are included there is little hope of the letters ever reaching here, because in this cigarette lacking community it is a great temptation. Actually the issue is quite sufficient for me, so don't bother about cigs.

I would give anything nowadays for a large – so large – slab of plain chocolate. And it would do me the world of good. So if you enquire at Kings' Street about registered parcels and the chances of them reaching me and they say they will (others probably won't), I would appreciate chocolate most of all. Of course, I would sooner have a letter from you than any of it.

But if I could have a letter from you and some chocolate. Oh! (But not in the letter). When I return home I shall have a whole world to tell you of. I can't tell you now for many reasons. One is the censorship. Not that I would tell you things which would not be true and which would be to show our cause faulty. No, but they could if separated from their perspective be used as counter-revolutionary propaganda. For that reason the censor would be right to strike it out (if he did – I would doubt whether he would). But this is a war – and most peculiar things happen under war conditions – and we are members of a proletarian army which has been in existence only some 15 months!   Personally I raise my hat to Republican Spain for its gigantic effort. Viva España!

And secondly I won't write them to you because in order to give you a true picture I would have to write many many pages. And thirdly when I return to you my viewpoint will be mature and you will benefit by my maturity (and you will benefit from my presence as well because I will love you with all my heart and with all my strength).

I have just been for a very nice walk for an hour or so in the sun. Out here even though it is middle November, the sun is warm but the wind generally cold.

Today the wind is wild. And today the sun seemed very markedly a winter sun. I walked with my "friend from Iraq" – really from India – who covered me with his own personal philosophy. And I feel too mentally weak (and also mature) to argue with him. You know my attitude towards philosophical conversations. But out here I feel only capable of studying military technique and I don't seem to have the brain power to do more. Still it will change when I come back to you.

I enclose 2 postcard copies of posters here in Spain. I don't think much of the Asturias one, but I do of the other. They are just to give you an idea of the many posters (as you saw in Paris) that surround us.

I have not been well this week although I have not reported sick – I am passing through a stage of fatigue and my system is jibbing against adapting myself to my new conditions. So that you must pardon me if my letters show a decline in intelligence. If they do, blame the war. But it is always difficult to know when one is in a state of great change, whether one's intelligence is dulled or is shining. It is the same here. I do not know whether you are sighing with the triviality of my

letters or whether they are helping you to get an insight into a different phase of revolutionary activity – namely the active military phase.
I have been reading Coriolanus and I must say it is not an outstanding play. Romeo and Juliet, which I read before Coriolanus, moves me very much. But in Coriolanus there occurs no fine lines, no great interest. At what period of Shakespeare's life was it written?
What more is there to say? I must remind you that I love you with my whole self and that I have been completely – with both my mind and body – faithful to you since I left you in Paris. And I hope always to remain so.
Of course I miss woman's company terribly; I have had no company with any woman since I left you and men's company is lacking in some sweetness that a woman can add; at least you can add. Still there is nothing to do about it.
Oh, the Base Commandant asked me if it would not offend my dignity too much to remove the fuzz; so I have shaved and had a haircut and smartened up.
It is getting dark and is time I left this room; so all my love to you sweetheart – I think of you often and always love you and miss you.

Hasta la vista
Ivor

When reading Ivor's letters, it is impossible not to feel slightly voyeuristic and intrusive when he refers to the more intimate matters between he and Juliet. It is easy to forget that his writings were not written as historical testaments but were originally love letters from a newly married husband to his beloved wife. Sexual matters are rarely taken into consideration when studying military history. As Ivor's early letters to Juliet show, the couple enjoyed a strong physical relationship from the beginning, something that challenges Twenty-First Century preconceptions. Few memoirs make any reference to any physical longing felt at the front line however. Sculptor Jason Gurney describes his outlook before he went to Spain thus,

> Given this obsession with the human body, it was not unnatural that I should have delighted so completely in sex. For me it was the logical outcome of everything that was wonderful and beautiful about the human body. (32)

He recalls how his pre-war life consisted of "roaring around the clubs and parties in a welter of drink, sex and nonsense." However after being in Spain just a short while these feelings had been suppressed and almost forgotten. He later says,

> It was a strange thing that ever since I had left London I had not thought of women at all, except for a mild flutter with Angelita in

Madrigueras which had been more sentimental than sexual. My whole life had been involved with women. They were the most wonderful things in the world for me ever since I had left school, but for the last few months, I hadn't even thought about them. (164)

Unlike the majority of volunteers who hailed from a more puritanical culture that might be considered a part of their working-class roots, both Gurney and Ivor had lived in a more 'enlightened' and 'liberated' environment. Intellectualism and sexual liberation are commonly found together. Ivor often makes self-conscious references to his background in many of his letters and was obviously aware that it differed greatly from the majority of his comrades. For example with his humorous comments such as "University/Comrade Hickman BA" he shows he was aware of the cultural gulf that existed. Ivor would have been a man uncomfortable in the more bawdy conversations of his working-class comrades, feeling somewhat "priggish" and possibly been thought of as naïve. His letters reveal the opposite to be the case though.

No 270, S.R.I.,
Plaza de Altazona,
Albacete, Spain
2 o'clock – Nov 28th, 1937 – Sunday

My dearest little love,
I have received one more letter and that was not from YOU, but from Scatten [one of Juliet's aunts]. *She wrote me an intelligent and kind letter in which she mentioned that you had spent a weekend with her, after leaving Manchester, and that you were very plucky (which I am sure is true) and also that you were working hard. Of course she assumed that I had received your letters, whereas as yet I haven't received one from you – Still that pleasure is in store.*
I do hope that you receive this letter by our wedding day. As I would like you to know that this first year of our marriage has been the best year (in every way) that I have ever had in all my life. And I wish you to realise that although I came out here to Spain after being married to you for only 10 months, still I look forward to many more years spent with you and by your side, years as happy as this last one, I am not of course looking forward to my front line work but already I have been at this base 6 weeks and the time has gone like wildfire. We get up at 5.15, lights out at 9, but even so there seems no time in the daytime to devote to anything other than our military studies. In many ways I am glad of this. It prevents my imagination from running rife and it steadies me down.
So that the weeks will become months, I shall go up to the line and with luck return. Different and difficult jobs will come my way; I shall be partially successful and eventually I shall come home. I care only about two things – victory against Fascism

and my return home to you. Of course those two cover a lot and imply a lot. I don't mind how I come home provided it is not in disgrace and provided I am in not too bad a state. Actually now I am in much better health and I am beginning to get over my first difficulties. My cold has gone and my indigestion also and at the very moment I am writing this out in the sun under a tree. The countryside here is very beautiful at this time of the year. The browns and greens of soil are vivid the poplars and olives man– placed, the white houses seem so clean and the sky is a rich blue, without a cloud. The colours are in some way I have not yet fathomed different from those in the South of France. I think that perhaps they are as vivid but not so varied – I cannot help feeling as I have so often felt on holiday. With the mass of the English working class "holiday" seems to signify hilarity. But being more fortunately placed economically than they, it signifies a sense of rest and peace and blue sky for me.

Do you remember those apple trees which were in blossom and the beeches; near Stamford's Park and the Bridgewater canal? Strange that we said we would perhaps never see them so again. Still we will, with good fortune, see many other good things. When this war in Spain is over, and perhaps long after it, we will visit Spain and the South of France – together.

Well, now, sitting out here in the warm sun – and it will be December in 2 or 3 days time – and I have that feeling of holiday and rest. You would love it out here sitting by my side under this tree and looking over towards the village. And I should love you to be here too. And yet 150 kilometres away there is a war on and Franco with the many thousand troops liberated from the north is thinking of an offensive this winter or next spring. And we are training our many many more reserves and thinking of our offensive this winter or next spring.

This soldier's life has the effect on me of making me rather fatalistic in outlook and in a way more critical of rubbishy speeches. Oh, by the way, Bill Rust spoke to the whole base on Friday. I was very disappointed with this speech, because he said very little new, he reassured us that masses of the British working class were looking to the British Battalion with pride and hope, and if we die, we won't die forgotten. I am too much of a realist to mind that attitude. I know that of the million Englishmen sacrificed in the Great War, very very few are remembered now.

And so it must of necessity be with us as a mass. So a sort of fatalism and maturity comes out of this. I often think of my return to ordinary (and with you marvellous) life, when I shall be so mature. Men of my age and intelligence won't somehow be so mature as I will be. Firstly they won't even then on the average be married, and secondly they won't have lived through this war in Spain. And then of course, even out here I feel very mature when I place myself against other comrades. And yet of course sometimes I feel stupid and childish and find myself self conscious in my conversation. And then I am learning to be one of the "quiet ones." And I feel that is needed here in the Officers School particularly. Many of us have had some previous experience and that makes a few very argumentative and in effect disruptive – It makes them academic and extremely irritating. If we had a bourgeois discipline of course this would not matter. But we haven't – yet!

I have become extremely friendly with an American comrade from Omaha, Nebraska, who is also at the school. I like him for many reasons, he is quiet, a trifle naïve, good *natured and basically cultured and last but not least because he is an American. I must say I like the Americans here very much. I am outgrowing my bias for Americans and am beginning to understand them more. He is of course my first American friend. We hang around together (when we have any spare time) perhaps a bit too much. He was an assistant in a grocers store and later a gate clerk at a club. And he is intelligent, easy to talk to and he doesn't philosophise. I can say what I feel to him; which is good. I am much happier here at the school than I was in the company because I am being very well instructed (with certain gaps) and because there is somehow more common ground between us all here.*

Scatten wishes me well in "my crazy but very gallant adventure" maybe it's crazy; we'll see. Gallant – no, efficient I hope, but not gallant. Let her think it is gallant though if she wishes. But there is one thing it is not and that is, adventure. This war business is no damned adventure. I think I realised that before I left, didn't I? And now I am waiting news from you and about you. The news from Pat's letter and from Scatten's letter about you is good. "I am glad she is working hard." That sounds good to me. And she adds that you have to be the brave one, Juliet, not so much me, because it is hard for you who are left behind – So my love I hope you will not worry too much about me and will be able to do some good work while I am away. I would love you to be able to continue with you training and finish it while I am away. So that when I come back – and we leave England? – You could be fully trained. But perhaps this is just my wishes being father to my thought.

I often think now about our holidays and how we – or at least I – had need for danger; and the Point of Ayr do you remember the beautiful day we walked along the sands from Prestatyn and do you remember Rhyl buoy, not so far from the surfline? And then I think of Fool's Nook and the Clond (a beautiful name for a hill) and Bosley Locks and our little boat and Bunberry and also is it Gainston? And the entrance to Chester and the distant Welsh Hills.

This reminded me the Pied Bull and the Cathedral and all this is so often vivid to me. I am sorry to give you the rather thankless task of quietening those friends of ours who want to hear from me. But they must understand that I cannot get my notes written up and my Spanish develops too slowly, so that I am unable to get off much to them. But I will try – I am in Spain so I say "manana."

You must excuse the paper but paper is very scarce here and it least it is better than a 20 leaf letter which type I hope you have received regularly up till now.

All my love to you my beauty and unless no other letter arrives before Christmas, this letter must be my letter of Christmas greetings and my New Year wishes. May 1938 be a great year for both of us and may the end of it see a victorious Spain and us in the U.S.S.R.! And may it be for you my love a year which will not be in its early months too unhappy.

Christmas for me will be spent here at the base, taking it easy and eating well. I hope some at least of the parcels for me will arrive. I wonder where you will spend Christmas; at any rate I hope you will spend it very happily. Remember that my training goes well on into January and then there is the delay before being attached to a line unit.

And I must tell you that in many cases have reports been published in the Brigade

and also in England of the death of so-and-so; obituaries have been written and much misery caused – only to find that they had the initials wrong or that the man was on long leave and the company records were destroyed and he was written down as "missing." It is a difficult thing to keep check on all the men in Spain, very difficult, so don't be too upset if you were to receive news about me unless it is completely and unconditionally confirmed. As my name is fairly uncommon there should be no such confusion in my case, but with Jones and Scott's and Thomases it is a very different matter.
Now I must settle down to my notes –
All my love to you my sweetheart –
Hasta la vista –

Yours ever,
Ivor

Bill Rust was born on April 24th, 1903, and was a British communist activist and newspaper editor. Born in Camberwell, Rust began working at Hulton's Press Agency before moving to the *Workers' Dreadnought* communist newspaper. He joined the Communist Party of Great Britain shortly after its foundation, and in 1923, joined its executive as a representative of the Young Communist League. He attended the Fifth Congress of the Communist International in Moscow.

In 1925, Rust was one of twelve members of the Communist Party convicted at the Old Bailey under the Incitement to Mutiny Act 1797, and was given twelve months imprisonment. In 1930, he became the first editor of the party's newspaper, the *Daily Worker*. He served two years before becoming the Communist Party of Great Britain's representative in Moscow, then after a stint as a party organiser in Lancashire, he became the *Daily Worker*'s correspondent with the International Brigade. Rust returned as editor of the *Daily Worker* in 1939, remaining in the post until his death in 1949.

In this letter, dated November 27th, 1937, writing from the Officers Training School, Ivor describes how he has become "extremely friendly with an American comrade from Omaha, Nebraska [...] he was an assistant in a grocer's store and later a gate clerk at a club." In the following letter, dated December 5th, 1937, he again makes reference to his "American Friend Albert." Born on June 2nd, 1914, Albert Foucek was an accountant and member of the Communist Party of the United States of America. He left America on board the Britannia and arrived in Spain four months before Ivor in June 1937. He was attached to the 15th International Brigade Mackenzie-Papineau Battalion (Canadian) when it was training. Along with Ivor, he later attended Officer Training School and was made an instructor of rifles in the training camp. During the retreats he joined the Mackenzie-Papineau

Battalion and was reported 'killed in action' on the April 3rd near Gandesa.
No. 270, S.R.I.
Plaza de Altazona,
Albacete
Dec. 5th 1937 – Sunday

My Dearest Little Love,
It is 2.30 on a cold Sunday afternoon – Sunday our free day – and so in almost a routine now I sit down to write to you and I hope that you will get my letter sooner or later. I have not yet received one letter from you which is irritating but perhaps I shall be lucky enough to get one by Christmas. If I do, it will be my best Christmas present and just what I am looking forward to getting. But still, even if I don't get a letter till April – a terrible thought – I shall not be too upset because I have confidence in you and your courage and I believe you will pull through.
Censored [...] we believe that many of our letters and particularly parcels are never allowed to leave England. If that is the case, then to hell with the –s who arrange that, if they do.
What I particularly want is for you to receive news of me fairly regularly. Then you will be sure of my condition and will be able to let the others know occasionally and will not suffer too much yourself.
We are settling down as a body in the new Officer's Training School. I must say Spain is full of interesting group processes, of how men take shape as a group. And I have just been out for a walk with my American friend Albert and a man who came over on the same boat as him. This man is demoralised by war and he just couldn't stand it all. But although I ought to have been more sympathetic towards him, I could not easily restrain myself and he angered me. He of course couldn't stand our "schoolboy enthusiasm." Yet Albert who had been here for the same length of time has no trace whatsoever of demoralisation about him. It depends so much on the individual, his nerves and his willpower.
Oh, yesterday and the day before I have been very pleased with myself. Albert has been to a special snipers class here in Spain and is a very good shot and knows his stuff; when first we fire 3 rounds at 100 metres and we both get three bulls. Equals so far.
So later at 150 metres we have 3 more rounds. We must mark our shots after we fire each one; that is, when we have fired we mark down on a piece of paper where we think the rounds went. So I marked down my shots and when I got the score back from the butts I had three bulls where I said. Poor Albert, he had 1 bull and 2 off. The feeling of pleasure received from shooting straight is great. Do you remember our shooting at Zennor? And our excitement? And so it is here on the range. I wished that I had been firing at a Fascist because it would have been 6 out of 6 – except that they would have been firing at me; which might have unsteadied me!
Then I had a strong desire to be a sniper, to wait my chance and get my man and take great pleasure in the technique of sniping. Then I wondered how I could have arrived at that feeling, and I realise of course, that my training is technical and I'm looking at this business more and more as a technique. Thank God for that.

It is very cold today and in Spain there seldom seems to be a fire in a house – and I am behind in my notes and in my Spanish so I will stop. Forgive this brevity, but although I feel well, the weather is cold and not good for writing.
I have left you 8 weeks today! It amazes me to think of it, and on Friday we shall have been married for a year! This thought and knowledge gives me much pleasure and I hope it gives you that feeling too.
I look forward into the future for the time when I see you again and sleep in our most beautiful bed, between sheets and in the warmth of our previous pleasure. I didn't realise how handsome our front room was and how beautiful our bedroom. All my love to you and a longer letter next time I write.
A kiss from me to you.

Love Ivor

It appeared that Ivor's time spent as Company Sergeant Major in the Cadets Force at Peter Symonds School was not time wasted.

From Ivor Hickman, 270 S.R.I., Plaza de Altazona, Albacete
Christmas Day 1937

My dearest and most precious love,
Today is Christmas day and I am having a most excellent day. Why? Primarily because of your astute efficiency in arranging for me to get as many as SEVEN parcels! You will I'm sure to be pleased to know that they are marvellous and that last night 4 of my friends (a Spanish Columbian, an Irish American, a Canadian and a Middle-West American) came with me to a private house. We had sardines as hors d'oeuvre then ox tongue(!) and potatoes and onions fried by the Spanish woman, then bread and cheese then dessert – figs, nuts and raisins, chocolate, petit fours and wine. Can you imagine such a magnificent meal! We left feeling happy, satisfied and very well fed. And many more such meals lie ahead.
The clothes, socks, gloves etc are also just what I wanted. My hands have been feeling the cold a little and so goodbye now to any such troubles.
But the greatest pleasure of all is that via Kings' Street I have received 3 letters from YOU! I have learnt so far that you went to Steep and so on, Ipswich and then Cambridge – near the Aemito Ward.
I was so very very pleased and excited to hear from you. You are indeed a very marvellous woman, my love, and very brave. You will always remember – won't you? – that even if I don't always say so, my lovely chamois I admire you with all my heart and love you so too.
And you say that you may be coming to work in Spain! You are an amazing woman, really. Aren't you frightened of these bloody Fascist bombers that drone about over Spain and drop bombs on our towns and villages? Our air force is OK and keep them off but even so, as you know, defence against enemy planes is a tricky job even

though we have a well equipped air force to oppose them. Even so, the damage they do is primarily in the way of demoralisation and not in actually destruction. Not that the loyalist people are demoralised by them but their nerves are strained – naturally. It is your own decision of course if you come. I would be proud of you if you came; proud if you stopped in England. As I know so little of your feelings (I must, because the postal system is so bad) I cannot decide for you. And anyway why should you take much notice of what I say?

The change of life you would undergo would indeed give you a revolutionary understanding you could not get in England. And I can notice even now (although I have been here for so short a time) in your phrases the difference between what you will be and what you are. I'm sorry that sentence went askew in the middle. I mean that already I can notice that you lack a sense of perspective in a revolutionary sense. So do I Christ knows. And also I know that without your living under revolutionary conditions or without you going through an immense mental maturity (without the concomitant economic change or physical change) you can't get that perspective. Nor can any human being.

One thing I wish to do when this Spanish business is over is to go to the U.S.S.R. and live there with you at any rate for a time. Because even though I have been here for such a short time, my idea of transitional revolutionary action is entirely altered. And so I want to see a stabilised revolutionary society to throw away my old ideas once again.

I'm sure you could do useful work here in Spain, and also I am sure you could too in England. If you stop in England, you will in your spare time (what a hope!) not forget your direct political work will you? Out here I feel a trifle ashamed of my laziness at home, of my lack of political understanding and of my lack of previous political experience. I don't mean to say for a moment that I feel less politically conscious than many comrades here – I don't – but even so most of us lack much; which doesn't excuse me.

If you come out, you of course will very seldom see me. No doubt I will be able to get a leave sometime in the distant future (not too distant, now that time goes so fast here) and see you. What a thought! But for most of the time we will be miles apart. I know that the reason why you want to come is not silly and sentimental; very far from that. If your coming would mean I could see you – how marvellous; if not – well I wouldn't see you and that would be all. Although I would feel marvellously close to you all the same – you working with the children, while I was working with the army! But as I say, you do as you please and as you decide is best for you. I know nothing of the work you could do, but I'm sure you could do much fine work either here or in England. You're splendid, really! Your letter of your cooking life – dated Nov 1st – is interesting and stirring. The children sound great and you must love contact with them. And your experience of community life is great for you too, but compare it with life, say, in a productive unit in the U.S.S.R..

By the way, your last letter was in your superbe (sic) parcel – before I had letters dated 15 Oct, 27 Oct and 1 Nov. The Spanish mail is bad, or perhaps the British authorities stop many letters to me in Spain when addressed to Spain. Anyway I have received no letters from you via the ordinary mail i.e. presumably addressed

270 S.R.I. Albacete, etc. They might or might not come. I hope they do. In the same way that I hope this gets to you. But it may not. If not, it's a pity.

I got parcels and letters from you, Mother, your Mother, Sarah, Joyce (with a lovely ginger cake), socks from Dora, books from you, letters from Ray, Jean, Joyce, Mary etc.

Oh, thanks very much for the Sonnets and the rest. What a beautiful little edition the Sonnets is. I shall take it around with me and read it often and think of you when I read. And I shall read as many of the other books as I can, except that I am very busy at the school and when I go up to the front – I suppose sometime in February – I shall have to discard all but the absolute necessities. But I won't discard the Sonnets. I am indeed a happy man.

Harry Pollitt came out here a few days ago and in his wake brought all these parcels and letters God bless him! And he brought a parcel for every Englishman – cocoa, milk, sugar, soap, tea, chocolate, razor blades, a tinned Christmas pudding and so on. We shared all this among the school without national bias. Good. The complete lack of chauvinism in this school is fine and an experience.

But now let us talk about our military victories. Teruel is ours! And at the very time that Franco's smashing offensive was supposed to come! The Internationales did not make this victory either; it was the Spanish Republican Army and they deserve all the credit. This is a marvellous achievement which reminds the world that our strength is growing day by day and Teruel marks another stage in this war – the beginning of a series of offensives by the Government forces. This is a land of hope. But to return to Pollitt. He gave us a most excellent speech. Moving, informed and critical. The political leaders from abroad almost invariably miss the feeling of us out here. We are too sophisticated and we are not interested when we are told we are sacrificing everything for our cause. Why mention that? But Harry Pollitt struck the exact pitch of us out here and as somebody suggested "What about having him as Brigade Political Commissar?"

I often think about the old house and I was struck by conscience when you described your return there. I'm glad Kathleen Corfield had her baby son without too much pain – and is fine now. My poor Chamois in the house packing up. I ought to have been more sympathetic and have helped you in the packing. But you know how unreliable and unkind I can sometimes be.

Now I must close as I have been appointed chairman of the socialistic self-help instructors and I am responsible for a new technical board (wall newspaper). Also my squad has to clean the machine gun and also I have been asked for an article on the student movement in England. Which makes me very busy but as I feel so well I do not mind the work at all. Also there are party meetings – not today – and so on. So my love distribute your letters between 270 S.R.I. and 16 King's Street. Then I should get one or the other. Only ever send parcels by King's Street. I believe this good advice. Well goodbye my Chamois – I am thinking about you today and I am sure you are thinking of me.

All my love as ever to you my beautiful and kind creature,
Ivor.

And many many thanks for the tobacco and cigarettes. I am smoking it in your little Irish pipe – delicious – a kiss for you. Ivor

Jason Gurney was not so generous in his appraisal of Harry Pollitt. Having been wounded in the hand, Gurney was in Albacete where he was to attend the Medical Board when Pollitt arrived on one his many visits to Spain.

> I had never seen Pollitt at close-quarters before. He was a smallish balding individual, with small dark eyes that looked as though he had never smiled in his life. He was neatly dressed in a city suit with collar and tie. We had been warned that he was coming to see us and everyone was full of expectation that he would bring a message of encouragement and joy. On the contrary. He had evidently come down to bawl us out. The general line of his argument was that we needn't think that, because we had served in the Battalion and had been wounded, anybody owed us anything. Quite the reverse, we had been given the opportunity to serve in this glorious cause and that should be enough for anyone. (Gurney, 1976: 183-184)

He goes on to say how Pollitt described the men as "the raw material" for a revolution that was being fought for by the "real revolutionary workers" in the Party offices. Pollitt finished his address by issuing a series of veiled threats against "shirkers and malingerers." Many of the men he was admonishing had a few weeks earlier been fighting for their lives on the battlefield at Jarama.

8

The Calm

New Years Day, 1938!

My dearest and most precious love, so it is 1938! I thought of you at midnight last night as we saw the New Year in – a New Year that holds very much for both of us and for our Spain.

Sunday 2nd Jan 1938
That was all I wrote last night. I was too tired and so went on to bed.
I received two more letters from you, but I have discovered why I only got your letters via King's Street. Because you wrote on the letter, 270 S.R.I., etc but you omitted my name. Now 270 S.R.I. covers a few thousand men, so that I was very lucky to get any of your letters. But someone noticed my name and enquired at the school – publicly – if anyone named Ivor or Peter Rabbit was at school! It really was extremely amusing and in a way flattering. Many thanks for your letters dated Dec 19th and Dec 12th. You sounded a little tired and disappointed in the thought that your letters might not reach. Now it should be better – and incidentally I might be able to get some more that came to our base and then went away "insufficiently addressed" I'm very sorry to have been ambiguous but it never occurred to me that you wouldn't include my name.
We had our preliminary examination a few days ago and I was placed first, so far, so good. I am told that I am almost sure to be asked to stay at the base as an instructor. It would mean responsibility and I believe I could do a good job. But what I want to know is – if I am fairly highly placed, don't they need me (as far as any individual is ever needed anywhere) at the front. I have been conducting some voluntary classes in military topography with some success. And I have been very busy on a military wall-board I am trying to organise. Now I've never taught topography in my life but still I can do it alright.
What I want to do is to go on up to the line and join the Anti-Tank Battery and there learn to apply my knowledge of mathematics, of military topography, of artillery, and of the duties of the infantry officer (that I have learnt here) to these particular guns. They are new guns, with peculiar characteristics and I feel that with practice

I could learn to handle them very competently. Let us hope I get up there and can do a good job there.

I still have a great deal of my Christmas fare yet to eat – most of my tins are as yet unopened. Good. Joyce's cake is nearly finished but Mother's is as yet untouched. My pipe tobacco is still going on well. It is very very nice to smoke a pipe again and I enjoy it very much.

Sunday Jan 9th 1938

My dearest love,
I have neglected you for a fortnight but you must excuse me because I have been very very busy here, what with the last week of school and so forth. This morning I went to see the commander of the base and he told me that it was a party decision and a military order that I stay here at the base for a few weeks – or months? – and take my first step in responsibility by being in charge of a technical group of men – maybe scouts or snipers or something and that if I shape well I go up to the line in charge of this group – Jesus!
I have met a small arms expert here and we work long together discussing machine gun trajectories, indirect fire and whatnot. Ballistic co-efficients and more! This is grand because he knows his small arms backward. However let us forget small arms for this letter.
The commander says that I must be developed. This problem of my political and military development will if things go OK start making a man of me (except that I felt a man when I went to Metrovic and when I married you).
The weather here, Jesus! ("Jesus" is my predominant expression nowadays – quite expressive; you can't get the intonation by post I regret my love). We had quite deep snow at New Year, followed by severe frost. This made the snow very beautiful but it made us cold. Then the sun – quite hot at midday – melted a little snow day by day. Then in a week the thaw came and the snow is gone.
We are in our outday training stage advancing across country and dropping into the snow, firing, running like hell, down, firing, up and on. Sweating and panting and warm at last. Something like it will be in action. As you eject an empty cartridge it drops into the snow. Then to get it out you pick it up and pull, because it has frozen in immediately. Sunny Spain!
I wonder how you are and what you are thinking about – last night at a concert someone played on the violin – "What am I without thee?"
And I wonder how everybody is and how they are living. Where the hell has Allen got to? The States? (Excuse the hells and so on but this is a military school and we all curse fairly roundly. Why not?)
I feel excited today. Why should I? I don't know. Tomorrow I am going out to eat at a private house. Potatoes and onions fried in olive oil and fried bread and wine. It is a change from the rather soup-like meals we get in the mess hall. And to think the Labour Movement is only just beginning to move! The lousy sons of bitches! (As you can see my contact with Americans is having its effect). Perhaps after all they're not lousy sons of bitches – but why don't they do something?

Franco does not seem to have been too successful lately; does he – despite his apparent superiority. And as the base commander reminded me – wait till we take the offensive all along the line. Then my technical training will help just a little.
Well my love I must close. It is getting near dinner time and I must finish my work on the wallboard – inspect my sections rifles and then attend two voluntary lectures in the afternoon.
My little love when this business is over and I am back with you! God, it's marvellous to think of. And I hope your work goes well.
When we get back to our old way of living – we will make up for this separation period. After all we are only 23 and with luck there is a long time yet, at least there is going to be if I know anything I can do to ensure it.

Hasta la vista and every thought and feeling for you, my only love
Ivor

From Ivor Hickman,
270 S.R.I. Plaza de Altazona, Albercete.
(Don't forget my name on your letters will you?)

Thursday, 3 Feb. 1938

My dearest love,
I'm very very sorry that I have taken such a long time to write to you but I have been extremely busy as you will read.
At the end of the Officers School I came out second in the exam which was in tactics, topography, rifle, light automatics, heavy maxim machine gun. A Spanish comrade did better than me.
So we had a good banquet and so on.
Then I was transferred as an instructor to the N.C.O.'s school and after 3 days there I was beginning to settle down, giving lectures on scouting and patrolling and whatnot when I was called to the Base Commandante and he told me he was making me the Commander of No.2 Company, the specialist company.
So you'll be interested to know that I am an unconfirmed teniente (full lieutenant) in this army and am in charge of 120 men. We are divided into four groups, snipers, Dikteroff light-machine-gunners, Tuckeroff light-machine gunners and sappers (field engineers). The Dikteroff section is Greek and a slight problem.
The nationalities in the company are interesting – American, English, Scotch, etc, Spanish, Greek, Yugoslav, Russian, Canadian, Negro comrades, an Iraquian (Sic) and more. When it gets to this stage, nationality does not count for much.
I find oddly enough that I am up to the job; I eat now in the Battalion (Officers) Mess and the better cooking there gives me more energy and so more courage to face my company.
Jesus Christ, there are some problems! Terrific problems which reflect the newness of the organisation of this army and of this base.

Then to cap it, I go and get a dose of 'flu on night manoeuvres and so spend 3 days in bed here in the office – with a headache and sensitive eyes and a sore throat just listening to all the complicated problems that my negro adjutant has to solve and unable to help him out.

Then I get up, feel weak as a lamb, see everybody and tick everybody off right and left – my section leaders I tell them exactly what I think of them – and on and on. I realise that I am in many ways very aggressive and forceful but inclined to be lazy. Everybody comes under my criticism and I am kind to nobody. God, this life is developing me!

So tell mother in case I don't write that I am now a Lieutenant commanding a full company of instructors at the base. That might please her a little.

But my sweetest love it means I am neglecting you – you must forgive me for this but if you could stay – invisibly – in this company you would realise what work there is to be done.

Sunday Feb 6th 1938

Now my love I am fully well again – my legs don't feel weak, my eyes don't feel supersensitive. But even so there hangs on my two feelings; one of deep regret that I have neglected you so disgustedly and the other the feeling of walking on air, of unreality.

I really am sorry my love that I have neglected you so badly. My only excuse is that the energy I have used up has not left me much to write with. Please forgive me and remember that I love you with all my heart and am so very very proud of you. Mother writes and hopes that as we grow older you will forgive me for inflicting such a hurt on you as I have done by coming here to Spain. I know – oh so well while I am out here – that it is you who have to bear the pain. I feel disgruntled with war, tired of this base, but my difficulties and troubles are nothing really. But with you I know the difference and I am sorry.

Perhaps this feeling of being out of touch with reality is a result of 'flu, perhaps as a reaction against my energy and my new work, perhaps because the political work is not sufficiently strong here to touch me in this predicament. Of course what it really is, is that this war is a test and I am naturally feeling the strain.

It is terrible to feel tongue-tied to your love, but that is how I feel now – I am sorry but it is so. Do you remember how I was tongue tied in your room at Newnham? Still I learnt to overcome that and I'll overcome this tongue tiedness soon enough when I come back. Nearly four months since I've been here! And I expect that I shall remain here another two months training a new specialist company and then after another six months here all told (!) go up to the line. I shall be glad to go, but somebody's got to stay – I am being developed like hell by this work, so I don't struggle like a mad thing about it but use my energy elsewhere. My love, I want you and I love you above all things. When we are together again I will show you how I really feel and I will try to make you realise how much you are to me. No other woman here or anywhere else interests me.

Ivor

Ivor graduated second in his class from Officers Training School and on January 16th, he, along with his fellow English-speaking and Spanish graduates took the following oath,

> We, the graduates of the Second Officers Training School, hereby pledge with all our hearts to carry high the standards of the 15th Brigade of the Spanish Army; we pledge to continue our studies in order to carry to completion the training of our units within the Spanish Regular Army; we pledge to carry into our work a crusading spirit for the improvement of our technique and the application of the military principles we have had the opportunity of studying.
>
> We pledge an eternal fight against fascism wherever it may be found and in whatever guise it may hide; we pledge to the international working class that we will fulfil the trust they have placed in us; we pledge to the working masses of our countries, our mass organisations, that we will carry out the mission for which they sent us to Spain.
>
> We pledge to carry out our tasks at the front in a militant and disciplined manner, to aid in the defeat of Franco and his foreign allies and thus deal a deadly and lasting blow to fascism; we pledge in the rear and at the front to bring this war to a quick and successful conclusion."[1]
> (See: Appendix 1)

In his letter dated February 3rd, Ivor mentions his "negro adjutant." This touches on one of the unique aspects of the International Brigades; the equality between African American and white volunteers.

In Spain, the African American volunteers found life starkly different to their lives in America. White Lincoln Battalion members recall how Spanish women showered the Black volunteers with smiles and flowers. "I never felt more like a man" reported Luchelle McDaniels while Tom Page would later recall "how sometimes a whole town would turn out when they heard there was a Black man around." From infantry privates to officers, the American Lincoln Battalion was the first fully integrated US Army. In addition to this the leadership resolved that African Americans would have an opportunity to prove their capabilities and leadership abilities. In the unit's first battle at Pingarron Hill in the Jarama Valley, the Lincoln Battalion faced a baptism of fire without air cover or artillery support. Alonzo Watson was killed by a sniper thus becoming the first African American to be killed in action in Spain. Twenty-three year old machine gunner Walter Garland was twice wounded, commended for bravery and was promoted to lieutenant

Andrew Mitchell: Ivor's "Negro Adjutant", from Pittsburgh, born December 27, 1902. During the Great Retreats, Andrew Mitchell was killed (some time between March 30 and April 2, 1938) leading his company that was retreating from Gandesa.

together with fellow African American Oliver Law. Often African Americans demonstrated raw courage and unusual battlefield skills. Doug Roach had a reputation as a man with "infectious enthusiasm" who could "carry a heavy machine gun over the hills of Brunette when others were too exhausted to walk." Luchelle McDaniels, known as "El Fantastico", could hurl grenades long distances with either hand. Legendary Lincoln commander Milt Wolff recalled of Walter Garland,

> Whatever I learned about the Maxim machine gun he taught me. But more importantly [...] he instilled in me the conviction that we could go out there and take on the whole bloody professional fascist armies and kick the shit out of 'em. The impact Spain had on the African Americans was strong. Salaria Kea discovered "divisions of race, creed and nationality" lost significance when they met a united effort to make Spain the tomb of Fascism.

One of the most famous African Americans to serve in Spain was Oliver Law who was to become the first African American to lead an integrated military force in America's history. Born on October 23rd, 1900 in west Texas, from 1919 to 1925 Law served as a private in the 24th Infantry, a black outfit stationed on the Mexican border. After leaving the military, Law moved first to Bluffton, Indiana, where he worked in a cement plant and shortly afterwards moved to Chicago where he drove a cab for the Yellow Cab Company. The onset of the depression forced Law into the ranks of the drifters and hobos before he landed a job as a stevedore and joined the Longshoreman's Association. Following this, Law opened a small restaurant. When this failed he went to work for the Works Project Administration. While he was out of work, Law joined the International Labour Defence and in 1932 the Communist Party of the United States. These political activities led him to frequent run-ins with the Chicago Police Red Squad. During one confrontation Law was severely beaten up. Shortly before departing for Spain, Law was arrested while leading a protest rally against Italy's invasion of Ethiopia. During this period Law married Corrine Lightfoot, sister of a prominent member of the Communist party. Law was one of the earliest American volunteers sailing for France aboard the SS Paris on January 3rd, 1937.

In Spain, Law's previous military experience was highly valued and he soon garnered a reputation for superb leadership qualities. After the reorganisation of the Battalion after the disastrous assaults at Jarama on the February 27th, Law was promoted to Commander of the Machine-Gun Company. During the trench warfare that characterised the Jarama front, Law continued to advance in rank. He was selected as Adjutant to the Battalion

Commander. An abortive attempt was made to form a regimental system within the brigade which resulted in Lincoln commander, Martin Hourihan, being transferred to the regimental staff and Oliver Law was promoted to the rank of Captain and was chosen to replace him. Law led the Lincoln Battalion during the initial days of the Brunette offensive. On July 10th 1937, during the fourth day of the campaign, under controversial circumstances, Law was mortally wounded while leading the charge on Mosquito Ridge.

In a letter to his family dated July 29th, 1937, Battalion member Harry Fisher recounts in detail what is taken to be the 'official' version of Law's death.

> On July 9, we went over again. It so happened that the fascists had attacked too. We were about a thousand meters apart, each on a high hill, with a valley between us. The Gods must have laughed when they saw us charge each other at the same time. Once again Law was up in front urging us on. Then the fascists started running back. They were retreating. Law would not drop for cover. True, he was exhausted as we all were. We had no food or water that day and it was hot. He wanted to keep the fascists on the run and take the high hill. "Come on, comrades, they are running," he shouted. "Let's keep them running." All the time he was under machine-gun fire. Finally he was hit. Two comrades brought him in spite of the machine guns. His wound was dressed. As he was being carried on a stretcher to the ambulance, he clenched his fist and said, "Carry on boys." Then he died. (Fisher, 1937)

This is the version that is recalled in the Battalion's history. However, William Herrick, a Lincoln Battalion veteran who later became a fierce anticommunist, began to circulate a story that Law was killed by his own men. In anticommunist circles this story continues to circulate as truth. In an interview in 1986, Herrick stated thus,

> This friend of mine and I spent some time with a couple of fellows from the Battalion, shooting the breeze, playing cards, drinking wine, and all that. He and another friend of mine, a black guy who happened to be an extremely good soldier, should have been the commander, began to tell me. And it turned out that Law had led the Battalion, at least the part under his command, into a number of ambushes. And they felt they could no longer abide him, he would just destroy the rest of them. So they got into battle position and at one point there he was, he hove into sight somehow, and there were a group of them, and they all looked at each other, they nodded, and he was shot. And

it was a pretty nasty thing because he bloated up, they danced around him, he was in a coma. Somebody said they pissed on him. Later on they refused to bury him. He lay there for days. (Berman, 1996a)

Herrick's claims are strongly refuted by veterans and scholars of the period but highlight the controversy surrounding progressive appointments such as Law's.[2]

Meanwhile on the US home front, the African American community gave their full support to the Lincoln brigade. Opinion polls at the time showed that around two-thirds of the American public supported the Republican cause. Committees to support the democratically elected government were formed in Harlem and national figures such as Lena Horne, W. C. Handy and Reverend Adam Clayton Powell Jr played prominent roles in fund-raising efforts. Famous African Americans toured the war zone and at a meeting in London to raise funds for the Spanish Republic, actor and singer Paul Robeson announced his support saying that an artist "must elect to fight for freedom or for slavery." Subsequently Robeson and his wife toured the front to sing for the antifascist troops. (Anon. *African Americans in the Spanish Civil War: The War in Spain*, ALBA)

Ivor's adjutant was Andrew Mitchell. Mitchell was born on December 27th 1902. When he volunteered to join the International Brigades, he was working as a driver in Pittsburgh. He departed for Europe, on the SS Berengeria, on July 21st, 1937. In Spain, after attending officer training school, Mitchell was assigned to one of the Battalions of the 15th Brigade on the Aragon Front. While at the front he became ill and was evacuated to Murcia. After he recovered Mitchell took command of a training company. When the front broke during the initial stages of the Retreats, Mitchell led a company to the front. He was killed between March 30th and April 2nd, 1938, during the retreat from Gandesa.

By mid February Ivor was nearing the end of his time in the training base. His impatience to be transferred to the front line is obvious.

From: Ivor Hickman,
S.R.I 270, Plaza de Altazona, Albacete
13. 2. 38. Sunday

My dearest little love,
So they have gone and I remain behind.
Some others too, but very few. More than seven hundred of the comrades went up to the front yesterday afternoon, loaded into camions, 50 in each, singing and laughing, armed with huge tins of marmalade and bully, and loaves of bread. My negro adjutant, Mitchell, and I loaded them all up. First, second, third, fourth, fifth

company, recruits, service company, south American contingent, veterans, kitchen staff, Spanish comrades from the officers training school, and finally the estado mayor of the column.

Today the base seems deserted. God knows why they strip the base of such a number – when our new recruits come in, there will be only a few men left here ready to instruct them. We are going to have some work to do! I asked to go up but no! I was to remain and instruct. So I shall be here working like hell for another 2 months until April or May and then I shall go up. My chances of ever getting to the Anti-Tank Battery seem small but one never knows. The British are sadly in need of officer cadres and it looks as if I am booked for the infantry.

Although the Personnel office has me down for the Brigade Staff.

I still feel very ashamed of myself my love for not writing to you for 3 weeks – now I have a little peace, a lull, and so I write on this Sunday as ever. I wrote last Sunday too, telling you that a month ago I was made an unconfirmed lieutenant and given a company of 120 men to train. Yesterday I handed them over to another commander and they left. I believe that my negro adjutant and I did quite a bit to improving (sic) their instruction and so making them a greater force against the Fascists. We only had 3 or 4 weeks with them but we saw a change. Of course everybody in charge of a unit thinks they improve – at any rate they did some good work in the field, on manoeuvres – attacking villages and towns, advanced guard for the Battalion at night and in a dense mist and so on.

We had enumerable difficulties but not comparable with what we will get forming a new company of training instructors to train others. At present we have a nucleus of 7 men and they must turn into 120.

I often think of Colin and his unit. [Juliet's elder sister Mary was married to Colin who commanded a Sikh Regiment in India] There is little or nothing in common between our young army and the Indian Army. Our problems and our fighting are so entirely different. When I come home again I would like to meet him and discuss the military side of life here and astound him.

A year ago yesterday – when the largest draft that every left the base went to the front – was the anniversary of the first action the XV Brigade saw. And in those days it was wicked. Just sheer conviction and ghastly waste of life stopped the Fascists then. Now it is different. We are developing a well-trained and disciplined brigade, where lessons are being learnt and our men's lives saved.

But still let us talk of something else.

It is very difficult to think of anything else nowadays. Always the same – military and political, military and political. When I come home I shall be able to tell you so much. But now what can we talk about?

Poor old M, he was white in the gills when he clambered into the truck. He won't be able to stand it and I feel sorry for him; although when he was a section leader under me, I bawled him out and told him exactly what I thought of him. Then when he had to do a job under me I had no sympathy for him. Now when he is no longer responsible to me I am sorry for him.

No, you've got to stop back here and train the others and develop yourself. Next time you will definitely go up. Thank God for that. So my love you need have no fear

for me for another 2 months. First it was 2 months from October, then 4, now 6!
I wonder how you are – you must put my name on the envelope, otherwise I may very very easily not get your letters. Are you happy or miserable? Or neither.
I miss you terribly. Except that I am so busy it would make me miserable. But it is always some question or instruction, of discipline, of food, of something. Why is so and so doing so and so? When does the canteen open? How many men here? Does the sniper section know the figures on the chart of the Russian rifle? Why is the Tuckerhoff firing low? Mitchell, send a runner.... Mitch, see about the guard. No, OK Mitch, go on out. Comrade, you must realise that so-called 'bourgeois' discipline is necessary in an army. Don't the field exercises show it so well?
Have you got your flank guards out Sergeant Barr? No! Then why the hell not... see about it, Mitch, will you... it's quarter to six, Mitch, time we got up – b – it! – Tienes naranjas, camarada? No hay! Manana, manana, manana.
My love, every ounce of my love is for you. This life makes me realise how much you mean to me. More than anything else really. When I come back from this beautiful but damn land, I'll show you.

All my love to you, my sweetheart –
Ivor

From: Ivor Hickman,
No. 270 S.R.I, Plaza de Altazona, Albacete –
28 Feb '38
9 at night

My dearest little love,
Once again I have neglected you for as long as a fortnight. Now with the reorganisation caused by the draft leaving, I am – or did I tell you in my last letter? – Chief of instructors of the Base. This means I plan the programmes of instruction for everybody ~~Censored~~ *present, later* ~~Censored~~ *supervise the instruction and check on company commanders etc. Any important discussion I am in on, any change of personnel. I am now half the time in an office with a Spanish comrade, who types most frantically; half the time out checking up on the companies, on the special group of instructors on the anti-gas school, on the first aid school, and so on. Bearing in mind the formation of an N.C.O's school and a heavy Machine-Gun Company. And after all that I shall be going up with the next draft – definitely. The weather was beautiful today – six of us went out on the range and checked 25 rifles. My shooting, considering how little practice I have had is not bad – 6 cans group at 100 metres for 4 shots.*
I really am very busy. Up at from 6 – 6.30, breakfast at 6.45, parade at 7.30, officers call, a dash out or dictation to Jamie, 12 lunch, a break often interrupted, 2.15 instructions, 6 cena, and most evenings till 9 or 10 spent in discussions and arrangements. It makes the days go fast and life if nothing else is not boring.
But it must seem boring to you – I received another of your letters my love a few

days ago. As you say you have to fight against the same people as me – I hope that gives you some consolation. You must forgive my neglect but really I am very busy and always jotting down notes in my notebook – and seldom feeling like writing. I start tonight and the adjutant comes in and starts talking about the individual reports of the special group of instructors. What can you do?
It is 9.25 – which is late for a base in Spain and I must go to bed. But let me say this – for God's sake don't think that I don't love you because I write so seldom. On the contrary I love you like hell and I always will. And I think of you many times every day and I am very proud of you. As Jack, the adjutant said today "what marvellous weather, all I could do with now is a Spanish senorita!" "I prefer shooting" I said – and I meant it – Damn them. I've got a job to do. But wait till I come back to you!

Love – all my love to you – Ivor

From:
Ivor Hickman, S.R.I. 270, Plaza de Altazona, Albecete,

This was to be Ivor's final letter before he was granted his wish and was sent to the front line. The Battalion records indicate the following assessment of Ivor,

> Sound politically. Very well educated. Expert in mathematics. Attended Officers School and graduated second in examinations. Excellent influence at school. Then made Chief of Training Staff at Tarazona. Responsible for mapping out Training Schedules. Weak in handling men. Slightly nervous. Suitable for technical or theoretical work at Estado Mayor.

9

Baptism & Retreat

On the March 9th the British Battalion was resting in reserve north of the town of Belchite, which the XV Brigade had fought over the previous summer. Unknown to them a massive prototype blitzkrieg was being planned by the Nationalist High Command along the Aragon Front south of the Ebro from Fuentes de Ebro to Seguro de los Banos. With massive artillery and air support the line was broken and Republican units forced to retreat rapidly and in disorder. By the March 15th, six days after the defence of Belchite, the British Battalion had retreated to Caspe. Here they were forced to fight a rearguard action against the 14th Bandera of the Spanish Foreign Legion – Peter Kemp, one of the very few British volunteers for the Nationalists at that time was serving with the 14th and later described the battle as his "bitterest engagement of the war" (cited in Baxell: 103). The British Battalion commander, Sam Wild, the Communist Party organiser, Joe Norman, quartermaster Robert "Hooky" Walker and Communist Party representative Harry Dobson were all captured but managed to escape. A desperate attempt to defend Caspe was made but by March 17th, it was encircled and the Battalion and other defenders were forced to abandon the town. Two days later, Republican reinforcements arrived and managed to temporarily halt the Nationalist advance. The retreats were a time of chaos for the British volunteers. Bill Alexander would later describe the march as "hell for the Battalion." (Baxell, 103) The column was constantly strafed by Nationalist aircraft and as the volunteers broke ranks to take cover, organisation crumbled. Some were left behind while others became mixed up with other units.

On March 19th, the base at Albacete was closed and transferred to Catalonia. The Battalion, now regrouping in Batea, had yet another commander, George Fletcher, while Sam Wild recovered from his wounds in Barcelona. The Battalion soon numbered six-hundred and fifty men as many sick and wounded volunteers responded to the emergency and returned to their ranks.

The following series of letters to Juliet are from this period.

21st March 1938

S.R.I 51, N.,
Plaza de Altazona, Albacete
My dearest love,

At last we have left the base! After 5 months work there I have gone on up to the front and become a gunner in the Anti-Tank Battery, a battery of three guns. From chief of instructors at the base, to a gunner! This is a unique army Censored *we are* Censored *kilometres behind* Censored *. The whole brigade has had a very tough time and everybody has been exhausted. But now after* Censored *rest they are better.*

Every now and again we hear the distant roar of artillery or avion bomb – this front is an active one – and periodically we have to hide when we hear the avion coming – lying still under the trees so as not to be seen. But otherwise nothing except sleeping feeding and keeping warm concerns us. The guns are away at the arsenal being repaired – they were damaged to varying degrees in the last action. So I am the only one in the battery who has not yet been under fire – now I feel frightened of nothing. The casualties – for your information – are nowhere as great as in the infantry or at least have not been so far in this war. The international situation is amazingly direct and critical. News is hard to get here but we feel the Fascists are winning the first round. Even now they have lost nothing but the time will come, and if we can get materials it will come in Spain. It all as ever rests with the British people.

I have not received any mail from you for a long time – cigarettes and mail from Mona and from Mother, but not from you. I believe this may be sabotaged in England. So occasionally send your mails via Dunster. Mother's notes always seem to get through, but yours lately have been held up somewhere. I'm sorry about this – very sorry, but if you occasionally try via Dunster and if these get through then I will let you know if it is any use.

Don't be too depressed about the mail. Remember most letters turn up sometime – even if three months overdue.

And don't be miserable about me. The open air is beautiful, the countryside wonderful – I often think how fine it will be one day to make a walking tour with you over this countryside – and the food plentiful. So my love remember too that I love you and only you and want you and only you. And when I come home again to you, you will understand how much I have missed you.

Perhaps it won't be very long before we are home – and then!!
All my love as ever to you my beloved,

Ivor
My new address:
Ivor Hickman, S.R.I. 51 N, Plaza de Altazona, Albercete

March 26th 1938

My dearest love,
We are ~~Censored~~ in this beautiful country of hills and rocks, white roads, vineyards, almond blossom and wheat. Eating well, sleeping and bathing in the sun. So that I have time to write at leisure but my brain has stopped. I read Workers, Imprecor, Labour Monthly, Spanish papers, L'Humanite and more. And I have met for the first time a graduate from Cambridge – one who used to teach music at Bedales. Miles something. [Miles Tomalin] *He knows Margot Heinemann but cannot remember ever having met you.* [Margot Claire Heinemann (1913 – 1992) was a Roedean-educated British Marxist scholar and leading member of the Communist Party of Great Britain (CPGB). She joined the CPGB in 1934, spurred by a desire to play a part in opposing the British Union of Fascists. She was romantically involved with John Cornford, while at Newnham College, Cambridge where she read English.] *At any rate it is pleasant to talk about corners we know, trees, parties, Newnham, Steep, the music shed he built and whatnot.*

29th March 1938

Tomlin (sic) is the name that goes with Miles – perhaps you know him?
The weather and the country is perfect. The sky a perfect blue without a cloud – mountains in the distance, mountains across the valley, fir trees encroaching on the rocks, terraced vineyards and olive groves encroaching on firs and so down into the valley. The colours are very rich – the basic colour of the sandstone buff, in fact almost exactly as Van Gogh portrayed the Arles country.
Very often an almond tree in blossom, vineyards, a field of green corn reminds me vividly of Van Gogh's painting. It is not possible in the galleries at home to realise how he catches the impression of these things so accurately.
All that I wish is that there were no more war and that I had freedom and you. Later we will go on a walking tour through some of Spain through I have gone (sic). It would be cheap, we could sleep sometimes in the open (as of course I do now) sometimes in a village, and wander up the valley, over the mountains – all for just a few pesetas. Perhaps when the war is over we'll do that together. You would love it. The flowers are varied and beautiful, daffodils, poppies, wild anemones,

Just a day after Ivor wrote the above, the Nationalists launched a second offensive in Aragon, south of the Ebro River. The weather was poor with low visibility and heavy rain as the Battalion was ordered to take up defensive positions beyond Calaceite towards the front lines. The Battalion formed up just before daybreak and began marching along the sides of the road leading towards Calaceite. No.3 and No.4 of the Machine-Gun Company followed while No.1 Company led the way. At first light the men began to dig in beside the road but the order was quickly countermanded and once again they were ordered to advance as quickly as possible. As the Battalion approached a bend in the road beyond the town disaster struck. As outlined briefly in my chapter on the birth of the British Battalion (p.72) a number of tanks appeared heading towards them. Thinking that they must be Republican troops, the men carried on marching regardless but he tanks drove between the two columns either side of the road and opened fire. Though the outnumbered Battalion managed to set up two heavy machine-guns, disabling one tank and forcing the others to retreat, the Battalion suffered heavy losses, including the death of Battalion commissar Walter Tapsell and the aforementioned surrender of many of the Major Attlee Company. The situation was further exacerbated with the arrival of yet more tanks that approached from the previously Republican-held town of Calaceite. David Stirrat was one of the Battalion's heavy machine-gunners and recorded his recollections of the ensuing drama,

> The first thing I knew we were getting machine gunned from a tank that was sitting in the middle of the road. It was only about 100 yards away from me. Apparently the column had marched right past these tanks. There was a general melee. (in MacDougall: 268)

With little delay, Stirrat set up his heavy machine-gun by the side of the road while another gun was set up on the other. Both fired determinedly at the tank but, lacking any effective form of anti-tank ammunition, they could only look on as the tank continued to advance. Then, suddenly,

> ...the tank went on fire anyway, whether a shot got through one of the slots. The crew jumped out on to the road and ran up the road. I don't think they survived the journey, put it that way. By this time some of our fellows had been getting wounded. We were getting attacked from the right flank. When I looked round the other machine-gun had completely disappeared. Groups of prisoners were beginning to appear in front of us under the guard of the Fascists. They obviously had us surrounded and our fellows were getting captured. (in MacDougall: 268)

Another tank appeared on the road in front of Stirrat and he defiantly continued firing, forcing it to pull over to the side of the road. With this, the attack on the Battalion's right flank slowly relented as he continued to fire numerous shots in its direction. To add to their misery however, the Battalion then came under further attack from the air as a Nationalist plane appeared and began to strafe them. The attention they were getting from the enemy seemed unrelenting.

> We pulled away from the road and away towards our right flank. And this of course cleared the road and the tanks poured through in a column. There were tanks and armoured cars just swept right past us. That was the first indication I had of the strength of the opposition. I believe it was the Italian Black Arrows, Mussolini's Black Arrows, whom we were fighting at the time. They were Mussolini's crack troops. (in MacDougall: 268)

The majority of the Battalion who managed to evade capture were either on patrol or in the Machine-Gun Company to the rear. They were forced to retreat south away from the road to avoid further attacks from both ground and air, thus allowing the Italian armoured column to advance rapidly towards Calaceite. The survivors found themselves disoriented, leaderless and in small groups that left them precariously vulnerable and ill at ease. As Stirrat continues,

> There were maybe about thirty of us left in this group by this time. No officers or nobody in command. I was the only one that had this gun. The situation was hopeless. So we discussed what to do. I decided that the only possibility of anyone getting out was to split up and every man to attend to himself. One guy wanted to make a last stand. Other people wanted to surrender. But the option I chose was to go my own way. (in MacDougall: 268)

Removing the lock, the principal part of the mechanism from his gun, Stirrat began to make his own way back. A short while later he joined up with fellow Brigader Donald Weston who was armed with "a bloody big axe." After many hazardous days avoiding the Nationalist troops and forced to live off the land, the two men eventually swam the Ebro to the safety of Republican-held territory. On arrival both were hospitalised, Weston being repatriated back to England – suffering from the trauma of the engagement he had become, "very vague and couldn't make his mind up even about having a haircut" (cited in MacDougall: 273) Eight days later Stirrat was back with the Battalion. Like David Stirrat the remainder of the volunteers made their way back to Gandesa where they met up with the rest of their comrades.

By April 2nd, under the command of Malcolm Dunbar, the Battalion took up positions southeast of Gandesa. Reinforced by around 50 Spanish soldiers and a small tank, they held off the Nationalist attacks for the day, then, covered by volunteers from No.4 Company under the command of Walter Gregory, withdraw later the same night. After a thirty-two kilometre forced march in the direction of Tortosa, they arrived at the Ebro River at Cherta. Many were forced to swim the wide and fast-flowing river. Finally after a journey of seventy-two kilometres and three weeks after the bloody fighting at Calaceite, the Brigade returned to Republican held territory.

British Brigader Bob Clarke describes his journey back to the Battalion,

> The next morning found us a good many miles on the road to Reus. About 10 a. m. we were ambling along, wondering whether to have a sleep or to find means of satisfying our appetites when an approaching truck looked very familiar. Yes, it was one of the Fifteenth's. In a few minutes we were perched inside and bowling along to Reus. This truck had been sent out along with a few others to scour the highway as far as Tortosa and to collect all Fifteenth Brigade men. We three made up about a dozen who had been found before the truck had gone more than a few miles, and before long about thirty English and Americans were crammed in, looking in a near state of exhaustion. As we neared Reus, which looked a large place, we noticed a car following behind us and as we drew nearer one of the Americans shouted a cheery greeting and we were surprised to hear a reply in English. The American recognised one of the car's passengers as Ernest Hemingway, the author. We all joined in a rather difficult conversation as we rolled along. As if by some invisible force not a single man harped on his experiences, but we all stated that it would soon be our turn to drive back the enemy. Damn it! We wouldn't admit any signs of lack of faith in the Republic's ultimate victory, not even to men sympathetic to our cause. (88)

In one of those strange little coincidences that often seem to occur in war, Lincoln Battalion volunteer Alvah Bessie makes reference to possibly the same incident in his *Spanish Civil War Notebooks*. Bessie states,

> April 3: Sent as guard on truck (4 a.m.) to look for other men of XV Brigade. Went through Tortosa, down Mediterranean shore and up into the mountains. Found some men. Very few Lincoln Battalion men yet found. (Only 4 of scout group reached Mora with us.) Peasants evacuating north. All towns empty. Fascists driving to the sea at Tortosa and elsewhere – expected to reach it shortly. Came back up toward Mora

with about 300 men. (Met Hemingway and [Herbert] Matthews – who gave us Chesterfields.) Slept in bus. (Bessie, 2002: 25)

The Battalion, now under the command of Sam Wild, then began a period of deserved rest and recuperation. Their strength was boosted by the arrival of a new batch of volunteers and, unable to find replacement guns for those abandoned by the retreat of the men of the Anti-Tank Battery, with typical understatement, Ivor writes of this period,

April 8th 1938

And I lost the next sheet somewhere so you must excuse that. Lately the Brigade has been busy and when I return I will tell you of many experiences that my comrades and I have had. I have had an easy and safe time. I have had my first shelling and sniping and so on – it was really quite exhilarating. Now we are able to get letters written and so on. Only I haven't got any more writing paper.
I had my first horse ride for two or three years this morning – Just for an hour or so on a cavalry mount. A light field piece is firing shells at those damned fascists. Over my head. Today I met a man from Wittgenstein's class, one Hutchison who has been out here 20 months.[1] *I am OK and very healthy. All my love to you as ever. I love you more than anything in the whole world.*
Ivor – From: Ivor Hickman, S.R.I. 51N, Albacete, Spain

10

Chabola Valley

The spring and early summer was a period of relative tranquility for the Battalion. Immediately after the Retreats across the River Ebro, from early April the Battalion initially held positions on the north side of the river in the mountains between Garcia and Ascó.

On May 20th the XV Brigade was based at Tarrega, in reserve for an attempted offensive to retake Lleida, but by June 1st they had returned to the Ebro and set up camp near Marca at a camp they nicknamed 'Chabola Valley' (*Chabola* being the Spanish word for shack or shelter). The camp sat near the road between Marca and La Torre de Fontaubella in a beautifully lush green valley. George Wheeler was one of several new volunteers to arrive at the "hidden wonderland of huts and lean-tos" established in the valley. (Wheeler: 53) As he was to later recall in *To Make People Smile Again*, he was placed in No.4 Company and immediately began to construct his own Chabola.

> Insufficiently equipped as we were, it was hard work under a hot sun. But by taking it in turns and with perseverance we felled two fir trees, which we dragged back to the valley. Trimming off the smaller branches, we used the trunks as supports, leaning them against the terrace wall, while the lower ends were sunk into the earth. We laced smaller branches across the main supports, and soon had the basis of a good, sound structure. Inside there was ample room for the three of us and our belongings. (54)

It was around this time that Ivor was transferred from the Anti-Tank Battery to a new and vital role within the Battalion. He writes to Juliet to tell her the news,

April 24th 1938

My dearest love,
I received your letter dated April 15th on the 21st – 6 days! Excellent.
And your letter moved me very much and made me strong for you – Oh Christ – that my love was in my arms. And I in my bed again.
But to tell you what I am doing – I am temporarily attached to the British Battalion as a Battalion observer, in fact a cabo unconfirmed (or corporal). So I am part of the Battalion headquarters staff and my job is to observe the enemy – i.e. see but not be seen. And I am armed with a rifle (to be used only as a last resort) and a pair of field glasses. It is an observer's job to know as much about the enemy and our own troops as possible; positions, areas of companies, gun emplacements, etc. It involves missions independent of the main body, which means more scope for initiative and more concentration. Also it is very tiring sometimes. Yesterday – no, the day before, I went round for 8 hours with a Spanish officer and mapped the trenches and gun positions as occupied by another Battalion – over a long front along 1 or 2 words censored. Then on getting back I started for an observation post in the mountains and walked and climbed in the dark until about 1 – and then settled down for a marvellous sleep on the mountainside. Before it was light I was up on the mountain top observing and with another comrade observed for 12 hours – until about 5. Looking thro' glasses at Fascists at 2–3kms for 5 – 6 hours a day is tiring. We couldn't see them on the hillside with the naked eye but with the glasses (magnification of 8) they showed up.
So a hike back to the Estado Major, food, report to the Bn. commander and then glorious sleep. Today I am resting. Possibly the artillery will get onto the fascists tomorrow and destroy a fair number of them – Good.
Yesterday I received a parcel from Mother, chocolate and so on. So that today I am feeling a bit worse for wear as my tummy is not used to ½ lb of chocolate at a time. My reason for gluttony was that I did not want to carry around any more than absolutely necessary as weight matters. Because I carry log tables, rules, a level, a rifle, 80 rounds of ammunition, 1 or 2 bombs, Shakespeare's sonnets, socks, underclothes, 2 pairs of sandals, rifle cleaning kit and oil, a spoon and a cup, a Spanish grammar, letters, notebooks and perhaps a reading book – all in and around the old pack. And of course one or two blankets rolled over my shoulder. Altogether I feel the complete soldier. And I generally wear two pairs of trousers, one of which has no flies the other no backside.
I forgot; and my towels and toothpaste, soap and string. Always talking about myself – I apologise.
You say were going up to town to see Mary before she went to India to marry Colin. I smiled when you said her sudden decision was because (or partly because) of her fear of a world war breaking out.
Why did she wait till now to realise that? Why is it obvious now and was not many years before? And again surely her wish to marry is independent of a world war, isn't it? When I read your remark I felt a little cynical, but perhaps I misunderstood. Being out here and seeing most excellent men, some of them my friends – here today

and dead tomorrow and I don't turn a hair or have the slightest trace of feeling, makes me a trifle more severe towards others. But still I am glad of that – of my conservation of emotion for other things – primarily for my love of you. My love will be richer and deeper because I am more real and I am learning to drown my old stupid ideas and whims and becoming sane and I hope more valuable to myself and to the world. Not that I have any individual value to the world. So why be a stupid little romantic ass?

These feelings are a reflection of my life – I don't object to the bad conditions, to the food and to the lice – (I have not got many – this warfare is open warfare not trench warfare thank God) nor to the killing. Because the war is no more horrible than the war that is always going on – at least now I know that in time I shall assist in the killing of people whose class interests are not mine. Whereas in so called peace time hypocrisy predominates. And I don't believe that death is too great a penalty for the ruling class – damn them. If they get me in the process – alright and damn them. Because if they do get me – I don't see why they should if I bear in mind my training – Shell Mex and Metro Vics and the church and the army and Cambridge and more are all to blame (if you can call it that) nearly as much as the Fascists. So don't let yourself or anyone else forget that, darling, if you can. This is not a letter of hate but a letter of fact.

A few days ago I received a letter from Elizabeth. I wrote to her one day during the period of forced idleness I underwent when I first joined the Brigade. She says she will try when she is home (at Geldeston, near Beccles) to come and see you. She has always wanted to meet you. And she says if she can be of any assistance to either of us she would like to be. Incidentally she writes Thomas is engaged to a Hertford girl. Poor old stupid Thomas. He was stupid really, wasn't he? I wonder if he sleeps with his fiancée? I doubt it. "Let's put it off and the flavour won't be spoiled." What a fool, being frightened of sleeping with a woman, I bet he is frightened even now. Of course, not of her breasts, but more? Tut, tut. And Mother writes and tells me Tex is blasé about sleeping with women – talks of it as of his dinner. What fools I had for friends!

So it comes about that of all the people I've known well, you are the only one left who is not a fool. Mother is in many ways antiquated – I feel that so much when I get her letters out here. I used at one time to put a great deal on friends – I don't now. So there is only one individual left in my world and that is you. Because you have beauty and culture and understanding. And because I love you. You know, I can remember your body so well, I can almost remember the touch of your thighs. Almost. Wait till I get home, I will love you and bite you (you will object to that but I don't care a damn) and make you happy and give you a son or a daughter or more. Don't get worried about me, will you? An observer's job isn't dangerous. He shouldn't fight but should see, see, see. And when I return to the Anti-Tank Battery I hope to be an observer there too.

Now I must finish. I hope you will enjoy this letter and what I have to say in it. Excuse it if it is priggish.

As I have told you so often – but let us hope that the oftener the firmer – don't forget that I love you more than anything else, anybody else – more than everything. And

when I get back I will show you what that means. And then God willing, you're coming with me wherever I go. And we going (sic) to work together, live together and love together. Viva! 'Ola!
My love, you're a marvellous creature and so damned beautiful.
Ivor –
Ivor Hickman, S.R.I. 51N, Barcelona, Spain (n.b. change)

Once again the intimacy of Ivor's letters emphasises the fact that these are the writings of a newly married yet effectively estranged husband, however deeply in love, thus highlighting the personal sacrifices made by both he and his many comrades. In the secluded valley of ramshackle shelters, thoughts of life in England must have seemed a distant memory.

In a letter to a close friend, Ivor further described his work as an observer with the Battalion,

26th April 1938

>*...Excuse me for sounding priggish, but wouldn't you be really surprised if meetings and so on did change the world right there and then? If we win in Spain, God knows how much good will come of it. Fascism is powerful but that is no reason for not going on fighting...*

I ought not to be writing now, but I ought to be wandering over the countryside marking trenches in our sketchmaps. Because now I am an observer in the British Battalion and have temporarily left the Anti-Tank Battery. Observing the enemy is a fascinating business. I watch through glasses all day from some high point, for example a mountain 15000ft. above the plain, and see fascists in houses and on the hillside and watch them sunbathing, collecting breakfast, sleeping after their siesta, lighting fires...So the brigade informs the artillery and if the artillery wants to start a war they are shelled quickly and accurately...Then the fascists answer back with their artillery and blast away at a town of ours. We shell their batteries and so on, until at last both sides get tired and everything dies down... [The recipient of these letters is identified only as an intimate friend. They were reprinted in the eulogy to Ivor written by C. P. Snow in the *Christ's College Magazine*. No 144. (1939). p47]

During their time in Chabola Valley the volunteers underwent various training 'programs'. They learned how to strip and assemble their guns under the cover of darkness; there were courses on the operation of Soviet produced 'Dyegtyaryov' and 'Tokarev' machine-guns; 'full-scale' training schools were set up for corporals, sergeants and officers. It was here at the Cabo (Corporal) school in the main square of the village of Marca that Ivor received his observer training. To this day the red painted lettering *Intendencia* (Stores) for the 15th Brigade, are still visible above the door next to the carpenter's shop were the training took place. As the classes were of

The role of the observer, for which Ivor Hickman was commended, wasn't dangerous, he thought. As he wrote to Juliet, the observer "shouldn't fight but should see see see."

mixed nationalities most of the training was conducted in Russian translated through interpreters. This led to the whole process being a rather lengthy and complex affair.

Another feature of life of the International Brigades in Chabola Valley and indeed throughout the war was the phenomenon of the 'war tourist'. Prominent politicians and delegates from various groups took advantage of this lull in the fighting to visit the volunteers. Future Conservative Prime Minister Edward Heath and was part of one of these deputations. In his autobiography, Heath would recall the events,

> In the summer of 1938, together with three other Oxford undergraduates, I received an invitation from the Republican government of Spain, which had then been involved for nearly two years in its civil war, to spend two or three weeks in Catalonia, the last great province remaining under its control. I was invited in my capacity as chairman of the Federation of University Conservative Associations. My colleagues were Richard Symonds, a socialist from Corpus Christi who joined the United Nations secretariat after the Second World War; Derek Tasker,

a Liberal from Exeter College who was later ordained and became the Canon Treasurer of Southwark Cathedral; and George Stent, a South African from Magdalen, who was probably the furthest to the left of us all in his political views. For all of us, it was to be our first taste of war.

We were to witness a conflict which aroused, in our generation, passions every bit as fierce as those stirred up by the war in Vietnam thirty years later. The struggle between the Republicans and General Franco's fascists had gained particular international significance because of the intervention of Germany and Italy on Franco's side, and the refusal of the Chamberlain government to do more than isolate Spain. Moreover, many of our contemporaries had gone off to Spain to fight, the majority on the Republican side, and many had lost their lives. My sympathies were firmly with the elected government of the Spanish Republic simply because it was not a dictatorship, although it was somewhat to the left and was supported by the Soviet Union. (Heath: 1988, Electronic Edition)

Future trade union leader and pensioners' rights campaigner Jack Jones, himself a volunteer in the British Battalion, met Heath and would later recall that "In a sense, we remained friends from that period onwards because we had a sort of common bond." (2008: 82) Another group of visitors who would later become household names in the post-war world was the leader of the Indian Socialist Party Jawaharlal Nehru together with his daughter Indira Gandhi and journalist and politician Krishna Menon. These fellow fighters against British imperialism received an enthusiastic welcome from both the British and Irish volunteers. They were greeted with cries of "Long Live Indian Independence" and descended upon by a hoard of autograph collectors. Visitors were treated to demonstrations of military skills and expertise including a display of the accuracy of the Battalion's machine-gunners. Nehru said of his visit "In the army I found not only efficiency and discipline, but also comradeship between the officers and the men." (Rust, 2003: 170)

After the prolonged weeks of training at Albacete, the period of relaxation did not appeal to Ivor. In a letter to a friend, he described his frustrations,

9th June
It's raining and I'm in a peasant's house, which is the Estada (Sic) *Mayor.* [Estado Mayor – Battalion HQ] *I'm feeling a bit miserable but thanking God I'm not out in the rain like most of the Battalion.*
I'm miserable because I can't help thinking of the future when if I'm lucky I'll return to civilisation (if civilisation or I exist when that time is due) and start at my A.B.C.,

from there through the three R's to long division. Will I ever get over long division? An immense barrier, you know.

Oh God, war is a bore, so dull, such an aches, such a pain, and so stupid. For the moment you have something important and valuable to do, that's OK. Possibly visit a town, OK. Possibly a climb up a mountain and a resultant view, OK. Otherwise boredom on boredom. A military maxim reads so truly: "Organisation is merely to assist in restraining the confusion."

The process of rest and rebuilding during this period was aided by the re-opening of the Spanish border with France. This not only led to the supply of much needed arms to the Republic but also allowed easier access to Spain for new recruits. Despite the list of defeats suffered by the Republic, around 35 men arrived in April and a further dozen in May. By the end of May the Battalion could boast a strength of around 650 men of which around a third were British.

While the majority of the Battalion were busy training, Ivor, in his role as an observer, was often away from the Battalion. He recounts his exploits in the following series of letters. His fatalism and realistic appraisal of his possible fate is apparent throughout these correspondences to his friend.

17th June
...Yes, I'm alive all right and with luck will remain so. I'm afraid I can't write to you if I am unlucky, so you will have to assume that I am OK until you hear from somewhere that I am not. Even then I wouldn't believe it if I were you, because quite a lot of men out here have had memorial meetings held for them and then read of them in local rags...I stand a moderately good chance of going back to England (that's quite honest) but somebody's got to be killed and this death business isn't dealt out fairly or honestly. Anyway, it's not really important. It's important to me because I have so many things to do yet.
Your misery is bloody and I'm sorry. Yet I assure you that if you heard the screech of an aerial bomb, you would suddenly find you had much to live for. Or I hope to God so, anyway...

19th June
I don't know why I haven't got on with this letter but I haven't. I have been reading a lot, which is quite a change for me; somehow reading is almost impossible.
I received two letters at the same time as yours; which tell me Juliet has been having a holiday and is now at Dunster with mother. God, Dunster in June!
The military situation is critical, very critical. In fact the whole world situation is so immediately critical that we haven't time to inspect every possible intellectual approach and work it out. And your arguments are a retrogression. But I won't argue. I doubt whether I will argue about politics again very much. I know that what you say is wrong, and I realise too that if you were here you just couldn't think like that...

I guess I'll be OK. Don't worry. Before long the whole world will have to get used to premature and unnatural death.

The following letters to Juliet are more concerned with more practical matters in England rather than in Spain.

June 23, 1938
It is a long time since I wrote to you but what with an observer's school and observing the fascist fortifications and so on I have been busy and what not and separated from the Battalion.
At present I am sitting in the shade of a white rambler in the yard of an evacuated hotel, writing at a table, maps around me, waiting for a fool who's got the maps I want so – good God – when was it last I wrote to Juliet? Hell, I ought to have written before. So here goes.
First, I'm so glad to hear that you have been and let's hope still are enjoying yourself at Dunster. I would like to have been there too with you my love. A future time.
How's Mother and Pater? And Dunster? Your Mother and Jean wrote me telling me that you had visited them – Guildford now? – and soon went on to Dunster. Your mother who wrote me a rather silly unreal letter putting individual wants before anything else independent of what it is, wars or god knows what. Any finally she tells me Mary is at a hill station and now has a bull-terrier of her own!
She also told me what was much more important, that you were very tired and beginning to feel the strain of the anxiety and worst of all – you had bad nightmares while you were there. Oh, hell. How long has that been going on? You remember I asked you before but you did not answer. I am sorry I am not with you to stop them. Or was it because you were tired and run down, or possibly going back to your life before I jumped into it? I don't think it is fundamental, because think of the simplicity of the cure – but hell, it's important. What can I say? I'm sorry, very sorry. I hope that the rest will improve it.
I also got a letter from Jean telling me much of her local news – next month school cert. for her, poor kid. And tell me is Mary married, thinking about it or what? A hill station sounds cool; it's getting hot here. My "front" i.e. down just past my navel is a good brown, because I wear a kind of shirt which can be undone right down. So I undo it and pull it out over my trousers. Hence the colour.
Also I am getting fatter. My face is fatter than you have ever seen it – really because of the food and the out of door life I lead – sometimes too out of doors. And last night I slept on a bed – without a mattress – and slept beautifully. After having slept on the ground etc for 3 months, it is magnificent to return to such luxuries.

3rd July 1938
Here I am again, not writing to you again until this date, a Sunday and a rest day thank God. I slept in this morning, a thing I haven't done for ages. And the weather has been consistently beautiful, if a trifle cold at nights. Now I am lying on a blanket, with my trousers on, writing to you.

I received a letter with the Foresters name on, but whose handwriting? I was very pleased to get your letter and to hear of Helen and Dunster and so on. Chamois, your letter was a beautiful one and made me happy for many days. Thank you so much for it. I realise that you alone are the only person who can keep any contact out here with me. Mother's letters don't strike a sympathetic note very often – I mean they irritate me because they sometimes seem so unreal to me out here. And Elizabeth, who has written to me twice, deserves to have her backside smacked for talking and thinking as she does about Communism and the Soviet Union. (It is interesting how intellectuals tend to Left-wing Communism and Trotskyism on one hand and dilettantism on the other). Your mother never did write a letter to my satisfaction and Jean is young. Pat's OK, but seldom writes, quite naturally because I seldom write to her. Mona writes to me sometimes, otherwise nobody does. So you see I haven't a very big correspondence. But as you so well know even that is not covered. It is from you that I look forward to mail and from no one else. When I see the mailman, it is your letters I think of. Obvious though, when you know that I am in love with you.

Fighting Fascism is often times a joke. When we were observing we were drinking the best vino of the town with our feet up on a stone table, under a huge shady tree for hours during the day. All within enemy machine gun range, but there weren't any guns or any fire.

There were 7 of us but somehow we managed to get rations for 21, and we went out from the deserted town and dug up vegetables, potatoes, onions and brought in fruit, pears, apples, and so on. And on the Fascists side we could see attractive Spanish women maybe working in the fields, maybe driving a burro out of town in their territory, the burro loaded with chairs and mattresses and god knows what. The quiet of the front was only broken by the very occasional machine gun fire on the right flank and once by 2 planes which few right over us but kindly passed on and dropped 3 bombs in some fields near the next village. So this is the glorious fight against Fascism. I sometimes laugh when I read the Worker about the I.B., more often the line annoys me. To some, not all, but even so some, this life is a holiday. I myself have other ideas of holidays.

Nowadays I am still British Battn. Chief Observer and I instruct the Battalion and Company observers and also the reconnaissance scouts of the Battalion. This means rather a lot of work because the 3 groups are at different stages of training. I have a responsibility next under a Company Commander but I am only a Cabo (Corporal)! This army to say the least is unconventional.

For the last 3 weeks we have been very short on tobacco – 15 cigarettes and 1 Spanish cigar (ooh!). So, we resort to leaves off the nut trees and today we had 'butt' (i.e. the end of someone else's cigarette) between 4 of us. As someone put it "not quite the thing for a Christ's man." But DON'T send any out in my letters because the bastards somewhere are sure to rifle the letters and I'll never smell them. Keep the money. Why should you supply those bastards in the post office with cigarettes? Oh, by the way, if you ever come to Spain bring a huge quantity of cigarettes with you because they are worth approximately 5 times their value and in Barcelona, change them at the prevalent rate (take care to find it) at approx. 50 pesetas for

20 Players, i.e. 1,000 ps. to £. The English sailors in Barcelona live like lords on a package of cigarettes! And a cigarette will get you anywhere and everywhere in Spain. I somehow feel you must be damaging somebody by such a transaction, I mean the 1000 ps. to the £, but I can't see who.
And talking of money reminds me – how are you going financially? Let me know how things are shaping in this respect.
I ought to have asked you more often but I don't know why I close my eyes to some things. Anyway let me know, won't you? And don't pay any of my old bills.
Forgive me for not writing to you oftener but I do love you more than anyone in the world and I want you more than anything in the world and I'm going to have you too.

My love to you my sweetest Chamois.
Ivor
PS. Yes, Pat must go to a good school, I will write to Mother about it, oh when is your birthday, September the what?

From Ivor Hickman,
S.R.I. 51N, Barcelona, Spain

PPS. Please send in you next package a Hugo Spanish Grammar for a friend of mine and 2 slabs of Pears Golden Glory soap for me. Even when we have any, our soap is poor quality and won't lather.

Ivor

Hygiene was, and is today, a constant problem on the frontline. As George Wheeler recalls,

> My limited experience as a soldier had already taught me one important lesson. If you wanted to keep clean, you had to get to the wash tubs early. And this I did on my first morning in Chambola Valley. I was disconcerted to find that the only washing water available was in three small buckets. By the time my turn came the water was almost black with a thick layer of scum. Shortage of water was to be a constant theme during my time in Spain. (54)

The lack of facilities led to a further common problem suffered by soldiers from the earliest days of warfare. Lice. Wheeler comments,

> We were also becoming typical soldiers in another less positive sense. We were lousy. I had reasoned that if one obeyed certain rules of cleanliness, these loathsome creatures could be kept in check. But with little water and no chance of a bath it was impossible. It was an

everyday sight to see men delousing their shirts and pants, and a sense of revulsion never left me. (57)

Although in his letters Ivor makes light of the hardships he was suffering, there is evidence to show that he was not as removed from the squalor as his letters to Juliet would suggest. In his unpublished memoirs, Billy Griffiths notes the following,

> Our food was quite monotonous. It hardly varied – bread and coffee for breakfast, carrabunces for dinner and lentils for supper [Carrabunces, which were similar to split peas] However, there was some slight advantage in being attached to HQ. After dinner, and sometimes after supper, Monty Sim's batman brought out the scraps for disposal into an improvised bin. All eyes were fixed on him as he scraped the plates clean and when he had gone, there was a concerted rush to delve among the scraps! It was an undignified sight. These were cultured men. Hickman, the head of the observers, had led a sheltered life. Prep school, Public school, Cambridge, a degree and an apprenticeship with Dunlop then Spain. Joe Latus, a trawler captain; an American news reporter and so on. Yet the food was irresistible: a bit of liver or meat on a bone, perhaps a potato. It was a change. (Griffith, 1997)

However, these hardships were soon to be replaced by an even greater challenge for not just Ivor, nor the Battalion, but the Republican forces as a whole. As well as weapons drills there had been much training on the procedures for crossing rivers. It was obvious to even the newer recruits at Chambola Valley that a Republican offensive was becoming increasingly likely, if not imminent. In his last surviving letter before the Ebro offensive, Ivor hints at the "surprises" to come,

> *3rd July*
> *Still I haven't sent this letter off. But I have been away from the Battalion and very busy. And today is a rest day. The first I've had with the Battalion at any time. So this morning I slept in – what a pleasure...Heaven knows when this war will end. Nobody seems to know and nobody believes soon. I don't either. These next two months will hold some surprises... I'm lying under a hazel-nut tree, my head in the shade, my body in the hot sun. I have never been so brown in my life.*

11

Ebro

The Ebro River (*Ebre* in Catalan) flows across what is commonly referred to as the 'neck' of Spain, from its source in the northwesterly region of Cantabria, diagonally bisecting the country in an easterly direction until eventually, it opens out to become a broad delta on the Mediterranean coast in the province of Tarragona. Today, the Ebro is well known as Spain's most voluminous river and, measuring nine-hundred and twenty-eight kilometres in length, it is also its longest, flowing through through the cities Miranda de Ebro, Logrono, Flix, Tortosa and Amposta. The name itself is derived from the Basque words *ibai* meaning 'river' and *ibar*, valley. Historically, the significance of the Ebro cannot be underestimated as, for centuries, it formed a natural divide between Roman expansion in the north and Carthaginian expansion in the south following the First Punic War (264-241BC). Today, however, it is better known as one of Europe's most popular fishing destinations, and the Ebro Delta is also one of the most important aquatic habitats of the western Mediterranean too, boasting a large and diverse bird population; its importance to the ecology of the Iberian peninsular cannot be underestimated. In July 1938 however, the scene was quite different, the River Ebro becoming the backdrop for the largest and bloodiest battle of the civil war.

The Ebro offensive opened on the evening of July 24th, 1938 and, unknown to the combatants would mark the final phase of the war. The build-up to the offensive began with the Nationalist drive in March 1938, into the Aragon. An initial armoured thrust with the intention of following up the recapture of Teruel was followed by a ninety-six kilometre advance which forced the Republican troops to fall back and retreat. On April 15th, Navarrese troops victoriously cavorted in the waves at Vinaroz on the Mediterranean. The Republic was now split into two by the Nationalists and

President Azana resigned himself to an inevitable defeat. Although the way to Barcelona was open to Franco, he hesitated and attacked Valencia instead. Diplomatic methods had failed and the only course of action available to the Republicans was to go on the offensive.[1]

The strategic aim was to draw the Nationalists away from their assault on Valencia and to reunite the two halves of the Republic. The vital centre of Nationalist communications in Gandesa was a primary target. The plan would be carried out in four phases. The main thrust was in the central sector, where one division would cross the Ebro near Ribarroja and occupy the Sierra de Fatarella. It would then link up with a second which had crossed in the region of Ascó. The axis of the march would be the road from Gandesa to Flix. The second division was then to attempt to occupy the crossroads and Venta de Camposines before continuing on to Lavall de la Torre where they would establish contact with V Corps who should by then be positioned in the heights of the Sierra de Cabals. Meanwhile in the southern sector, one brigade was to cross the river at Benifallet and occupy the dominant heights on the left bank of the River Canaletas and the Sierra de Vallplana. They were then to link up with another division of V Corps that had crossed at Ginestar, then re-enter the Sierra de Cabals to link up on the right with forces of XV Corps. The unit which passed Ginestar was to surround Mora de Ebro and cut off the road from Alcolea del Pinar to Tarragona. The 42nd Division in the central sector was to provide a diversionary action by crossing the river to the south of Mequinenza and occupy the Auts Hills. This would prevent the Nationalists from forming a bridgehead south of the front. Other units would cross the river towards the right bank of the River Matarrana to cut the Fayon-Pobla de Masaluca road. A brigade would try to cross the river towards Amposta in the southern sector, cutting the Valencia-Barcelona road. This was to form a bridgehead for further operations.

The second phase required the forces that occupied Fatarella to advance in the direction of Villalba de Los Arcos-Batea. The units that occupied Venta de Camposines were to continue on the Gandesa-Calaceite and Gandesa-Bot-Horta axes. The occupation of the Sierra de Pandols in the southern sector would be completed after gaining the junction of the River Gandesa with the Canaletas.

The third phase would begin with an advance in the central sector to continue along the axis Pinell-Tortosa-Vinaroz, with the right flank in the Sierra de Pandols. Here it would link up with XV Corps and occupy the left bank of the River Magrane and Serbol. Once adequate bridges were constructed, artillery and armour would be transported to the right bank.

The fourth and final stage was to pursue the campaign as indicated by the High Command. The ambiguity of these orders are indicative of the

The River Ebro viewed from the crossing point of the British Battalion near Asco

complex nature of the overall plan specifically the river crossings. Observers, possibly Ivor himself, had infiltrated the Nationalist territory by swimming across the river and noting down positions and troop concentrations. Prisoners were interrogated and boats and equipment were hidden near the banks of the river.

Led by Juan Modesto, the Republican forces moved up to the River Ebro and during the night of July 25th, began crossing the river at 16 separate points along the eighty kilometre front.

First hand accounts of the offensive make compelling reading and for that reason it is worth quoting at length here the recollections of those directly involved. In his memoirs, *No Boots to my Feet*, Brigader Bob Clark describes the moment the Battalion were informed of the offensive,

> Bob Cooney was a rather boyish looking chap with very bushy eyebrows and hair that grew straight up. The announcement he made sent a thrill through all of us; "We are going to cross the Ebro." The words were astonishing to most of us. We hardly believed it possible, thinking all along that we would only take up defensive positions along the river. To re-cross the river was electrifying, especially as we were told it was

(Photo: J.W.)

to be an all-out offensive. How we laughed when we remembered it was only a few weeks ago when we had been taunted by the Fascists on the other side of the river who had advised the Internationals to get their running pumps ready as they would soon be coming over after us. The boot was on the other foot. We were even informed that the Republican High Command knew the names of the enemy Commanders on the opposite bank as well as the number of troops and where their artillery was stationed. This information had been received from peasants who, at risk of their lives, had swum the river on black nights and swum back again past the enemy's lines to prepare the people for the coming liberation. (97)

He continues,

> We all gave three hearty cheers and began to get ready to move. In a very short time we had left the valley and were trudging along a narrow tortuous path with an amazing number of trucks slowly crawling along loaded up with material for bridge building. The break of day found us skirting the edge of a dried-up river which was densely covered

with rushes over six feet in height, giving excellent cover. A tense feeling of excitement was obvious by the queer smiles on everyone's faces. Now and again we stopped to enable a labour squad, who were feverishly hauling huge coils of rope and carrying countless numbers of small boxes to be used as a light pontoon bridge, to pass. This is what we really enjoyed. The spirit of revenge permeated all ranks and we longed to wipe out the insults hurled at us from the opposite side of the Ebro. (98)

As the men readied to cross a Nationalist aircraft came into view,

> Suddenly the cry of "Avion" was given and we flung ourselves face downwards amongst the rushes, but only for a moment. The new tactic of the army was to fire back at planes if circumstances warranted it. The old method of lying doggo obviously immobilised troops and definitely played into the enemy's hands. We were in an ideal position for retaliation and a short time previously we had been equipped with a number of new machine-guns called *Brens*, made by the Czechs, who feeling themselves going under before the rising threat of Nazidom, had somehow contrived to send help to another democratic Republic in dire peril. These *Brens* could be used for high-angle fire and in a few moments we received orders to get ready to open fire. All at once, at about a height of three hundred feet, came a huge black-painted Italian bomber, evidently on reconnaissance. Judging by the plane's erratic flying, the pilot seemed to have an attack of the jitters. The view along the river must have upset him. No wonder! The sight of hundreds of ships' lifeboats taken off the decks of passenger liners in Barcelona's docks conveying thousands of troops across the Ebro, must have made him wonder if he was dreaming. One day the river was quiet with not a sign of movement anywhere, the same every day for weeks. Then that day the river alive with activity. As the bomber circled overhead, he banked steeply looking for a suitable target on which to unload his bombs. This was our chance. About three hundred rifles and machine-guns were levelled at the tip of his propellers and the order "Fuego" (Fire) came immediately. The plane staggered, lurched violently and rolled once or twice, the pilot almost losing control. But after a moment or so of turbulent anticipation on our part, we were disappointed to see him gain height and unload his bombs which fell like black eggs, fortunately on open ground quite a long way from where we lay. The plane roared for home, without wasting any time, to report his amazing story that the Republicans were across the Ebro.

> How the Franco High Command must have listened incredulously to his story, for I doubt if he got any pictures to prove it, but the severance of communications with their river command must have upset them considerably. (98)

Once the alarm had passed Clarke and the others continued with the crossing,

> In a very short time we regrouped and in a few minutes had reached the water's edge. An amazing site met our gaze. It was a roaring torrent, deeply discoloured with the brown clay scoured from the mountainsides away up in the Aragon. White painted lifeboats with numerous steel hausers stretched across the torrent were an unforgettable scene. The sun was well above the horizon and for a moment I thought that I was back home on an August Bank holiday and expected to see small children sporting on the shingle. It would have been natural to hear the hoarse cry of the boatmen; "Nice day for a sail", the cry of the ice-cream vendor and the hoot of the incoming ferry steamer. Truly, the Republicans had accomplished something even their foreign admirers could hardly have believed possible [...] I took my seat in a lifeboat that was marked for sixty persons. This number was well exceeded but in a few moments we were out in the middle of the river. Further up it looked comparatively calm but at that particular stretch it was rather narrow, with huge boulders protruding well out into the river, which made it extremely dangerous. It was a short but exciting trip. We reached the opposite bank eagerly scanning the surrounding hills for signs of the enemy. But the advance guards had done their job thoroughly and there was not a sign of the enemy anywhere. About half a mile up river a light field-piece was lobbing shells in a vain attempt to harry the crossing, but in a very short time this too was silenced and except for the yells of the "Marineros" (sailors) who were in charge of the crossing operations, it was hard to believe that we were invading enemy territory. With a grinding crunch on the shingle we scrambled out of the lifeboat and ran towards a small battered house. The walls were pitted with bullet marks and it was plain to see that the enemy had put up some resistance, but curiously not a body to be found. This pointed to the fact that the Fascists had got going quickly, not waiting for casualties. The country around consisted of small hills well-covered with vegetation. It was ideal country for a defending force, but an amazing stillness reigned. Not a single rifle shot disturbed the almost uncanny silence on that beautiful summer morning

but a distant low rumble suggested a bitter struggle somewhere on the pine-covered hills. (99-100)

Following the Canadian troops of the Mac-Paps, the British Battalion crossed the river to the south-east of Ascó in a number of small boats and on a rope suspension bridge a metre wide. Upstream tanks and other heavy vehicles crossed on pontoon bridges. Nationalist aircraft attacked the temporary bridges but on the whole the Nationalists were taken by complete surprise. There was an immense feeling of optimism throughout the Battalion. Runner John Longstaff (1994) summed the situation up thus,

> Battalion had crossed, and again no sound had come from any direction. No.2 Company moved quickly over fields and vineyards, fully alert. As the sun rose and light came, the platoons and sections found themselves on a road. The road led to Gandesa, where the British and other units had made one of the last stands against the advancing enemy during the retreats of March/April 1938. Still no sign of the enemy! "Where are they?" were my thoughts and those of many others. Even the equipment I was carrying seemed lighter. At last the sun was up, and it was a hot searing sun. The leading platoon was about 250 yards ahead with sections out on the two flanks. The company was well on schedule, having now been over the Ebro about four hours, and still I had not heard a single rifle shot. It was unreal. Were we going into a trap? Even the enemy's planes had not been seen. We pressed forward again and again. It was evident now that the Fascists had not thought it possible for an ill-clad, ill-armed army would attempt to cross the fast flowing Ebro and attack at the heart of the Fascist positions. (95)

By the afternoon the Battalion was within a one and a half kilometres of Corberra, a small town near Gandesa. Suddenly the element of surprise was abruptly ended. John Longstaff vividly described the moment,

> ...Rifle and machine-guns started firing. This time a strong force of Franco's Moors was firing from some low hills on the outskirts of Corbera. No.2 Company was still leading the Battalion. A comrade came running to Company HQ. The message he brought was that coming in from our right flank, and flying the Spanish and Catalan flags, was some unknown Battalion. I was sent back down the road to find Sam Wild who was studying some notes. He replied; "it will be the 13th Brigade." I quickly went up the road with orders to Comrades Gilchrist and Green to send out one of the platoons to contact the party on our

right. It seemed the 13th Brigade had the same idea as us and sent a small advance party. A few words spoken by each Commander and it was agreed that our company would now continue to advance along the flank of the road that led to Corbera and Gandesa. Further instructions were given to other Platoon and Section Commanders. The No.2 Company HQ was organised under a road culvert, which allowed winter rains to flow along the now dry riverbed. This culvert four months later was to be the site of the last fight of the British Battalion. (96)

No.1 Company was engaged in the search for the Moors at the rear, No.2 Company continued the advance on Corbera. There were no written orders, all instructions were given verbally. No.1 Company could be seen in extended order searching the foothills of the Sierra Caballs while No.3 Company was out on the left flank, the right being in the hands of the 13th International Brigade.

Acting in support of the 13th International Brigade, they successfully captured Corbera forcing the Nationalists to pull back to defend Gandesa. Next day the Battalion continued to advance on their main objective, Gandesa. By this stage of the battle the element of surprise had gone. The situation was made worse by the woeful shortage of armour and motorised equipment available. No.1 Company was detailed to mop up a detachment of Moors who were holding out near Corbera. Leaving the highway, they spread out in skirmishing order and began the exhausting task of scouring the pine covered hills. Many kilometres were covered but there was no sign of the enemy. They finally returned to the highway late in the evening were they learnt they were to guard the road from any attempted enemy action. In the hours of guard duty that followed there was little activity on the road, something that quickly led to concern and misgivings. Had the enemy blown the bridges? Where were the Republican tanks?

In the early hours of the following morning the sky became blackened with Nationalist bombers all heading for the Ebro. The Republican forces had only limited numbers of Anti-Aircraft guns on the opposite bank and were generally ineffectual against the number of aircraft they faced. Bob Clark remembers "the low, dull rumbling of many bombs hitting the ground made even the hill on which we sat tremble with concussion." (1984: 101) Over four hundred tons of bombs were dropped that afternoon in an attempt to wreck the bridges so vital to the Republican advance. Even if none were hit, the bombardment reduced the resupply and reinforcement to a trickle. One flight of bombers changed course from the river and began bombing a number of the surrounding pine-covered hills. Scores of bombs were dropped and within minutes the hillside was aflame. In the darkness the lurid glow illuminated the surrounding countryside. The Italian High Command appeared to have lost its sense of proportion and decided to carpet bomb the entire area with their unlimited supply of heavy bombs. It was a miracle that anyone lived through the ensuing inferno. As Bob Clarke's section continued watching the road they were dismayed to see that in a period of four hours only two armoured cars and one light tank passed their positions. They hoped that the Republican army were using a better road.

Nationalist reinforcements continued to provide fierce resistance with several units of German and Italian aircraft bombing the advancing troops with all the ferocity they had become known for. Bob Clark recalls the moment his section came under attack,

> A road to the left branched from the main highway and seemed to disappear away over the hills, where to I never had the opportunity of discovering, because after walking along it a matter of two or three hundred yards with two of the patrol, the distant sound of heavy bombers could be heard and we jumped immediately into the bushes off the road. In a few minutes the unearthly scream of falling bombs made me grovel into the earth so desperately that I believe the impression of my body is still imprinted on that particular piece of Spanish soil. My mouth filled with gravel and I felt that my backside was about as large as a barn, presenting a superb target to the Capronis. How near those bombs sounded! I suddenly remembered that the whole Battalion was very close to the crossroads and I felt sick as I thought that the bombs were being aimed at them, not just indiscriminately.
>
> After what seemed an eternity of indescribable suspense, the shattering roar of the missiles striking the yielding earth made the very hills around us shudder with shock. The air tasted of dust and even the sun was blotted out by the clouds of dust, soil and pebbles. For what seemed many hours the stones rained down on our heads. In what was actually a few minutes the air cleared and the Capronis sped on their way home doubtless to reload. (101)

The battle began to dissolve into a race between the Republican bridge engineers trying to construct the pontoon bridges and the Nationalist air force attempting to hamper their efforts. To further exacerbate the situation, the Nationalists had opened the lock at the Barasona reservoir, which increased the flow of the already powerful river. Meanwhile, the heat of the sun was starting to take its toll too. As Bob Clark outlines the situation,

> The sun had become almost unbearably hot and many men stripped to the waist. They had slung their bandoliers around their waist complete with a hundred and fifty rounds. We were looking definitely piratical and if any gentlemen of the press had been present, they would have had plenty of pictures for right-wing propaganda. Half-naked men, many with bare bayonets stuck in their belts, their bodies burned almost black by the sun, with badly worn shoes, some with *alpargatas* almost in ribbons, and badly torn trousers. We looked like what the French armies must have looked like in the early days of the Revolution. (101)

Approaching Gandesa the Battalion encountered batches of Moorish prisoners, the first they had seen for a very long time, being escorted to the rear. In his memoirs Bob Clark described the meeting,

> They looked rather fierce, chiefly because they sported black beards. They noticed our water bottles and begged for a drink, which was given. This gave me an opportunity to observe them more closely. Their ages varied from about 17 years to one old grey beard of well over sixty. It appeared later that he was the Battalion cook. They were dressed in rough khaki with white socks rolled just above the tops of their boots. Some of them wore a red fez while the rest had coloured handkerchiefs wound around their heads. They seemed rather surprised at their decent treatment, no doubt expecting to be treated with anything but kindness, knowing well enough that they were hated by the majority of the Spanish people. I visualised the treatment we would have received from these self-same Moors if the boot had been on the other foot, despite the quite pleasant smiles they gave us when we handed them our water-bottles. The most amusing sight was when they continued their journey and with broad grins gave us the sign of the clenched fist. (103)

It was calculated that five thousand prisoners were taken on the first day of the crossing. Amongst the captured Nationalist equipment were around half a dozen trucks loaded with large pontoons; proof that the Nationalists had been preparing to cross the river themselves in the near future.

The Battalion now held their positions in the fading light. Patrols and listening posts were set up and Company Headquarters was established at the dry riverbed. Morale within the Battalion was still high. However, in times of war, situations can change rapidly. Soon the Battalion would face one of its greatest challenges, Hill 481 or '*the Pimple*' as the volunteers would innocuously name it.

12

Hill 481

Hill 481 dominated the countryside for miles around and was the key to controlling the strategic town of Gandesa. Aware of its importance, the Nationalists had fortified the defences on the heights. The British Battalion's assault on the hill would continue for many days. George Wheeler would later recall the first assault,

> We were formed up into our squads, platoons and sections on a ridge facing the hill about one thousand metres from the enemy and waited for the order to attack. At last it came: "Over you go, lads! Almost bending double, we plunged over the crest. As each man went over he was, for a brief moment, a perfect target on the skyline before hurtling down the hill with bullets whistling all around. (2003: 69)

Wheeler was sent sprawling down the steep wooded slope losing his rifle in the process. Recovering it he eventually reached relative safety at the bottom of the hill. After reassembling they began to climb up to the Nationalist positions.

> From here onwards there was practically no cover and it was obvious that a final assault would have been suicidal. We opened up a steady fire, which they answered with a terrific bombardment, and it was all we could do to retreat to safer positions and hang on. (69)

John Longstaff arrived at Hill 481 full of buoyant optimism. However this was soon to fade as attack after attack failed to make any impression on the Nationalist defenders,

> The lads in the two sections, as soon as they started, came under rifle and machine-gun fire from two valleys. Lads could be seen falling; I don't know if they were killed, wounded or just getting down. The platoons came back, bringing some of their wounded. Since Lt.. Harrington's platoon, by using the ridge was almost two thirds of the way up the hill, it was decided that they, together with all of Company HQ and one other platoon, should make a further attack the remaining platoon would fire in the direction of the enemy position in the valley. The machine-guns would fire both at the top of Hill 481 and towards the end of the valley where the enemy had some well concealed positions, but able to fire at the back of us. The attack went in with the Company Commander leading his Company HQ lads advanced also up the Hill. We noted our dead we had left at our last attack. A withering, murderous reply of shells, rifle and machine-gun fire met us as we tried to reach the top. One comrade lay flat out, I looked him over, but the only blood was from a small wound on the head, he was dead. All the dead men, Spanish and Internationals, were buried again in shallow graves where they lied.
>
> New orders had come instructing us to go back to the start position. Our attack had failed. More British and Spanish lads were left for dead, and some were now lying wounded out in the open. The comrade with the small wound had, in fact, received an enemy's hand grenade on top of his head that had killed him. (1994: 99)

Fellow volunteer Morris Miller wrote a dramatic account of the assault for *The Volunteer for Liberty* newspaper.

> The first two days the Battalion lacked the support of Captain Paddy O'Daire's Company One, which was away on a mopping up expedition. With Company Two in reserve, Companies Four and Two (sic) attacked and succeeded in occupying the ridges facing hill 481. It was in this action that the grim list of casualties among the officers of the Battalion began: Maxie Nash, youngest section leader in the Battalion, was killed as he led his men over the top, and Company Commander Angus received a severe wound. Observers reported that the hill was heavily fortified and for the first time the action assumed a serious aspect. What had previously been regarded as a light action became a tough proposition.

Brigader John Dunlop tells of further dangers during the many attempts on the hill; "It was during an early attack on Hill 481 that we were being fired on by one of our guns, in the hands of the Irishman Ryan." (cited in

Hill 481 ('*The Pimple*') dominated the countryside for miles around and was key to controlling the strategic town of Gandesa (Photo: J.W.)

MacDougall: 162) Subsequently Dunlop and his fellow Brigaders discovered a drunken Maurice Ryan fast asleep beside his machine-gun, together with a spent belt of his uncharacteristically erratic fire.

Ryan had always been a bit of problem in the Battalion. Described by his contemporaries as a "larger than life character," (Downing, 2010) Ryan was a tall, burly and fearless extrovert from Limerick. On Pandit Nehru's visit to the Battalion in Marsa, Ryan demonstrated his skills with the machine-gun knocking chunks out of a tree across the valley. Often amiable and amusing, Ryan was a source of disciplinary problems within the Battalion. Eugene Downing recalled one such occasion,

> When I was on sentry duty at the Battalion headquarters he was placed in my care until the following morning on a charge of being drunk and abusive. He just lay on the ground and went to sleep. The following morning he used his charm and powers of persuasion to induce me, when I was going off duty, to fetch his mess tin when I returned to the camp and bring it back to him. To me this was above and beyond the call of

duty, but he succeeded in getting me to do it. (Downing, 2010)

On this occasion no amount of Irish charm could extricate Ryan from the serious position in which he found himself. Military discipline, especially during a battle, had to be observed and Ryan was court-marshalled and sentenced to death. While in Mataro Hospital, Downing heard the details of Ryan's demise,

> Sam (Wild) and George Fletcher had taken Ryan for a walk and informed him of the decision that had been taken. He responded calmly; "You wouldn't do that Sam would you?" But he was wrong. He was shot in the back of the head. (Downing, 2010)

Despite the manner of his death, fellow Brigaders, including Sam Wild, always included Ryan's name in the Roll of Honour. Although somewhat troublesome, Ryan had previously given good military service. British Battalion Brigader Jim Jump went so far as to write a poem in his memory entitled "To M. R."

Meanwhile the Battalion continued their efforts to take control of the heights. After discussions between Bob Cooney and Alan Gilchrist, more Maxim machine-guns were placed to give covering fire for further assaults. The platoons were weak after three murderous attacks and many experienced volunteers lay dead or seriously wounded. Such was the heavy toll reaped on the Battalion that Brigade headquarters sent men to act purely as stretcher bearers. John Longstaff later wrote of the next phase of attacks,

> John Angus called Section and Platoon Commanders together and it was decided that the HQ Unit, together with Jack Nalty of the machine-gun crews would fire at the Fascists at the top of the hill. David Guest had found this position and observed that a barbed wire defence now existed on Hill 481, and that the enemy's position was under the supported shelter of logged and sandbagged roofs. Thus, hand grenades were needed; we had none. Again the lads attacked, but our forces were now too weak, and again the enemy on the two flanks had control of the three sides of the hill. It was now apparent that if our lads could only get about half way up the hill then the Fascists could not use their machine-guns. However, when our forces climbed higher up the hill, the enemy could throw his hand grenades, they had plenty, down on our lads. Our wounded comrades had no respite as the Fascists continued to throw grenades down the hillside. (100)

Over the coming days and night No.2 Company had mounted nine attacks to no avail. The men were getting further and further away from the summit of the fortified hill. Longstaff continues,

> We could hear them strengthening their position, the enemy, night after night we could hear them digging, chopping down wood to make roofs over their shelters, and of course they were getting relieved. They had a roadway at the back of them where they could bring transport up to almost a quarter of a mile. We had no transport. We had to climb or walk everywhere. You couldn't carry your picks and shovels in any case there were so few of those that round this position they were making what we called sangers. Now a sanger is a small rock fortification. You built up a rocky wall in front and a rocky wall at the back. This was to stop, if you possibly could, shrapnel that had gone over the other side of your position from facing backwards onto the back of you. Now these sangers, obviously there were great gaps in the rocks and metal, especially bullets would soon break through but, at least to a point, you were a bit safer and there was specific little parties going out at night time, scratching, digging, making new positions or burying your mates or, at times, carrying a wounded lad over to the roadway in the hope that some transport would pick them up. We were in that position for a fortnight and do you know I can't remember how we got fed up there. (104)

On the same theme, Bob Clark writes,

> The supply of water became a pressing problem although the food question was also a difficult one, mainly consisting of captured tins of food manufactured by a well-known English firm. (106)

The assaults revealed worrying elements about the entire Ebro offensive; the intelligence was faulty; the supplies were inadequate for a prolonged engagement; and the casualty rate far higher than expected. Miller's report continues,

> On the second day, Company Three, commanded by Cipriano went forward to within 20 meters of the top of the hill and engaged in hand grenade combat with the enemy. That night with the help of the Listers on the left and a group of the 13th Brigade on the right, the Battalion carried out a night attack. The Listers succeeded in occupying the ridge, but the peak of it remained impregnable and they had to retire. (1938: 8)

Among the casualties suffered by the Battalion on the assault on Hill 481 were mathematician, scientist, author and philosopher David Haden Guest and Oxford rowing blue, Lewis Clive. Guest had been working as a lecturer at Southampton University prior to volunteering. Before he left he wrote of his decision to volunteer, "Today we have certainly entered a period of crisis, when the arguments of 'normal times' no longer apply, when considerations of most immediate usefulness come in. That is why I have decided to take the opportunity of going to Spain." (Stevenson, 2011) In his memoirs volunteer John Longstaff wrote of his impressions of David Guest,

> To me David Guest was a man well worth knowing, a kindly man. He should never have been a soldier; he wasn't suitable to face the rigours of front line fighting. He was an academic, both in the shape of his body as well as his ability. He was totally like that [...] David had a high degree of intelligence. I believe, if I think correctly, that he would have been one of the leading statisticians. Another ability was to get people to do jobs that they didn't want to do and probably that was his best ability, his organising ability. An excellent speaker, very very quick on the uptake of the political situation. In my view he would have been a better Commissar because of his ability to explain but he was also a staunch anti-fascist [...] he would certainly have been a brilliant scientist. (86-87)

He goes on to describe Guest's death,

> I had been sent on a message to tell him to come off this particular hill that he was on because we had discovered by this time that the enemy were shooting at his back. Now David was probably the only man that I knew at that time who had a pair of binoculars and a compass that his mother had bought out for him. I got to Johnny (Connors) and shouted to him no more than about three or four yards away "Come down David, you've got to come off that hill, they can see you." I dare not go up any higher because there was a point where I would be observed. "Just a minute" he said, or words like that and the next thing I knew he was falling backwards and he was dead. He was shot clean through the head. I was no more than nine or ten feet at this stage and Johnny Connors and me pulled him down. We couldn't even bury him because we had no spades or equipment. We just had to cover him up with a little blanket he had and buried him that night. (Longstaff, 1994: 102)

George Wheeler described the death of Guest as "a grievous loss to the

David Haden Guest: Fellow Wittgenstein graduate and "a man well worth knowing"

working-class movement." (2003: 80) His name is engraved on the memorial plaque in Southampton alongside Ivor's.

Lewis Clive was born on September 8th, 1910. He was a godson of Conservative politician Neville Chamberlain and rumoured to be a descendent of Clive of India. On leaving Eton, he rowed for Oxford in 1931 and 1932. After winning the Silver Goblets and Nickalls' Challenge Cup at Henley in the same years, he was selected to compete in the coxless pairs at the 1932 Los Angeles Olympics together with Hugh Edwards from Christ Church, Oxford. The pair scored a comfortable victory in the final at Long Beach, California. He was later became a Labour borough councillor for St Charles ward of the Metropolitan Borough of Kensington and was also a member of the Fabian Society. Shortly before the crossing of the Ebro, Lewis Clive was taken ill and was transferred to hospital only to return to the Battalion in time for the assaults on Hill 481. John Longstaff was a runner for No.2 Company at the time and was at Battalion HQ with Sam Wild when Lewis Clive reappeared,

> …Sam Wild, the Battalion Commander, gave me a couple of fags and told me to sit down and get my breath back and along came Lewis Clive. "Hello John" "Hello Comrade" I said, "I thought you were ill" "No I'm all right John." Then with Sam Wild and Bob Cooney came up and it was obvious who was going to come back with me, it was Lewis Clive. (Longstaff, 1994: 101)

There was a gap of approximately forty-five metres which was under constant observation and fire from the Nationalist defenders and Longstaff warned Clive of the danger and the need to "run like hell" to cross this point. He illustrated his point by informing Clive of the death of David Guest. However, on this occasion Longstaff and Clive managed to traverse the area without attracting any enemy attention. They returned to the Company HQ where they found nearly everyone either ill or wounded. The lack of transport and harsh terrain still occupied by the Moors meant that the stretcher bearers were unable to carry the wounded over the mountains. Longstaff recalls,

> There were talks with somebody I didn't know and in less than half an hour he's dead, killed a few yards away from where Guest was killed. He had taken no notice and done what he wanted to do and observe and he was shot, just like David Guest had been only a few yards away. He was buried like all our dead, in a shallow grave at the foot of Hill 481.

Harry Dobson from the Rhondda:"What *a* man; steel-willed and *a great* personality!

That graveyard got bigger by the day. (Longstaff, 1994: 121).

Frank Deegan's account of the incident confirms Longstaff's appraisal of Clive's recklessness. He remembers Clive as a "giant of a man, absolutely fearless...he marched around encouraging his men, ignoring the heavy gunfire from the enemy." (1980: 50) George Wheeler was with Clive when he was killed. He describes the "great loss" thus,

> Lewis Clive re-appeared and asked about the activity in the fascist lines. It was a hot, sunny day and, as usual, my shirtsleeves were rolled up. At that moment I felt splashes on my forearm, and glancing down, was astonished to see they were splashes of blood. Turning I saw Lewis reel and fall. Someone below said "What a ghastly sight." I slid down from my firing position and saw that the top of his head was severed completely and, as he lay there, the brain was spilling from its case. It was indeed a ghastly sight. (2007: 77)

The attacks on the hill continued regardless. Morris Miller continued his description as follows,

> By this time the boys were thoroughly tired. Night and day they had made herculean efforts. To add to their difficulties, water was kilometres away and very rarely could details be spared. Moreover, communication had not yet been established with the Intendencia, though Bob Cooney, Battalion Commissar, had succeeded in getting up a small amount of tinned stuff which had been captured from the fascists. Still the boys carried on without a murmur and when Paddy O'Daire and the First Company joined them they went forward uncomplaining. All the third day the battle went on. Morris Davis, Commander of Company Four, was severely wounded and Harry Dobson was killed. On the fourth day, Company Two and Company Four combined under the leadership of Catalayud and Johnny Powers and on the fifth day, the last and most severe attack on the hill began. All day long it went on with the leading men only twenty meters away from the top of the hill and the rest of the men not far behind. The air was thick with bullets and the fascist shells were landing in our forward positions. When Battalion Commander Wilde gave the order to withdraw, the last attack had ended. (Miller, 1938: 9)

Frank Deegan (1980) poignantly recalls the mortal wounding of his friend Harry Dobson and the bravery and self-discipline he displayed while being stretchered out,

> At that time one of the stretcher bearers was a casualty. The remaining one named Gibson from Sunderland asked for someone to help carry Harry down. I was ordered to assist young Gibson. I felt very sad seeing my good pal lying on the stretcher; it was obvious he was seriously injured. On the way to the doctor who was a few miles further down the valley, Harry kept asking for a drink of water. We were afraid to give him some. Although we were not expert first aid men, we knew one of the main rules was to give no liquid to wounded men. This could endanger their lives. He pleaded, saying he would only wet his lips. We gave way, letting Harry hold the water bottle himself. True to his word that's all he did – wet his lips. What a man; steel-willed and a great personality. If I had been in his position, I would have tried to drink the lot. Shortly after reaching the doctor he died. I felt I had lost a great friend – one who by his courage and humanity had inspired all who knew him. (49).[1]

A conference was held at Battalion Headquarters and a message subsequently sent requesting that anti-tank guns be brought up and used as artillery pieces to bombard the Nationalist positions in the valleys and on the hill itself. No such weapons were available however, as the British Anti-tank section had been disbanded and the Divisional Artillery units were meanwhile being used in other sectors. With an understandable degree of bitterness and frustration, Bob Clark wrote of his despair regarding the lack of adequate artillery,

> How we longed for the sight of artillery pieces or even one solitary anti-tank gun. I firmly believe to this day that the arrival of half a dozen anti-tank guns would have cleared the Fascists from the surrounding hill positions, which would have paved the way to capture Gandesa. But these guns never came. Even the tanks that we had seen were more of an armoured car type, although fairly heavy, but almost useless against an entrenched enemy. (106)

Regardless, a fifth attack was planned. No. 3 Company was to attack the ridge while the machine-gun battery, now strengthened to four Maxims, would provide covering fire; two would sweep the valleys while the other two would fire at the hill's defences. No.1 Company would work their way around the base of the hill to attack one of the strong points in the valley. Bob Clark would later describe his feelings while waiting for the order to attack,

This was the real thing, I thought, as along with the Major Attlee Company I lay in a slight ditch waiting for the expected order to storm Hill 481. What a queer feeling it is waiting to go over the top! My senses seemed unusually dull as I contemplated what chances I had of coming through alive. I had a feeling that it was not very important if I did not, but the vision of the postman handing the fatal letter to my people at home upset me considerably. If only to prevent that, I tried not to think of such a possibility but concentrated my thoughts on which part of my body the bullet would strike. (107)

Sam Wild was with No. 2 and No. 3 Companies when the attack took place. Again, frustratingly, the onslaught failed. No. 3 Company got almost within throwing distance for use of hand grenades, which would have been of some benefit, but there were no grenades to throw. either. To risk climbing higher would mean that their Battalion machine-guns would have to cease covering fire for risk of shooting their own troops. Without wire cutters or explosives, the men would be exposed to the hill's defenders too. During the inevitable withdrawal Lieutenant Bill Harrington was wounded. The order came that no further attacks were to take place that day. For the first time in four days the Battalion cooks arrived that night with hot food for the weary troops. Eating in silence the battle-shocked volunteers peered at each other looking for missing comrades knowing that the next day would, in all likelihood be as vicious as that day.

Sent out to reconnoitre later that night, John Longstaff happened upon a grisly find.

> I was told to go to a nearby hill to see who occupied it. Someone had said No.1 Company was in position. A Spanish comrade and an International Brigader called Blair, not George Orwell, would go with me. We had to cross one of the valleys, so we took care crawling and hiding among the vines. We came to an open patch; the area stunk of our dead and those of the enemy. The moon was high and full, shining brightly. The ground seemed to move, a black patch had come and disappeared, the three of us waited. I looked at the sky but no cloud was about. I was soon to know what that black patch was, which had now gone. A number of bodies lay bloated. I don't know if they were our lads or the enemy. All I do know is a damned swarm of rats had been disturbed by us while they had been eating the bodies. I got up very frightened. So did my companions and we quickly departed from that foul place. While still going to our destination we met some of No.1 Company, the Major Attlee Company. They had sent out a patrol to find any of

our wounded and they told me that the hill I was going to being occupied by Moors and that No.1 Company was at the foot of the ridge we occupied. I was now becoming afraid; those rats, not death, had put fear into me. Reporting to the Company Commander, I gave him the information. He could see I was shivering and, no doubt, thought I was cold. I must have dozed, and had some sleep, with a blanket well over my face. How much I wanted to get out of that rat ridden, stinking place I cannot express suitable words. (Longstaff, 1994: 106)

The Battalion's position came under heavy shell fire killing many and wounding among others Company Commander Walter Gregory. The Battalion shifted their positions from the ridge to the reverse slope and dug in. Sergeant Joe Harkins replaced the wounded Gregory as Company Commander only to be killed in the next attack on the hill some six hours later that morning. Bob Clark vividly contributes his own recollections of the brutal assault,

> The sun was almost overhead when once again we began to move. Creeping cautiously forward, hundreds of the British Battalion advanced close enough to make an attempt to rush the height. On the right side of this hill we had excellent cover until we reached a point about two hundred yards from the crest. On the left the cover for the advance was even better, but near the top a murderous cross-fire came from Gandesa itself and from a number of heights on either side. Nearer and nearer we crept when suddenly the cry *"Adelante"* (Forward!) was given and Britishers and Spaniards, among whom were youths of seventeen years, with loud yells clambered over rocks past trees which the leaves were dropping like a day in a park in autumn cut by a thousand bullets. (Clark, 1984: 107)

The entire hill became a death trap of bullets and mortar fire. Earth and stones were lethally cascaded amongst the advancing troops. As Clark continues,

> I found that I had reached a position from where I could see the enemy machine-gun posts. But the fire was overwhelming and it became imperative that I should lie flat on my face for a few moments. Peering cautiously around during a slight lull in the firing, I noticed a dip in the hillside which would give a measure of protection. Slowly crawling along on my belly, I gained its slight protection. Glancing around I was aware that signs of our attacking force were nil, although the enemy still

kept lobbing heavy mortar shells on to the sides of the hill. My nearest companion, a chap from Leeds, who was crouching behind a boulder about twenty yards away, signalled to me that he was coming over. In a few minutes he had joined me and we debated our next course of action. It was apparent that if we as much as raised our heads above the skyline we would be dead men. Yet it seemed hard lines that the enemy was so near that we could have thrown a grenade plumb into their post. The rest of the Republicans must have suffered terrible losses to get so near. (107-108)

Taking cover in a 'funk-hole', Clark contemplated the long wait until dark and the opportunity to escape when suddenly,

> ...an explosion covered us with dust and stones and I had a feeling of eating a large quantity of dust and seeing a black cloud close by. When the cloud had disappeared I found that my right arm had suddenly gone limp and despite all my efforts I could not use it. Turning to my companion I informed him that I must be wounded. He looked at my arm and decided that a few pieces of shrapnel had probably entered it and advised me to make my way back down the hill, as I would probably lose a lot of blood if I lay there. (108)

Even in such extreme occasions Clark's English sense of modesty nearly cost him dearly, for at precisely the moment that he decided to make his move,

> ...my blasted trousers slipped down as the buckle of my belt came loose and as I was endeavouring to pull them up I felt a numbing shock and found that I had stopped a bullet in the same arm. Later I was to find that this was not quite correct. The bullet had gone clean through. It was a pleasant surprise to me. I felt not the slightest pain, just a dead numbness and the irritation of attempting to use my right arm but finding it useless. My trousers were hanging down over my boots and try as I might without presenting too much of a target, I could not pull the damned things up. What a predicament! My ridiculous modesty would get me into trouble. Who was worrying about seeing my hairy legs? So off the trousers must come if they impeded my progress. (108)

Precariously sliding down from tree to tree, Clark eventually reported to an NCO who advised him to be careful as his white underpants presented rather a fetching target for the enemy. The advice came too late for Clark however. As he relates it, the next thing he knew he felt he had been,

...hit in the face with a sledgehammer. Jumping about five feet in the air I felt a terrible emotion of seeing a searing wall of flame followed immediately by a dreadful darkness. (109)

At first thinking himself blind, he lay on the grass, his life flashing before him. A heavy melancholia descended on him and he thought bitterly of the irony of being blinded within feet of safety. Slowly it dawned on him that the warm sticky blood was from a head wound and not from his precious eyes. Relieved and in a semi-conscious state, he was found by Battalion members and taken to a field dressing station. He was eventually taken back across the Ebro and sent by ambulance to Barcelona. While on the journey he witnessed the full extent of the failing advance.

> Hour after hour we rolled along the main highway passing numbers of trucks, many laden with ships' lifeboats. This confirmed my opinion that the majority of the bridges had been destroyed or were badly damaged. (110)

The role of the Battalion Observers such as Ivor was vital on Hill 481. Runner John Longstaff's job was to send messages directly to the Battalion from the Divisional Observer. The Battalion Signaller would send the same information to the Brigade who in turn would send it to the artillery. The proficiency of the Battalion Signallers made up for the somewhat laborious method of communication. Longstaff describes the work of the Divisional Observer during one Republican artillery bombardment on Hill 481,

> The Observer, the officer with the rank of Captain, was looking through his binoculars and checking his map, noting where the few shells were exploding. More messages went out. During this second lot of messages the ridge we occupied was machine-gunned and bits of rock and deflecting bullets came showering down. The enemy was looking for the Observer, but he was doing his job well, observing from behind a stone wall and only looking out when he could hear our few shells going over our heads, that would be when the enemy would have his head down.
>
> Another attack had gone in, but with the same result. Hill 481 was a hard, hard nut to crack and getting harder as Franco had again, during the night, poured in still more of his troops and had strengthened his positions around 481. Just prior to the attack I had crawled up to the Observer's position. I took over while he went a few feet down the ridge

to have a smoke. I shouted to our lads as they attacked, and though they could not hear me with the noise going on, at least I was getting something off my chest. I next started firing my rifle but the Captain came and stopped me. He correctly pointed out that I would be giving his position away. Despite the attack by the 13th Brigade they had not got any further than we had done. (Longstaff: 109)

Listening posts were set up and patrols sent out night after night, while the troops dug in deeply for fear of Nationalist tank attacks. On August 3rd, the Battalion launched one last desperate and unsuccessful attack on Hill 481. The failure to secure Hill 481 effectively halted the advance in that sector. The Republican forces gave up their attempts to capture Gandesa and took up defensive positions. The British Battalion was moved into reserve on August 6th. A day later Ivor wrote to Juliet recalling the events of the previous week.

August 7, 1938
My dearest darling love, it's weeks – 6 or 8 weeks – since I wrote to you. You must forgive me – we were immensely busy for all that time culminating in 15 days of action around Gandesa – you read of our crossing the Ebro, amazing thing and pushing on till Gandesa where we met our first really organised resistance. Last night thank God we came out of the line and this morning, the first thing I do, is to write to you.
This indeed has been a tough and tiring action and we left more people behind than we wanted to. We all have been practically dead beat and living for 15 days on dry rations (with the blessed exception of a hot meal on the last few days) – which is enough to upset anyone's stomach.
So much has happened that I don't know where to start. It took a long time to dawn on me that we really were going to cross that river. At last the orders came through and followed 2 terrific days of map-making and map reproduction (that is included in our job). Then we moved down to a banranco near the river and waited. A brigade had to go across before us and they got across in boats without a shot being fired. Then the light came and we moved off, over the sand into boats and across the river, gaily coloured boats and the river so swift and green. And a pontoon bridge made of barrels was soon rigged up and I went across on that.
The scene was strangely gay; as I felt, like the seaside on a holiday. The enemy artillery fired haphazardly at the hills around, our artillery was firing at a town about 2 kilometres farther up the river and then an enemy plane turned up, flying recklessly low, dropped 6 small bombs on us, strafed us a little and then left us as we all fired at the damn thing and frightened it off.
Then started a long hard march in the dust and sun, of some 15 kilometres. Everywhere were signs of hurried leaving, horses left about, piles of clothes thrown off, deserted guns, rifles, food, camions. Our only trouble was the enemy avion which that day gave us some very near squeaks with their heavy bombs. The concussion

with bombing is very great but bombing is not really dangerous because it is so inaccurate. The planes hover around overhead and drone away. Then suddenly a screech, a second or two and the explosion.

After a day spent in cleaning up the terrain behind the first eschelon, (sic) we moved into the first eschelon near Gandesa and there we met our real resistance. We were fighting in the mountains, through woods and schrub (sic). And we had our share of enemy artillery. And down below we saw Gandesa and of course we observed what was happening there.

The Fascists were in a bad way but at last they stopped us, we had only rifles and machine guns and only later artillery and tanks so that of course sooner or later we had to be stopped because of their superior equipment.

Many and varied were my experiences, observing the enemy at close quarters, being sniped, being shelled, attending staff meetings and thieving the Brigade Commander's delicious peaches, being shelled at night in a wrecked and burning village. Not boring exactly, but I hate it all. I shaped up very well – surprised myself, wasn't too afraid of shells and mortars. And was goddamn cautious. I did not risk my life unnecessarily once. Because I have my life to complete, my life to live with you my beautiful love.

Lying out in the open, among lavender plants that smell so beautiful, I missed and wanted you and I regretted so very much my not writing to you. But this life is not conducive to consideration for others, in fact it is deadening. But now when I write to you I think my letter must sound rather horrible – but it is not the bombs etc that get me, it is the boredom. (Even now a damned 'plane is manoeuvring overhead trying to find the troops just behind the lines (i.e. 10 kms or so).

It is practically 10 months since I left you in that boulevard in Paris. May I soon touch you and love you and see you again. I think I should burst with feeling if I saw you again now. Here I haven't more than shaken hands with a woman for 10 months and then if I were to meet and have the most beautiful woman in the world! By not having you I have found your true worth. But later by God I'm going to taste it.

I have many many things to tell you but this morning I feel weak and listless. I will get over that with rest and cooked food.

I have received one most beautiful letter from you. It made me so happy to read it. And you talk of coming to Spain. Will you really be coming? I should love to see you and love you again. And God I will love you when I see you again!

My love, don't be nervous about me, will you?

I am not particularly cowardly but hell! I am cautious. I do not believe in recklessness nor even in lionheartedness. It is amazing how incautious some men are, particularly when they get tired. Some walk on skylines or paths, take dangerous shortcuts, but I don't, I walk round.

The next day

Yes, I have met him – *Casey, by name*. [Charles Frederick Casey was born on November 21st 1915 in Norwich. He was unmarried and previously had worked as an Insurance Clerk. He was a member of the Labour Party and the Communist Party of Great Britain. He was also one of the last volunteers, arriving in Spain on July

8th, 1938, whereupon he was appointed a Political Commissar at the Montblanch Training base in Catalonia. He was with the Battalion in September. However there is no record of frontline service.] *Directly he arrived at the Battalion (how many t's and l's has it? – or better Battalion) he made enquiries for me and soon found me, unshaven and my hair matted and everything very dirty. He said he would not have recognised me from a photograph he had seen – which one? – where I had "so much hair." Quietly I hoped he wouldn't have recognised me in this dirt.*

Then fell to us the difficulty of talking about you. Naturally, how were you? You were tired before you went away and in high spirits and very fit when you came back. What did you talk about nowadays? He was vague. I couldn't ask him things I wanted to – "Did you ever sneak a look at her breasts?" "and her thighs?" So I had to content myself with "How much Spanish can she speak?" and "What does she do?" and then, nearer possibly, "What clothes is she wearing?" Here, he said he didn't notice clothes much but he liked you best in your blue trousers (the envy of several) and blue jumper – with your black hair parted in the middle. Also you like motorbike rides. Strange how patchwork it all is as a description of you, but for all that very moving to me who knows you better than anyone else in the world knows you.

He told me how glad you were to receive a letter from Ivor; which made me feel guilty because of my neglect in writing to you.

Casey seems a very likable man – he mentioned Margarita with regard to his having learnt Spanish and explained that he had learnt much listening to her – "because all women like to talk."

And to do, sometimes? I somehow felt sorry for him, I don't know why. He tells me that he wished he had come out when he first decided to – December 1936 – but his mother persuaded him not to. He would have been dead by now if he had.

I very much enjoyed talking to him but later when I see him again and again he will remember small things about you that will bring me much pleasure.

It is strange how one is very slightly shocked when one hears of a comrade's death but there is no feeling of sorrow. Some of them excellent men, too. Two of my friends [Lewis Clive and David Guest] *– one an Oxford Blue and the other a Trinity Hall man and previously a pupil of Wittgenstein (the second in Spain I've found) – both idealists were killed outright by putting their heads up and being lionhearted. However idealistic you are, you should obey the rules and not take unnecessary risks. Don't think that most people are killed by recklessness, they aren't. They are killed in the normal course of their duty.*

Now I close, looking forward to your next letter with great appetite. Sooner or later this business will end and I will come back to you.

Don't forget how much I love you and want you.

All my love to you my Chamois darling,

Ivor

A day later, Ivor wrote to a friend further detailing the events,

8th August
I have just picked up someone's fountain pen which is very comfortable to use after using stubs of pencil all the time. First, many thanks for your last letter, which I received in the middle of the last action around Gandesa, which we have just pulled out of. The Battalion has had a very hard and tiring action, with losses more than we wanted. We crossed the Ebro in boats and on a pontoon bridge, as second echelon; and after cleaning up small groups of Fascists, left stranded by the rapidity of the advance of the first echelon, we entered the first echelon and took up a position on a heavily wooded and very complicated (topographically) mountain range. Gandesa was down in the valley on our right, only two kilometres away. So near and yet so far! The Fascists had time to form some line of resistance and soon got up their technical equipment, and their avions, and their artillery. We were forced to use only rifles and machine-guns for the first two or three days, because the main bridge sank or something. Later our artillery and tanks and very occasionally our avions came up to assist us. Then we had a gruelling experience of seven assaults upon a hill. [Hill 481]
——Yesterday I——a most beautiful river, swift and wide. Only a fortnight ago there were Fascists on one side and us on the other. Now we can—— and feel.—— after it. We collected from the fertile plain, which runs parallel to the river, apricots, tomatoes by the ton, apples, vino, olive oil – so this morning we had fried bread and fried tomatoes, which makes a change. The food problem in action is hellish. We had to live with dry rations (i.e. corned beef, sardines, and bread) for a week or so. Our first hot meal was a great pleasure – an immense pleasure. Our observation service worked satisfactorily and despite the action has not been destroyed...
I smiled at your obsession about my death. Yes, I'm alive on August 8th and should remain so. I'm very cautious and I don't believe in recklessness; nor am I brave, but I try to observe properly, which is to see but not to be seen. Observers get more artillery and more avions than the infantry, but the infantry gets the filth and the machine-guns.
...Anything different is interesting when compared with this boring existence. So write and tell me anything. What I don't like is immature wallowings, but now having other difficulties than before, I am intolerant of those who are suffering difficulties that I myself once had...
It is strange to think that on Bank Holiday we were fighting hard around Gandesa.
...So what can a man do? Well there is no paper answer, otherwise there would be no major problem.
I don't know if it does me any good to see a wrecked and bombed village and men lying around, covered with flies, rotten and stinking. Or to see a shell land among a group of men and throw one man most gracefully – like a doll – some twenty-five feet into the air, slowly turning, so elegant, and then plop-plop on to the ground. It and worse can be seen on the films any day...
I have enjoyed writing this letter as is obvious, I expect, by its content. Excuse some of it, but remember the extremely dull unemotional life we live out here. Even now an avion has been droning overhead for a quarter of an hour, trying to observe us and then bomb us.

Taking advantage of being away from the frontline and having a lull in his observational duties, Ivor wrote to Juliet again beginning on August 10th. This letter offers a fascinating selection of 'thumbnails' describing Ivor's impressions of his comrades and fellow observers.

August 10th 1938

My dearest love,
I wrote you a letter two days ago and now I am writing you another. For three reasons – firstly, because I want this to be different, secondly because you deserve many more even than this one, and thirdly because my other letter maybe delayed by the censor because of references to our recent actions. And I hope that is not true because if the censor cuts out things then the contact between us is broken down a little. Even the existence of the censor does this to a certain extent and after all I can't write about things which are often the most important things locally, for example of the inefficiency of Comrade X – what ought I to do? Or why did the Brigade Commander order us to do so and so? And on forever. Not that they would particularly interest you, but they do interest me and are often momentarily important. They give a truer picture of my everyday life too, but it can't be helped. The censor does not cut out bits of – how shall we put it? – an intimate nature; which is one blessing.
August 11th 1938

Now the morning has come again – one more. The time in Spain goes so much faster than it did at home. I look forward to sleep, partly because the time goes quickest and also because it is the most comfortable time. Of course even at home I preferred the evening.
Now I am sitting in our shack, Orte one of the Spanish observers is frying in olive oil tomatoes and corn beef. Latus, a Hull fisherman and George Buck, a Lancashire lad, are as ever arguing furiously about the tanks and armoured cars that did or did not get out of the retreat from Belchite (Franco's first phase in the drive for the sea). I haven't told you who we have in the Battalion observers. We have some very good men, who are learning (like me) points of observation, topography and so on. George Buck, a thick set tough guy from Nelson, near Warrington, a moulder in an iron foundry, 22, extravagant in the extremes in all descriptions (his numbers are like the Old Testament), has been through all the campaigns of the Battalion – except Teruel, when he was at the O.T.S with me – from the early Jarama days. George has immense energy and enthusiasm, which despite some 18 months in Spain has not lagged. When I met him first at the O.T.S. he was suffering from a morbid obsession with death. He relished all lurid descriptions of death in its many forms found during war. But now fortunately he has outlived it. Sometimes he in his excitement grips your arm in his immensely powerful grasp and sometimes even bites you with his sharp teeth. As I say to him – although he does not understand why I say it – "do this to your woman and more besides. Then you won't bother us." He just smiles

pleasantly whenever women are mentioned which of course is quite often – and says nothing. One day he dropped a remark "I only kissed one woman once; she was a girl in Woolworths and worked at the celluloid counter and was burned to death when it caught fire."

Now there is Joe Latus, another thickset but bigger man, 26, arguing still with George. Now it is the 8th Route Army, partisans, army in the Japanese war, and so on. He is a fisherman from Hull, a Communist of long activity (George oddly enough is politically nothing), heavy in his actions, slow, reliable in his way, upset by avion. He is typically a fisherman – I am sure he is an excellent fisherman. Whereas George by his very nature can stand this business without qualms, Joe has fundamentally to resort to political matters to prop him up, without his political convictions, he would be a bad soldier. George who is an excellent soldier would be one quite independently of whether he was fighting with the I.B. or the British Army.

Then Phil Boyle, an Irishman from the mountains of Donegal, a master joiner, an excellent soldier with a sneaking regard for liquor, as cool a customer under fire as anyone. "three – sixteenths that one!" (i.e. that shell missed us by 3/16 inch). "Five – thirty – twos – Time we started thinking about shifting, eh?" His age which is in no way obvious makes him more mature. At 14 he was fighting in Ireland against British imperialism and he has that Irish ruthlessness. Never does the liberal or sentimental occur to him. If he shoots a man, a Fascist, it would never occur to him that that Fascists might have a wife, a mother, children. "He is a Fascist, I kill Fascists, Fascists kill me. Nothing more." This resoluteness makes him a pillar of strength, yet without priggishness. (That weakness is so very easily come by in men of political resoluteness).

Then comes Bill Leakey, a fat fair Englishman, a one time Coldstream Guardsman, who deserted that job with a consistent and vivid hate of the British military machine. An excellent man politically, very willing and very gentle, who as he says has not received letters from his young lady since he came out here. He comes from Bath, one of the few Party members in Bath, with a healthy hatred of most that Bath reflects. Bill had an accident in the last action, falling down a bank and hurting his leg.

And the last of the Internationals, Jack O'Connor. A small and slight man with a good Party record, a weak stomach and noticeably high cheekbones. He has been many things from being rather gay to being for 6 months on the Aldwych underground going backwards and forwards from Holborn to Aldwych. He is a wit, a broad Cockney and likable man, who incidentally receives Woodbines from his Dad every day practically. Viva Dad! (as he says). He is ill today unfortunately with his stomach. This food of course upsets everybody in turn but he suffers more than the rest of us. And when a man has a bad stomach, he feels miserable and everything seems miserable.

Now our two Spanish comrades, Claudio Orte and Rafael Garmendia Gil. Orte, one of the best looking Spaniards I've seen – which says a lot, is a nice fellow with a rather marked aversion for artillery and avion, neat, smiling, quiet and receptive. Food bothers him a lot – he always has one eye glued on the food at mealtime. He can move over country very stealthily. In fact he is rather like a great and handsome cat. Rafael is as different as you could imagine. Almost demoniacal, dark skinned, supple, witty, much younger than Orte, he talks quite a lot of very broken English. "If my mother could see me now! Anti-fascists, territory, shut up..." A nice fellow again, very quick and intelligent, from Barcelona, where I'm sure he has his girl in every street, so to speak.

The language difficulty is no difficulty at all really. Sometimes the Internationals are a little intolerant of the Spanish comrades for that reason and sometimes because the Spanish ask for it. As you can imagine some of the national traits are not conducive to efficient soldiering. But the same applies to us, a great mob of wild emotionally-starved Internationals. So we must sometimes appear.

In fact our moral standards sometimes surprise me. I don't suppose the XV Brigade in all its history has had to deal with more than two or three rapes. And most of the men have remained celibate ever since they arrived in Spain. Some of course on their trips to Barcelona have had whores there, a mere handful have had woman in other capacities, otherwise nothing. Spain, the land of Senoritas and luscious living is limited to a few cities like Barcelona and Madrid, but even there there is another side. Undoubtedly Spain is a beautiful country and its women are beautiful – nada mas. (nothing but, Ed) Did you ever receive my letter about the "casa de puta?" – I hope the censor was not feeling puritanical and destroyed it.

Casey has just passed. A day or two ago – or did I tell you? – he had his first taste of war while he was down in the valley picking tomatoes for a meal, an aerial bomb missed him by some 20 metres. It probably fell in sandy soil and so was of little danger but I guess it made a big crack for all that. It did not seem to upset him much but his courage is a built up courage whereas for example Boyle's is well nigh innate. The afternoon has come and I feel sleepy. I think I am justified in closing this letter now with a 7 on the top of the page! Unusual for me.

I wonder how your arrangements about Spain are going on. Casey got a letter today saying that You – Julietta and someone else had gone round collecting with the returned ambulance. So they call you Julietta! I used to sometimes, do you remember Chamois?

Now I must sleep, I am lazy and tired. I hope this letter will give you pleasure, particularly if it arrives close to the other one. I miss you like hell and wish you were with me. Ten months! Hell, it's been a long time, although God knows it's gone quickly enough. When I get back to you!

Don't forget I love and admire you more than I ever did before.

All my love you to Chamois dear –
Ivor

From: Ivor Hickman,
S.R.I. 161, Barcelona,
Spain

PS Just as I finished this, I got your letter telling me about your day in Ipswich. Yes, you are having a surprising time. Let us hope it will change fairly soon – when I come home to you.

I'm sorry there was such a gap between the "hotel" letter and the others, but it was because one never got through, was lost or censored. That always may happen. But my worst offence has been before and during this last action, which all of you are so pleased about. We were in that and it upset correspondence arrangements. But I promise not to be so unkind again if I can possibly avoid it.

I wish we were together again; I would love you and excite you and satisfy you, my beloved Chamois. And then we would lie so still together and so impossibly happy. With your beautiful breasts and thighs and triangle relaxed and free.

Oh, well, this war must end and I will come back to you my sweetest love.

I can hear the heavy guns away in the distance now, damn them. Sooner or later they must get hoarse. All my love for you, you beautiful creature. When we are together again you will remember that I promised to fill your belly, won't you? Oh hell and I will.

Love Ivor

The *very good men* described by Ivor in this letter hailed from a variety of backgrounds and may not to conventional eyes seem to be ideal comrades; drunks, deserters, IRA activists and ex-trawler men; a mixed bag to say the least but it is apparent that Ivor held them in high regard. Their individual biographies perfectly illustrate the variety of backgrounds of the "average" Battalion members. Joe Latus is described earlier in this book but the other men merit further examination.

George Buck was born in Lancashire in 1917/18 where he lived with his parents on Poplar Street in Nelson. An iron moulder by trade and member of the Moulders' Union, Buck arrived in Albacete on the April 14th, 1937. He was in the Battalion during the latter stages of the Jarama campaign and served at Brunette and Quinto for which he received the Spanish Navalperal medal for his conduct during the fighting there. He later served in the Ordinance section before being sent to Officer Training School on the February 28th, 1938. He was back in the Battalion on the April 27th, 1938. Shortly after Ivor's letter, Buck was given leave and left Spain on September 1st, 1938. The records of the Battalion list that Buck's conduct in Spain was *very good* and that he was *a comrade with most excellent record on all occasions, not much capacity for leadership and rather muddled politically, but entirely reliable in every way. Good Comrade.* George Buck died around 1954.

Phillip Boyle was cut from similar cloth as the famous IRA Brigader Frank Ryan. Boyle was born on October 5th, 1903. There is confusion over his exact birth place. In some sources it is listed as either Glenties or Calhane, Co Donegal while another even states that he was born in Renfrew, Scotland. This is actually plausible as many people from Donegal came over to England and Scotland for work as Agricultural labourers during the crop seasons. Whatever his birthplace, Boyle became a member of the IRA for ten years between 1914 and 1924. He was imprisoned at Strangeways Prison in Manchester from August to December 1921 for IRA activities and was subsequently released after the signing of the Anglo-Irish Treaty. After his release from prison, Boyle lived mostly in London listing his address on the repatriation forms as being Westwick Gardens, W12. Boyle arrived in Spain on October, 13th 1937, and joined the British Battalion in the December. He was wounded at Teruel on the January 19th, 1938, and was listed as being in hospital between the March 24th and the April 15th. A short while later he was charged with drunkenness and sentenced to extra guard duty and by being docked ten days pay. Boyle was also reduced to the ranks. He was last listed on the Battalion roll on the September 5th, 1938 before being repatriated with a group of British volunteers in December 1938. He died in London in the 1980s.

William Leakey was born on November 10th, 1914 in Bath. He served three years in the Coldstream Guards from 1930-33 before deserting. He worked as a store keeper and was a member of the CPGB and also the National Union of General and Municipal Workers (NUGMW). As far as is known, Leakey, one of the few later volunteers, arrived in Spain on or around the April 4th, 1938. By this time the Headquarters of the International Brigades had moved from Albacete to Catalonia so it must be assumed that he trained at one of the bases there.

He was posted to XV Battalion Staff where the observers worked and was subsequently wounded in the first action of the Ebro campaign during late July. He suffered a broken right leg and was sent to a series of hospitals in Mataro, Valcarca and finally Vich. From here he was repatriated with other wounded volunteers on the 18th December 1938. In July 1939, Leakey would write to Juliet (See: p.216).

Born on June 23rd, 1915, in Forest Gate, East London, John O'Connor was a railway worker and member of the CPGB and the National Union of Railwaymen (NUR). He arrived in Spain on the February 27th, 1938. By early September 1938, he was posted to the Cartographers section of the Estado Major of the XV International Brigade and served with Ivor and his fellow observers of No.2 Company. He was refused entry to the Spanish Communist Party despite his character being described as "Good." He was repatriated in early December 1938.

Of Ivor's Spanish comrades, there is sadly no known information other than Ivor's thumbnail descriptions

13

The Last Post

The first few days of August were fairly quiet. The fighting around Gandesa had eased and the ill-supplied Republican army were in no position to press ahead with the offensive. The only option open to them was to consolidate the bridgehead and await the enemy's next move. However, they did have one major advantage. Enrique Lister's V Corps were firmly entrenched in the strategically vital heights of the Sierra de Pandols. The Sierra de Pandols mountain range has many peaks of over 600 metres high, many of sheer rock face and hidden caves that offered a perfect observation platform for the defender. No one hill could be assaulted without the attacker being visible to defenders on another hill. The Nationalists, aware that they now had to fight along a new front, nevertheless made the decision to go on the offensive. On August 11th they launched a counter-attack in the Sierra de Pandols to the south of Gandesa. The defence of Hill 666 previously occupied by the 11th Republican Division fell to the 15th International Brigade.

George Wheeler's first impression of Hill 666 was of "a hill encircled in a ring of flame" that burned for two days. (2003: 89) John Dunlop records a similar sight,

> ...there was a lot of aerial bombardment on the crests of these hills. One night all the brushwood went up in flames. It was a kind of heathery growth on top of these hills that was set on fire and they burned for several days. We were watching that and thanking our lucky stars that we weren't up there. Little did we know that we were going to go up there! (in MacDougall: 163)

Lister's V Corps units had defended their positions with great courage but were driven back by the Nationalist incendiary shells. Somehow they managed to counter-attack and re-take the hill. The intervention of the 15th Brigade stabilised the line and prevented any further advance. Their success was not without losses as Billy Griffith would later write in his memoirs,

> One tried to avoid as much as possible the path and open ground because of the intensity of shell and mortar fire, which at times, came over at the rate of 40 per minute. Yet this was the only way to the British Battalion HQ, the Canadian positions and the frontline.
>
> I got caught twice, but each time was fortunate to be near a shallow slit trench. Morris was not so lucky. He was killed outright!! So also was the Chief of Fortifications for the Brigade (Egan Schmidt), who with his staff, was caught in a barrage not far from the Brigade HQ. He and three of his staff were killed and a number wounded. (Griffith, 1997)

Morris was Morris Miller the aspiring journalist who wrote so vividly of the assaults on Hill 481 for *The Volunteer for Liberty*. A year before Miller had stormed out of a family tea after accusing his uncle, a prominent Jewish timber merchant in Hull, of being "nothing but a dirty capitalist." After swearing his parents to secrecy, Miller left for Spain arriving on the September 24th, 1937. The following week he joined the International Brigade and took part in the Aragon retreats from Belchite before being wounded at Caspe in mid-March 1938. He was hospitalised but returned to the Battalion in May where he was named assistant political commissar under the chief political commissar, Bob Cooney. He was 23 years of age when he was killed.

John Dunlop vividly described the hellish landscape that the Battalion were ordered to defend on Hill 666,

> ...by the time we got up there there was nothing but blackened twigs of this heathery plant and just cracked stones. It was a very steep escarpment, the strata had been tilted very steeply. We were ranged along the edge of the escarpment and then up at the top the escarpment turned into a ridge which went off towards the enemy. We discovered a stone wall had been built up there for protection, because there was no possibility of digging trenches. It was just stone. There were one or two dug-outs further down the slope where some of us spent the night. (in: MacDougall: 164)

From the moment they arrived, the volunteers were subjected to aerial bombardment. Huge splinters of rock flew around while massive boulders kept rolling down the hillside. Movement was limited as the troops were

Aspiring journalist Morris Miller, seen here flanked by Lincoln brigaders David Gordon (left) and Edwin Rolfe (right), wrote vividly of the carnage on Hill 481. Morris Miller died not long after this photo being taken.

under fairly constant observation from the enemy aircraft. Stretcher bearer Frank Deegan was kept busy,

> Their artillery blew holes in it. Their machine-gunners and snipers notched up many casualties. Young Gibson and I were kept busy. One of the lads we carried down was Joe Moran from Birkenhead who had a very bad leg wound. I had had some fine nights out with Joe in Albacete scrambling for some of the near English beer. It was sad seeing him suffer. The journey to the nearest first aid post, some distance away, was very rough, up and down the hills. Every inch of the way was agony for Joe. When we returned to the front line Ted Edwards from Manchester, who was secretary of the Battalion, informed me, my pal Ernie Pilsen had been taken away wounded. I would miss him. He and I coming from the same neighbourhood, boyhood friends, and having been together in many a major action, made me feel very despondent. (Deegan: 52-53)

Brigader Tom Murray describes the grisly results of one such barrage of shell fire.

> It was a nasty situation. Well, I got up and here I found George Jackson lying stretched out. George Jackson came from Cowdenbeath and I think he was one of the recruits that I got to go with me when we went out there. Charlie McLeod of Aberdeen was lying with his head on George Jackson's chest. And Malcolm Smith of Dundee was lying about a yard or so away. All were dead by the blast of this anti-tank shell. (in MacDougall: 318)

The higher up the hill the troops climbed, the stronger the putrefying stench of the dead. It was a supreme test of the Battalion's self-discipline. As Longstaff recalls, the resolve needed to just to take up positions was immense,

> Silently the comrades walked and climbed upwards, every one with a serious expression on his face. I led the company up. It was rough going with all of us carrying a heavy load up a mountain. At each position, the correct section or platoon took over from the Spanish lads. We had had a hell of a job in getting to the top of Hill 666. Finally all No.2 Company was settled in. I had no information as to the positions of Companies 1, 3, 4 and HQ Company. The change over had been quiet and our men fully alert as they tried to see in the dark any sign of the enemy. The previous occupants had left and disappeared down the mountain. I had now to go down the mountain and get some signal wire, as I had to lay a field telephone. I had luck and managed to get some at Brigade HQ and away I went back up to get help in laying the lines from platoon position to Company, and then down to Battalion HQ. That night I reckon I had climbed more than the height of Mount Everest! (Longstaff: 114)

Wrapped in blankets, the troops passed a cold night on the bleak mountain top. They woke before daylight and prepared for the anticipated enemy attack. Rifles were loaded and the few grenades available were placed on rock ledges ready for action. They waited in complete silence, straining to hear any movement to their front. The enemy positions were very close, at some points less than forty-five metres from their own, while the main defences were a mere two-hundred and thirty metres to their front. As was the case on Hill 481, the Nationalists held the higher ground. As the men looked up the mountainside it was clear to see that there was a second and third defence line occupied by enemy troops. August 17th passed quietly with just a few shells firing overhead aimed at the Brigade Headquarters in the valley below. Sam Wild and Bob Cooney went over to the frontline American and Canadian positions and began observing the enemy lines through rifle slits in the rock walls. A feeling of anticipation passed through the ranks. They knew that when Sam Wild came to a position and began observing then attack was imminent. The options before him were a raiding party, a Company or even a Battalion attack. Wild decided upon the latter, a full Battalion attack was to be mounted later that night. All that day Section and Platoon Commanders from other companies crawled into the frontline. They took notes and estimated the distances to the various enemy positions taking careful note of any obstacles they would have to face during the advance. Night fell and the Battalion was provided with cold food and coffee before the attack. Once again an eerie silence descended. Section leaders and platoon commanders positioned their men in extended lines. No.1 Company was to lead, then the mainly Spanish No.3 Company who would be followed by No.4 Company and finally No.2 Company. Sam Wild and Bob Cooney climbed over the parapet and the four companies of men armed with rifles and bayonets followed in silence. John Longstaff recounts the unfolding drama that followed,

> Then it happened, machine-guns from the enemy fort blasted us. Away on our left we could hear men running on rocky terrain. Sparks were flying as the bullets hit the rocks near us. Paul and myself dived tight under a rock wall; all the entire enemy occupants needed to do was to throw a grenade over on to us. Silence again prevailed along our front. Where we going? I could see no movement. I listened. Was somebody moving backwards? Or forwards? No.2 Company's objective was the 3rd line of the enemy's defences, which meant going through No.1 and 3 Company positions, but only if they captured the 1st and 2nd defence system. Paul the officer was crawling towards me giving only hand signs. What was the score, I wondered? Then again all hell was let loose. Flares went up from the enemy's first line. Grenades were exploding, men were running, somebody was moaning, enemy or comrade I didn't know. We started to crawl away. Explosions went off about 15 feet away. The enemy in the stone fortress had thrown grenades, but not towards us. We crawled back, right to the foot of that fortress. More running sounds were heard, the enemy was putting up flares and bullets were hitting the rocks. The attack had failed. We could hear our lads clambering back over our positions. It was now getting lighter. The officer and myself, again without speaking a word, ran to our position, which was only 25 to 30 yards away. I was over in a flash and so was he. (116)

The battered troops retreated back to their lines and as daybreak came, they awaited a possible counter-attack. The Company Commanders returned from Battalion Headquarters having been summoned to explain the failure of the attack. John Dunlop recalls Sam Wild unfairly admonishing the battered troops at the failure of the night attack. In Dunlop's opinion the failure for the attack had familiar echoes from previous assaults,

> I think probably in matters of actual military tactics and so on in Spain we lacked trained officers. I think that's true to say that. For instance, the night attack that we made on the Sierra Pandos (sic) was an absolute disaster and it was because we didn't know what the devil we were supposed to be doing. There wasn't you know, a sufficient preparation for the thing beforehand. Well, this experience was similar to one prior to that when we were trying to take a crest at Hill 481 at night and were driven off it because we were unable to see the enemy. (Dunlop in MacDougall: 165)

Enemy shelling began once more and the volunteers flung themselves to the ground, hugging it as great pieces of rock and splinter filled the air. The defensive wall had been holed in a few places and many men were wounded by flying rock. By nightfall the Battalion was placed in reserve.

On the August 24th, the Battalion took over the positions of the Lincoln Battalion on the main height of the Sierra de Pandols. The Battalion came under attack from two Nationalist Battalions and suffered a massive artillery bombardment. The hard rock offered no defensive cover and the best that the Battalion could do was to try and keep a low profile and not attract the attention of the Nationalist artillery. Nighttime offered no respite either, however, as they then were subjected to a constant stream of Nationalist rifle fire, something that was frequently interpreted by the Battalion as a precursor to yet another attack. Finally, at dusk on August 25th, the XV Brigade was relieved by the 43rd Division and sent into reserve.

Peter Kerrigan, base commissar for the International Brigade at Albacete, wrote an article for the *Daily Worker* (See Appendix 4) in which he described the events in the Sierra de Pandols,

> On a hill two thousand feet high, which forms part of the famous Sierra Pandols, I sat yesterday outside headquarters and listened to the latest stories of the magnificent quality and endurance of our lads. You have to be on the spot to understand the character of the fighting which is at present ranging around this Spanish Sierra. To reach the line it is necessary to climb 1,500 to 2,000 feet up the mountain side along paths which only just qualify for the name. Footing is over bare

volcanic rock or loose rubble that flies down from underfoot, and up these same paths have to come food and munitions for the men.

The enemy have been furiously attacking in this region, but have been completely rebuffed, and the hill I have referred to was taken by our troops only a few days ago. Since then it has been held in the face of every counter-attack of the enemy. On the night of August 15 our Battalion was in reserve to another Battalion of the same brigade. The reserve position was very difficult because of the constant use of aviation by the enemy, but when the other Battalions attacked our Machine-Gun Company moved into action in support. During this period of the later fighting George Fletcher performed invaluable work in maintaining liaison under the difficult conditions. On the night of the 17th our men attacked in absolute darkness over unfamiliar ground under the most difficult circumstances. Not only was there no moon, but there were clouds.

In this action Lieutenant Commander Johnny Bowes [Lt/Company Commander Johnny Powers] showed outstanding courage, rallying the men and driving against the enemy. (*The Daily Worker.* Wednesday, August 24th, 1938)

After further praising Bob Cooney and reporting on the death of an American comrade (Paul Wendorf) who was killed by the same shell that injured Sam Wild, Kerrigan continued,

Another comrade who did a splendid job and has been singled out for special mention is the Chief Battalion Observer, Ivor Hickman. His was a specially difficult task, carried through with a high degree of courage. (*The Daily Worker.* Aug 24, 1938)

The citation records of the British Battalion confirm Ivor's contribution and bravery. "Chief of Observers. For efficient work, coolness and bravery under fire." And on the Battalion List of Recommendations, "His work was of the highest merit and he remained at his observation post during the fiercest bombardments and to whom is due the perfection of the Battalion's observation services." (*The Daily Worker.* Aug 24, 1938) In an undated letter to R. Robson, probably relating to the action on Hill 481, Harry Pollitt wrote, "Cabo Ivor Hickman. Co Sargento acting as Battalion Observer displayed great initiative, enthusiasm and interest in carrying out his duties. Strong recommendation with a view to making this Comrade a lieutenant."[1]

Fighting on Hill 666 in the Sierra de Pandols, near Gandesa. A near-barren terrain, the hard rock offered little defensive cover.

On August 31st, with characteristic modesty, Ivor makes light of the praise that he had received in his letter to Juliet,

Aug 31st 1938

My dearest love, I feel very well today and well rested after wandering around by myself on this marvellous country, picking figs from thousands trees, taking bunches of grapes from innumerable vines and testing pomegranates and finding them as yet unripe, I have come back to my chabola, (i.e. a hole in the ground covered by trees and beautifully shady) to sit down and write to you my love.
I have been thinking about you a very great deal just lately and I have been missing you terribly. George Buck went to England on leave yesterday and I gave him a note for you – very quickly written but enough to prevent there being any question of fraud. I wished like hell that I was in George's shoes. My turn will come later.
I got a mention in the Worker on the 24th – stupid because the whole observers organisation worked really well and deserved mention. As for 'courage'. The reporter did not know what thoughts are in my mind when the heavy artillery is going. And Pollitt came out just after we left ill-famed cota —Censored— and told us the difficulties there were with the Dependents Aid Fund, how pensions had had to be cut down and how £750 a week was terrific for the Worker to carry.
Carlos, who is OK and who finds war even more horrible than he had expected it,

showed me a letter you wrote to him dated – I think – August 2nd.
Tomorrow will bring in September! And you seem to make September a limit. Well, we'll see what September holds for us! Let's hope it will mean we will see each other again? Nothing like hope.
There is so much and yet so little to say. I sent that regulation card when I was very very busy. Don't forget the best exchange if you come to Spain is cigarettes, 100's of them.
Now I must close, excuse this terrible letter but the day has become hot and I feel restless. So as ever I love you more than anything in the whole world and I want you like hell.

Ivor
From: – Ivor Hickman, S.R.I. 161, Barcelona, Spain

Though she would not know it for some time, this was to be the last letter that Juliet would receive from Ivor.

14

One of Eighty-Nine

September 3rd marked the beginning of the next Nationalist attack. The Nationalists had reorganised to incorporate newly arrived units. Two Army Corps were now formed to aid flexibility. The first corps consisted of four divisions while the second corps was made up of three divisions. The two units were separated by the road from Gandesa to Camposines. The constant artillery and air attacks were wearing down the resolve of the Republicans whose lack of serviceable artillery and ammunition had hampered any opportunity for a significant advance. The first stage of the Nationalist offensive was to open with attacks in the Sierra Lavall de la Torre while another division was to launch an assault at the point between the two Republican Corps. Corbera was to be attacked and captured by another division. The second phase was to be a strike on the Republican 3rd Division from the heights of Gaeta while the 27th Division would be assaulted by artillery and aerial bombardment. By September 5th, Corbera was in Nationalist hands along with some of the nearer peaks in the Valle de la Torre and Sierra de Cabals. However, flanking fire had halted the progress of the advance and by the 6th; it had ground to a halt. The key to the whole defence of the front was the Sierra de Cabals so the Republican commander, Modesto, despatched the special Battalion of machine gunners to the Cabals peak. One division would extend their right flank to the northern slopes while another was committed to the central sector. Modesto launched the counter-attack on the 6th and 7th and utilising the reserve of twenty tanks and all the artillery available, stemmed any further Nationalist advance.

During this period the British Battalion were fighting on yet another hill in the Sierra Cabals, Hill 356 near "Sandesco."[1] Despite being outnumbered and under heavy attack from artillery and air, the hill was secured.

Events in Europe were affecting matters in Spain. During the negotiations that led to the Munich Agreement in September 1938, both sides promised a withdrawal of foreign volunteers. On September 21st, 1938, Spanish Republican Prime Minister, Juan Negrin, announced the withdrawal and repatriation of all of the foreign volunteers. It was Negrin's naïve belief that this gesture would result in the withdrawal of German and Italian troops from Spain. The fascist countries broke their promise and ignored the withdrawal. On the same day that Negrin announced their demise, the 15th Brigade was recalled to the front to replace the 13th Dombrowski Brigade at Sierra de Lavall de la Torre. Two days later, on September 23rd, 1938, the British Battalion under the command of George Fletcher were moved up to the front to take part in their last action of the war. The Battalion could boast a strength of only 337 men of which less than a third were British. George Wheeler was one of the volunteers that day,

> With a full compliment we left the valley and marched to face our final engagement with the enemy. What would be the outcome? Who would survive? There were many tracks leading off from the road, and there was some uncertainty on the part of our officers. Finally halting, it was realised they had blundered and we turned and retraced our steps. Identifying the correct path to follow, we at last reached our destination. The error had cost us considerable time and it was almost dawn when we reached our positions. (Wheeler: 117)

John Dunlop remembers the futile defensive position in which the Battalion found itself during those last hours of combat.

> ...we had been put up overnight on a hill which had defences already prepared for us by the engineers. But the defences were prepared on the wrong side of the hill. They were prepared on the forward slope of the hill, in full view of the enemy. They should have been prepared on the reverse side of the hill, so that the enemy would have had to come at us over the crest, and where also we would have been immune from machine-gun and tank fire. That in fact was the downfall of the Company, because on the very last day that we were in, not long after daylight I was in position on the right flank of the Company and we were strung round this hill in trenches, some of which were only two or three feet deep. They had not been dug nearly deep enough. We had very little cover indeed. (Dunlop in MacDougall: 166)

The morning of September 23rd began with a massive enemy artillery barrage. The Battalion HQ counted one shell landing every second along its front while 250 bombers and fighters harried the frontline with constant strafing and bombing. John Dunlop described the onslaught,

> We were attacked by air planes, by bombing. A large part of the hill was fairly sandy and dusty and it was very dry and dusty and with the smoke of the bombs and dust and grit that was flying around our visibility was very seriously impaired. (Dunlop in MacDougall: 166)

After five hours of this onslaught the Nationalists began to advance. Once again the rocky slopes left the volunteers with very little cover. Trenches less than a metre deep were dug in the vain hope of offering some protection from Nationalist snipers. To the left of their position was a high hill with almost sheer sides and in front of them, the hill gently sloped away. A thickly wooded slope that would offer the advancing Nationalists excellent cover lay to their right. As the dust from the aerial bombardment cleared the Battalion could see clearly the predicament in which they found themselves. Dunlop continued,

> ...it was only when it cleared that we discovered that the enemy were advancing up the hill over a brow below us. They had advanced to the foot of the hill in completely dead ground that we couldn't see. They had advanced round to our right, in between us and the nearest Company of the Battalion, which was a Spanish Company commanded by Felix Sais, and they were just moving down on the backs of these poor chaps who were strung in a sort of half moon battery position on a lower slope of the hill. They were just coming down on top of them from the rear. There was nothing we could do about it. (Dunlop in MacDougall: 166)

George Wheeler remembers those final hours before he was finally captured,

> We were woken by a massive aerial bombardment which was followed by ferocious artillery fire. Those of us in the shallow trenches could only lie there and hug the earth. The continuous hail of shells prevented us from looking over the parapet and we simply hung on, waiting for a respite. The bombardment seemed to last for hours, and then suddenly it ceased. A few minutes passed and I heard someone yell: "Look out, they're up here!" (Wheeler: 118-119)

The chaos that followed is lucidly described by John Dunlop thus,

The grit from the atmosphere had filled up the locks of our rifles and I got away three shots before my rifle jammed and even hitting the bolt with a stone I couldn't open it again for re-firing. So I told the blokes. I said, "Get out and down the back of the hill as quickly as you can." But only one of them took the opportunity and by that time we were having grenades thrown at us. So I thought, "Well, I can either stay here and just be captured or killed or I can try and get back to the Battalion and tell them what is happening." I stood up and got out of the trench and was immediately the target for grenades and was hit in the shoulder by one and I stepped over another when it was sizzling at my feet and got down the hill. By the time I had got down to the foot of the hill and was going up the other side of the hill I was being shot at. (Dunlop in MacDougall: 167)

Frank Deegan was shoulder to shoulder with John Dunlop during the attack and described the situation in his unpublished memoirs,

> Dawn was breaking when the men were climbing up to a hill position. Planes came over bombing and machine-gunning us. Fascist heavy guns were sending a barrage of shells. I as usual was last to reach the top. I jumped in a slit trench on the corner. There were about a dozen men already in it. The rest of the Battalion led by Johnny Power, one of three brothers from Ireland serving with the Brigades, had succeeded in reaching positions near the centre. The Fascists were in the surrounding olive groves. What a day! It was suicide to raise your head over the top. The enemy had the range within inches. After a few hours of heavy bombardment which brought many casualties everything went quiet. I looked over the top. About twenty yards away coming up the hill were enemy soldiers. They were shouting and beckoning to me; probably asking that we surrender. I had no intention of being taken by them. I wasn't a hero, but I preferred to die. My legs seemed rooted to the ground. Retreating had never entered my thoughts. Thinking it was hopeless I kept shooting at them. Suddenly the only one left with me, a young Scots lad named John Dunlop said, "Come on Frank, let's go." We jumped out, running down the other side. All that saved us was they had to climb the steepest part. We were on the descent. They threw hand grenades. Some exploded close to me. I fell and when I got up I was covered in blood. Luckily I could still run. Johnny was ahead going at a great pace. Further down I contacted the Fifteenth Brigade Headquarters. John Gates, an American who was the Brigade Commissar told me to keep going. I met some Spanish troops moving

> up. One of their first aid men emptied his rucksack of bandages, dressing my wounds, they were that numerous. I remember him saying, "*Muy Valiente*", (very brave), I thought how fortunate I had been to get off so light. I would have probably died in that trench if John Dunlop hadn't uttered those words 'Let's go Frank'." (Deegan: 54)

The British Battalion bore the brunt of the attack. The Nationalists now occupied the Lincoln's positions and subjected the Battalion to an intense enfilading fire. A small group of thirty-five British volunteers managed to put three out of five advancing tanks out of action before being forced to retreat. The two surviving tanks, followed by infantry, reached the *barranco* behind No 1. Company and inflicted heavy losses. John Power, the commanding officer, alongside a handful of men managed to fight his way out but the Battalion were sitting ducks. By now the Nationalist tanks and infantry were amongst the Machine-Gun Company. John Dunlop continues,

> And our Machine-Gun Company were on the brow of the hill behind us. I was absolutely drained of all energy when I was halfway up the hill towards their position. I thought, "Well, I'm not going to get there unless I try a trick." I deliberately waited till the nearest burst of fire came just at my feet, just a second or two after I had made the decision. As soon as that happened I threw myself on the ground and lay there as if I had been hit and killed. After a quarter of an hour there was no more firing at me and I got up and trotted up to the top of the hill before they started firing at me again. I got back to find the Machine-Gun Company just being pulled out. I thought that the whole of the Company had been captured but it turned out that later on when remnants of the Battalion got back together Johnny Power had got away. He was praising up to the skies a young Spaniard who had managed to hold off the enemy with a machine-gun. They were on the left flank of the Company and the enemy had not come up in front of them. They were moving along from where they had captured most of the rest of the Company. This young Spaniard had held them off with a machine-gun and they managed to get away in short rushes back, firing. But it was their machine-gun that had saved them. (Dunlop in MacDougall: 167)

Reserves led by George Fletcher were brought up but their numbers were too few. Fletcher and Cooney gathered a few machine guns and a few groups of disorganised men and consolidated them on a ridge three hundred yards back. Fletcher was the last volunteer to leave. The wounded were left were they fell until after dark when it was considered safe to try and recover them. Roderick McFarquhar, a former railway clerk from Inverness was in charge of a group of stretcher-bearers and led them forward. Under the rising moon they sorted the wounded from the dead and carried them back to safety. John Longstaff poignantly recorded his memories of those last days,

> Those three days and nights of the 21st, 22nd and 23rd September were as bloody as any other battles the Battalion had fought. George Green, one of my old Company soldiers who was wounded on Hill 481, came out of hospital still with his old wounds bandaged up, was to die in the last hour of the 23rd September 1938. Other comrades, Spanish, British and Irish had again left their hospital beds to defend the line. Such was the morale and the dedication those men had in fighting the just war of the Spanish people against the foul International Fascist Armies. George Green, Jack Nalty and many others died near to the old dried up riverbed. One of the last to be made prisoner was Walter Gregory who had left hospital still with open wounds; he was again No.2 Company Commander. (Longstaff: 125)

Peter Kerrigan would later describe the events in a letter to Harry Pollitt,

> I could give dozens of individual acts of heroism but what is the use. The list of citations which I enclose, tells in brief official terms of acts of deathless glory which were played out against a background of the cutting to pieces of our very bravest. I saw what No. 1 Coy. came through at Cordoba and I will never forget when I was told what our casualties were in those first 3 days at Jarama. But nothing can compare with the end of our Battalion. (Kerrigan, September 27th, 1938)[2]

On September 21st the British Battalion numbered 106 British and 271 Spanish. On their withdrawal only 173 men answered the roll call. Of these 74 were British. At 1.00am, the survivors of the 15th International Brigade withdrew from the frontline for the last time. Ivor Rae Hickman was not amongst them.

The exact circumstances of his death are unclear but it takes very little imagination to conjure up the carnage and chaos of those last few hours of action. The relentless artillery barrage and merciless rifle fire would have left little room for survivors. There are unconfirmed reports that Ivor was mortally wounded and was transferred to one of the make-shift hospitals where he later died but these cannot be substantiated. His name was also mistakenly entered onto the list of surviving volunteers to be repatriated.

However, in his unpublished memoirs *Proud Journey*, written in 1944, Bob Cooney makes brief mention of Ivor's fate, "Our observer Ivor Hickman was killed by almost the last bullet of the day while reconnoitring the enemy positions." (Cooney, 1944: Ch.27)

Cooney elaborates on these sparse details on one of the Imperial War Museum sound archive recordings. On the tape he states that Phil (sic) Hickman, Scout at the crossing of the Ebro, "got a wound which he didn't think was serious. Bobby Walker set off to help him get back, but he died before he could get to treatment." (IWM b)

In a squalid basement flat in Mornington Crescent in the London Borough of Camden, Juliet awaited word from Ivor. She had not been idle while he was in Spain and had been working, firstly as a supply teacher at Barking and Stratford school and then as a teacher at feminist and social campaigner Dora Russell's progressive school, Beacon Hill. Finally, through a friend, word reached her of Ivor's fate. It was a devastating blow which she would never fully recover from. A few months later she received the following letters from two of Ivor's comrades,

> *3 Grosvenor Ave*
> *Wyndham St*
> *Hull*
> *E. Yorks*
>
> *10th February 1939*
>
> *Dear Mrs Hickman,*
> *On my arrival in London from Spain last Friday I was asked by Comrade Ollerenshaw if I would get in touch with you as you wished to speak to me about Ivor.*[3]
> *I was with Ivor practically all the time he was in Spain and if I can give you any information regarding his work in Spain or anything I will gladly do so. He was a great comrade and with his devotion to duty and untiring work increased the efficiency of our Battalion immensely. His death coming as it did in our last hour of battle was a tragic end to the brilliant work he did. May I take this opportunity to offer my heartfelt sympathy to you in your sad loss. Anything I can do to help you is yours for the asking.*
>
> *Yours sincerely*
> *Joe Latus*
> *Observer 57th Battalion (British)*

33 Kings Mead St
Bath,
Somerset
2nd July '39

Dear Comrade,
Being at the Summer School at Capt. Scobells on Sunday and hearing your name mentioned, I made inquiries to find out if you had lost anyone in Spain, on the way home my father who had spoken to you told me you had, and I knew that you were the wife of Ivor Hickman. I was perhaps his most intimate friend while I was in Spain being with him until I was wounded. I feel compelled to add my tribute to the many others which I am sure you have received, he was the finest man I ever met in Spain, nothing else I could say would do him the credit he deserves. I hope I have not done wrong in writing this letter, but knowing him so well I felt compelled to.

Yours Fraternally,
Bill Leakey.

Shortly before Ivor's death, Juliet had begun working at a Basque children's home in Ipswich in Suffolk.[3] In 1937, a group of almost 4,000 children were evacuated from Bilbao in the Basque region. They embarked from Santurce, Bilbao, on the 'Habana' on Friday May 21st and dropped anchor at Fawley, at the entrance to Southampton Water, on the Saturday evening. The following morning, Sunday 23rd, they docked at Southampton. They were sent in bus loads to a camp in North Stoneham in Eastleigh which occupied three fields. By mid September, all the children had been relocated to residential homes across the country. After Ivor's death Juliet continued her work at the camp. Perhaps this work may have been a way of soothing her grief at Ivor's death and of sealing her bond with him. With her keen intelligence she soon picked up the Spanish language, her sister Jean recalled that "it came easy to her." (Moya, 2009)

In June 1942, Juliet married Leslie James Vaughan Shepherd, a school teacher and later an Inspector of Schools. By now she was working as an Educational Psychologist in Bradford. Although Juliet gave birth to two daughters, Sarah and Janie, sadly the marriage was not to be a happy one and Juliet left Leslie in the late-1960s and moved to Lewes in East Sussex where she worked as a Senior Clinical Psychologist at Chailey Heritage Hospital. Juliet died on September 26th, 1977.

15

Survivors and Premature Anti-Fascists

The battered survivors of the war would mark their departure from Spain with two formal events. On October 17th, 1938, the foreign volunteers of the 35th Division were paraded and reviewed at Marca. Malcolm Dunbar and Sam Wild were promoted to major while John Power was made a captain. Finally in Barcelona on October 28th, crowds numbering tens of thousands attended the final parade of the International Brigades. The emotional population expressed their gratitude for the brave sacrifices they had made. President Azana and Prime Minister Negrin made speeches and gave their thanks to the brigades but the event was to be remembered mostly by the emotive speech given by Dolores Ibarrui, the communist deputy, known to all of the Brigaders as 'La Pasionaria'. The following day British volunteer Fred Thomas wrote the following description,

> For an hour and a half we made our slow way through some of the principle streets in one long glut of emotional excess. I was not the only Brigader sometimes reduced to tears; we, who were leaving the fight, were yet receiving the heartfelt homage of the Spanish people. In the street of the 14th April the march ended, and then came the speeches. From a platform full of important people from many countries as well as the Republic, Dr. Negrin, Prime Minister, addressed us and the vast crowds. Then came President Azana followed by the chief of the Army of the Ebro. Finally we recognised the spare figure of the indomitable 'La Pasionaria' who quickly had the crowd roaring their approval of her every word. But we British were not near enough to hear much, so I have to wait until today to read her stirring speech. (Thomas: 114)

These are the words spoken to the 13,000 volunteers gathered that day,

It is very difficult to say a few words in farewell to the heroes of the International Brigades, because of what they are and what they represent. A feeling of sorrow, an infinite grief catches our throat – sorrow for those who are going away, for the soldiers of the highest ideal of human redemption, exiles from their countries, persecuted by the tyrants of all peoples – grief for those who will stay here forever mingled with the Spanish soil, in the very depth of our heart, hallowed by our feeling of eternal gratitude.
From all peoples, from all races, you came to us like brothers, like sons of immortal Spain; and in the hardest days of the war, when the capital of the Spanish Republic was threatened, it was you, gallant comrades of the International Brigades, who helped save the city with your fighting enthusiasm, your heroism and your spirit of sacrifice. – And Jarama and Guadalajara, Brunette and Belchite, Levante and the Ebro, in immortal verses sing of the courage, the sacrifice, the daring, the discipline of the men of the International Brigades.
For the first time in the history of the peoples' struggles, there was the spectacle, breath-taking in its grandeur, of the formation of International Brigades to help save a threatened country's freedom and independence – the freedom and independence of our Spanish land.
Communists, Socialists, Anarchists, Republicans – men of different colours, differing ideology, antagonistic religions – yet all profoundly loving liberty and justice, they came and offered themselves to us unconditionally.
They gave us everything – their youth or their maturity; their science or their experience; their blood and their lives; their hopes and aspirations – and they asked us for nothing. But yes, it must be said, they did want a post in battle; they aspired to the honour of dying for us.
Banners of Spain! Salute these many heroes! Be lowered to honour so many martyrs! Mothers! Women! When the years pass by and the wounds of war are stanched; when the memory of the sad and bloody days dissipates in a present of liberty, of peace and of well-being; when the rancors have died out and pride in a free country is felt equally by all Spaniards, speak to your children. Tell them of these men of the International Brigades.
Recount for them how, coming over seas and mountains, crossing frontiers bristling with bayonets, sought by raving dogs thirsting to tear their flesh, these men reached our country as crusaders for freedom, to fight and die for Spain's liberty and independence threatened by German and Italian fascism. They gave up everything – their loves, their countries, home and fortune, fathers, mothers, wives, brothers, sisters and children – and they came and said to us: "We are here. Your cause, Spain's cause, is ours. It is the cause of all advanced and progressive mankind."
Today many are departing. Thousands remain, shrouded in Spanish earth, profoundly remembered by all Spaniards. Comrades of the International Brigades: Political reasons, reasons of state, the welfare of that very cause for which you offered your blood with boundless generosity, are sending you back, some to your own countries and others to forced exile. You can go proudly. You are history. You are legend. You are the heroic example of democracy's solidarity and universality in the face of the vile and accommodating spirit of those who interpret democratic principles with

their eyes on hoards of wealth or corporate shares which they want to safeguard from all risk.
We shall not forget you; and, when the olive tree of peace is in flower, entwined with the victory laurels of the Republic of Spain – return!
Return to our side for here you will find a homeland – those who have no country or friends, who must live deprived of friendship – all, all will have the affection and gratitude of the Spanish people who today and tomorrow will shout with enthusiasm –
Long live the heroes of the International Brigades!" [1]

Their departure left many of the volunteers with mixed feelings. Although they obviously wanted to go home, there was a feeling among many of guilt at the 'unfinished business' in Spain. On the evening of the December 7th, 1938, 305 British Brigaders arrived back at Victoria Station, in London. They were welcomed home by a huge crowd including senior members of the Labour party, most notably its leader Clement Attlee.

However, many volunteers were still uncertain as to their fate and would have to wait a while longer to return home. Large groups of the British Battalion were taken prisoner both during the battle of Jarama in February 1937 and during the retreats of March 1938. There were also a substantial number captured individually throughout the war including several on the Battalion's last day of action. George Wheeler was captured on or around the day that Ivor died. He describes the moment thus,

> I made a movement to get at my rifle, but the fascists were there with hand grenades held aloft. Shouting "manos arriba!" – hands up! – they ran along the parapet throwing our rifles out of reach. There was nothing to do but surrender. (119)

The Machine-Gun Company captured in February 1937 at Jarama were under the belief that they would be shot out of hand. Leeds born Phil Elias was shot while reaching for his cigarettes and Londoner John Stevens killed by the same burst of machine gun fire. Another volunteer, Edward Dickenson, was shot through the head as he protested over the two men's deaths. The remaining prisoners were finger printed and interrogated then taken to Talavera de la Reina. Living in virtual squalor in an old factory building, the men worked repairing roads and burying the bodies of executed Republicans. Stomach and lung disease were common amongst the prisoners, some of whom still carried wounds from Jarama.

In May 1937, they were moved to Salamanca to face charges of 'aiding a military rebellion'. A military show trial sentenced five of the men to death and the remainder to twenty years imprisonment. They remained in the New

Model prison in Salamanca until May 1937, when Franco pardoned them in an exchange for a similar number of Italian prisoners from the Republicans. Twenty three British volunteers were released however, within weeks five had returned to the frontline.

The men captured during the fighting in the Aragon found themselves facing the same interrogators as their comrades had done the previous year. Indeed one volunteer, Jimmy Rutherford, was recognised as being one of the men captured at Jarama. This contravened his release agreement not to return to Spain and he was executed. Rutherford's death persuaded the CPGB not to allow previously repatriated volunteers to return to Spain to fight.

While at Saragossa the prisoner's were visited by several international journalists including Kim Philby from *The Times*. The Nationalists had recognised the propaganda value of the prisoners and were keen to exploit this. Again conditions were particularly brutal and sickness amongst the prisoners was rife. Irish volunteer Bob Doyle would later recall his treatment at the hands of the Nationalists,

> As I entered, I was surrounded by sergeants. "So, you refused to fall in!" they screamed. Before I could answer, four of them closed in and began raining blows on my back, shouting, "*Rojo! Rojo!*" (Red! Red!) and in their frenzy they sometimes missed their target and hit each other instead. I was wearing only a light khaki shirt. I managed not to scream, doubling up. I protected my face and head with my hands. Two had heavy sticks, another had a heavy strap and the chief guard his favourite 'bull's penis'. "What have I done to deserve this?" I thought, as my knees began to buckle, and I clenched my teeth. The beating lasted ten minutes. Sweating and panting, the four called for a soldier to take me back to the others where I had to stand to attention, facing the wall until everyone had been beaten. I could hear the shouts and blows as each was taken in. (Arthur, 2009: 194)

Despite this treatment the prisoners organised themselves setting up lectures and language classes and even wrote a newspaper, *The San Pedro Daily News*. By January 1939, most of the prisoners had been released from San Pedro and were made ready for prisoner exchanges with captured Italian troops. After the typically lengthy bureaucratic delays, the majority of the prisoners were released in February and April 1939. There were two exceptions. Welsh volunteer Tom Jones had to wait until March 1940 to be released while for Irish Nationalist Frank Ryan (captured on March 31st, 1938, at Calaceite) there would be no homecoming. Ryan had originally been sentenced to death but this was commuted to 30 years imprisonment.

Although a campaign was launched in both Ireland and Britain, Ryan was eventually taken to Germany where it was felt he might be useful to the Nazi regime. Frank Ryan died of pleurisy and pneumonia in Dresden in June 1944.

The British government's attitude to the returning Brigaders on December 7th 1939 was one of little sympathy for their plight. The Foreign Office even went to the lengths of actually attempting to charge the men for their repatriation. There are no records of any volunteer paying the demands although one volunteer was later to admit to doing so. These attempts by the British government to dampen the volunteers' return could not detract from the rapturous welcome that awaited many. Lou Kenton remembers arriving at Victoria station amid scenes of "such joy, the celebration, the tremendous enthusiasm of the crowd." (Arthur: 43) Volunteers such as Paddy Cochrane who had been repatriated after being wounded at Belchite went to Victoria to witness his comrades' return.

> In October 1938 I heard that the Brigaders were leaving Spain and I was amazed. I went down to the station to meet them on their way back but I mistook the day. I sat there and waited for them for a long time. Later there were lots of marches through London, and the Brigaders were always at the head of some left-wing movement or Labour Party march – and I felt proud to have been to Spain. (Arthur: 282)

Less than two years later the surviving Brigaders were given the opportunity to finish the 'business' that began in Spain. Many attempted to enlist in the army to join the fight against Hitler only to find themselves rejected and branded as "premature anti-fascists." Bernard Knox who fought in the French Battalion of the XI International Brigade on the Madrid front in 1936, describes the first time he encountered the phrase,

> I was taken aback by the expression. How, I wondered, could *anyone* be a *premature* anti- Fascist? Could there be anything such as a premature antidote to a poison? A premature antiseptic? A premature antitoxin? A premature anti-racist? If you were not premature, what sort of anti-Fascist were you supposed to be? A punctual anti-Fascist? A timely one? (Knox, 1998)

The government finally relented and many former International Brigaders found themselves once more in the fight against fascism. David Marshall transferred from doing clerical work in the Pay Corps to active duty with the Royal Engineers. He was in Normandy just after D-Day. Esmond Romilly, veteran of Boadilla and nephew of Winston Churchill, moved to Canada at the outbreak of war and joined the Canadian RAF. He was shot down and killed over the North Sea in 1941. Jack Edwards came home in February 1939 and within less than a year had volunteered for the RAF serving for the duration of the war. Irishman Bob Doyle served in the merchant navy, while union leader Jack Jones played a crucial role as an official for the TGWU in Coventry helping to keep the city's munitions industry functioning throughout the Blitz. George Wheeler served in Africa, while Fred Copeman played a his part in organising civilian protection against German air-raids. He was later made an officer of the Order of the British Empire for his efforts. Former Battalion commander Tom Wintringham had mixed fortunes during the Second World War. At its outbreak he applied for a commission but was rejected. In May 1940, after Dunkirk, Wintringham began to write in support of the Local Defence Volunteers, the forerunner of the Home Guard. On July 10th, he opened the private Home Guard training school at Osterley Park, London. Wintringham's training methods were mainly based on his experience in Spain. He even had trainers who had fought alongside him there, training volunteers in anti-tank warfare and demolitions. He also taught street fighting and guerrilla warfare. The British Army still did not trust Wintringham however, due to his communist past. After September 1940 the army began to take charge of the Home Guard training in Osterley and Wintringham and his comrades were gradually sidelined. Wintringham resigned in April 1941. Ironically, despite his activities in support of the Home Guard, Wintringham was never allowed to join the organisation himself because of a policy barring membership to Communists and Fascists.

Nearly seventy years on, the feelings of the veterans still reverberate with the passion and belief of their youth. In 2005 Sam Lesser recalled,

> Years afterwards there was an exhibition at the Imperial War Museum on the Spanish Civil War. We were called in, the people on the committee of the International Brigade Memorial Trust, for a chat with one of the deputy managers of the place. He said that they'd done their best but it was difficult to get the material. Their main concern was to have a balance. The moment I heard this word balance, I thought, well I didn't go to Spain just because I was interested in restoring balance or anything, I went because it was an opportunity to fight Fascism. I knew that if it wasn't beaten somewhere, my own country, Britain, and after all I was born in this country, my parents found shelter in this country, would be next. At the exhibition, we went in. They had a number of posters up, the Republican side and Franco's side. There was a sort of corridor on one side and then you had on the right hand side the Republican posters and on the left hand side the Franco posters

(which I thought was a bit arse about face). In there was a photograph, a painting of Franco. This was the day before the official opening, there was a private showing including the Minister of Culture, Tessa Jowell. When we saw this one of our chaps spat on the floor. Maybe it's because I'm an old man now but I get emotional about these things. After all there's been no shortage of wars that people have been involved in, but Spain has had this effect you see on all us who survived. After all a whole life has gone since Spain but it was something that lives with all of us through the years.

Bob Doyle succinctly summed up his feelings in an interview with Max Arthur in his book *The Real Band of Brothers*, "I have been back to Spain and on one of the visits I stamped on Franco's grave. Well, I have outlived him and most of the Fascists against whom I fought." (Arthur: 205)[2]

Revisionist historians and commentators have analysed, discussed and debated the reasons and motivations of the volunteers who fought in Spain. Many see them as puppets of Stalin, naïve idealists or romantic fools. Revisionism is a marvellous luxury afforded to those luckily enough to be gifted with hindsight. Personally I believe the the Irish born poet, Cecil Day-Lewis perfectly encapsulates the altruistic attitude of the volunteers from across the world in his poem *The Volunteer*.[3]

> *Tell them in England, if they ask,*
> *What brought us to these wars,*
> *To this plateau beneath the night's*
> *Grave manifold of stars.*
>
> *It was not fraud or foolishness,*
> *Glory, revenge, or pay:*
> *We came because our open eyes*
> *Could see no other way.*
>
> *Here was no other way to keep*
> *Man's flickering truth alight:*
> *These stars will witness that our course*
> *Burned briefer, not less bright.*
>
> *Beyond the wasted olive-groves,*
> *The furthest lift of land,*
> *There calls a country that was ours*
> *And here shall be regained.*

Shine on us, memorised and real,
Green-water-silken meads:
Rivers of home, refresh our path
Whom here your influence leads.

Here in a parched and stranger place
We fight for England free,
The good our fathers won for her,
The land they hoped to see.

16

Remembrances and Resurrection

July 4th 2009. Jubilee Gardens, London: It was a journey I had wanted to make for a few years but this year it seemed more important than ever that I attended. The International Brigade Memorial Trust holds an annual commemoration ceremony at the bronze commemorative sculpture to the 526 volunteers from the British Battalion who were killed in Spain between the years 1936-1939 (its creator was Ian Walters, who died in 2006 aged 76, was himself a committed Socialist who took part in Tito's public sculpture programme in 1960s Yugoslavia and, in the 1970s, worked with the African National Congress – he is best-known for his Parliament Square statue of Nelson Mandela and the statue of former Labour Party Minister Harold Wilson that stands in Wilson's home town of Huddersfield). Every year the surviving veterans, their descendents, activists, researchers and historians gather around Walters' memorial to pay homage to those who gave their lives fighting in the vanguard against fascism. For most of the men commemorated here, there are no known gravestones; they have simply become part of the Spanish earth that they fought with such desperate bravery to defend. The statue was erected in 1986 on the fiftieth anniversary of the outbreak of the Spanish Civil War and has been the annual focal point of remembrance ever since.

Standing in the shadow of the London Eye, the crowd slowly began to gather. A solitary purple, gold and red banded flag of the Spanish Republic rippled in the midday breeze while the sounds of the South Bank were muted by the gentle harmonies of Na Mara's Paul McNamara and Rob Garcia. The guitar and mandolin's contrasting notes playfully entwined within each refrain of the traditional Spanish music. I looked around the assembling audience hoping to miraculously recognise the unknown faces of the many people who'd been of such great help with my research; Alan Lloyd and Richard

In honour of over 2100 men & women volunteers who left these shores to fight side by side with the Spanish people in their heroic struggle against fascism 1936-1939. Many were wounded and maimed 526 were killed. Their example inspired the world. They went because their open eyes could see no other way.[1]

Baxell, Alan Warren or even Juliet's daughters Sarah and Janie who'd said that they planned to attend. Email had been the research method, fast, efficient but oh so impersonal, leaving me with my own constructed impressions of what these people looked like. I'd seen a photograph of Richard Baxell on the internet so had a vague idea of what he looked like. With this small nugget I scanned the gathering crowd and honed in on a slim dark haired bespectacled man casually dressed in a shirt and shorts. Unsure and slightly nervous, I walked over. "Richard?" I inquired introducing myself. My assumption was correct and through Richard I was soon introduced to many of the people whose invaluable assistance has made telling Ivor's story possible.

The commemoration was a dignified and fitting tribute. Comrades from International Brigade associations from across the world spoke of the past and future fight against international fascism. Patrik Helegson of the Swedish International Brigade friendship group spoke of the need to guard against the rise of the right in Europe today, a concern also addressed by the German and American delegates of affiliated groups. Sam Lesser was there, defiant and passionate despite his advancing years. To listen to Sam that day, it was easy to summon up the image of the devout comrade who gave up a promising archaeological career to fight fascism in Spain. One moment he was an aged wheelchair-bound veteran flicking through a tattered scrapbook; the next he was the firebrand, defiant and proud, standing at a microphone addressing the crowd with rare fervour and compassion. He decried Franco with a venom undiminished through the passing of the years yet in the next breath delivered a moving eulogy for his friend and comrade, Jack Jones who had recently died. Bob Doyle's son spoke with such affectionate honesty of his charismatic late father that it was impossible not to be touched by his words. BBC Radio London presenter Robert Elms told how he had been compelled to attend the ceremony. He wanted his young son to meet "real heroes" rather than the vacuous media constructed celebrities that are too easily described as such. Adding to the truly international flavour of the commemoration was Carles Casajuana, the Spanish ambassador to London and Xavier Solano i Bello, leader of the Catalan Trade Delegation. Both men spoke warmly of the debt of gratitude that their country owed to the volunteers. Wreaths and tributes were reverentially laid at the granite base of the sculpture while Na Mara led the crowd in renditions of *Jarama Valley* and *The Internationale*. Finally Marlene Sidaway of the International Brigade Memorial Trust made a short speech before asking the crowd to observe a minute's silence.

I stood in the silence looking at the wreaths reflecting in the granite base and read the inscription on the memorial (transcribed opposite).

Five hundred and twenty six men; five hundred and twenty six lives lost; five hundred and twenty six stories whispering to be retold. Ivor had been a forgotten footnote in an almost forgotten war. There was no one left to grieve his passing, no one to mourn the loss of potential of this gifted man. Reading his letters had given me a privileged insight into a stranger's life; his aspirations and insecurities, his humour and nobility had lent his ghost a tangible form. A very real sense of sadness had profoundly touched me while reading through his last letters to Juliet and I found writing of Ivor's death to be personally difficult to write. My mind had drifted back to childhood and to the first time I saw Robert Aldrich's classic war film *The Dirty Dozen*. The film tells the fictitious tale of a rebellious US Army Major who is "volunteered" to train twelve convicted military criminals for a suicide mission – to parachute into a heavily-guarded Nazi general staff officers' retreat to try and assassinate German officers on leave. To get his unorthodox assignment done the Major must convince Army brass to grant pardons to the men, then try to mould the twelve into a functioning military unit. In the climax of the film the character of black convict Robert Jefferson, played by Jim Brown, is assigned to run to a series of ventilation shafts and drop live hand grenades down the air vents while under intense machine gun fire from the surviving German troops. A sprinting Jefferson completes his mission but is shot and killed almost within touching distance of safety. Each and every time I watched the film I would hope that maybe this time he will complete his mission and finally reach the safety of his comrades' armoured half track and survive. Obviously time after time he buckles under a burst of machine gun fire and endlessly dies a hero's death. Writing of Ivor's death left me with the same feeling. I'd hope against hope that the ending would change with each reading and rewrite but life does not work in the simplified and naïve manner which Hollywood encourages us to believe in.

As the crowd began to disperse Alan Lloyd introduced me to Sarah Shepherd who along with Juliet's surviving sister, Jean Moya, had managed to attend the commemoration. My elation at the prospect of meeting someone with a direct link to Ivor was mixed with a slight trepidation. Although they were aware that their mother had been married before meeting their father, Sarah and Janie had not, until recently, read Ivor's letters and had not realised the loss that their mother had endured seventy years ago. The very nature of research can be intrusive and I had felt slightly uncomfortable when probing into the private and intimate details of Ivor and Juliet's love. However, both sisters had been more than generous with their help and I had tried to be as tactful as possible when discussing Ivor with them out of respect for their own father. More than anyone, I was especially pleased to meet Jean. Although she had only been around fourteen years of age at the time of

Ivor and Juliet's courtship, she still had known him better than anyone left alive. We chatted briefly but it felt inappropriate to probe too deeply at such an emotive time so we exchanged telephone numbers and she agreed for me to call at a later date.

The crowd had dissolved once more back into the metropolis and I was left standing alone in front of the memorial sculpture. Among the floral tributes sat two red roses. They were laid on the plinth in front of Cecil Day Lewis's beautifully inscribed words, their reflection giving the illusion of them floating ethereally inside the granite. I stood in silence and thought of Ivor Rae Hickman. By writing his story I had achieved what I originally set out to do. From the outset I had wanted to resurrect Ivor as a human being and not just as a name on a memorial. If immortality is suckled in memory then Ivor would live forever within me and within anyone who would take the time and reads these words.

17

Epilogue
A Personal Journey

"There's rosemary, that's for remembrance"
Act 4, scene 5, Hamlet by William Shakespeare

Catalonia. October 2009.

The scent of the rosemary is intoxicating, a pine and camphor cadence drifting across the abrupt limestone crags of the Sierra Pandols. Olive and almond trees dot the rich red earth of the Ebro Valley below. The Terra Alta is now a refuge of tranquility; a place of peace and contemplation; a playground for mountain bikers and hikers who explore the 'green routes'. The High Land is suffused with the Catalan temperament, light and shade, nuances of character that are subtle and unique to the region. The Knights Templar came; they built their impregnable castles high on the summits, pilgrims en route to Santiago de Compostela, wove their way along precipitous mountain passes, Greeks, Carthaginians, Franks, Visigoths and Moors all have come and gone yet the mountains stand sheer, stubbornly unchanged by the foibles of human history.

We stood on a ridge ripped from the summit of Hill 481, *'The Pimple'*. It was October 2009 and the air was thick with rosemary. Brutal reminders of the violence of the past littered the unforgiving crags and ravines. No metal detector was necessary. The rusted shards of grenades mixed with fragments of artillery shells and bullets peppered the peaks obvious to the naked eye; corroded reminders of the industrial-scale slaughter that was played out here over seventy years ago. A more poignant *memento mori* were the bones. Bleached chalk white by the sun and made smooth by the wind, the skeletal remains emphasised the fragility of mortality. We reburied them under small cairns. David Guest and Lewis Clive breathed their last here; Harry Dobson was carried from here severely wounded in the liver and taken to the cave hospital in Bisbal de Falset only to die there and to be buried along with sixty nine other soldiers in a mass grave. Others lay buried near the crumbling stone house that nestled in the dead ground at the base of the hill. The undulations of the landscape rolled from the Brigaders' former positions towards their mountainous nemesis. My familiarity with the site was both inexplicable but undeniable. I've read many volunteers' accounts of those terrible days in late July and early August 1938. The endless assaults, the air scorched by gunfire, the stench of the dead and dying, this was an unforgiving environment; the ground hard, the ridge precarious. Veterans tell of the aromatic scent of rosemary mixed with the stench of the burnt flesh of the dead, a grim Sunday roast. Even in late October my sweated brow betrayed the sun's autumnal radiance; I could barely imagine the toll that the strain of combat would take on a man in the apex of the Catalonian summer's sun. The nights could be cold, the mornings veiled in mist but by midday the heat could be oppressive. Below and behind us was a wooded copse. Sam Wild had nonchalantly leant against one of those trees while Peter Kerrigan, cigarette gripped between his lips, stared intensely into the photographer's lens.

In Catalonia time seems to drag her heels, unwilling to be rushed. Marca stands today much as it did then. The red flaking painted letters, "*Intendencia XV Brigada*", above the doorway of the old Brigade stores are still clearly legible; the theatre and dry dusty football field, scene of the tragic fiesta would still be instantly recognisable to those who were based here after the nadir of the great retreats. Chabola valley, the volunteers' 'shanty town', is now a patchwork of allotments and small holdings. Further down the road stands the old Papermill, Brigade Headquarters in July 1938. The roof and floors have crumbled, skeletal beams and joists remain but in essence it takes little imagination to picture Ivor sat outside writing to Juliet and waiting for discarded scraps of the officers' food. A short walk away, sheltered and secretive during Franco's time, is the grave of American Brigader John Cookson (seen opposite); a modest inscribed stone, profoundly touching in its humble simplicity and now symbolic for all of the other lost Brigaders.

Catalonia is slowly breaking the '*Pact of Silence*' which much of Spain naïvely clings on to. The past is being reclaimed and re-examined. With the Parliamentary approved creation of the *Memorial Democratic*, Catalonia has the first institution in Spain dedicated to putting into practice public policies aimed at recovering, commemorating and promoting memories of the Civil War. Their goal is to broaden knowledge of the period of the Second

The grave of American John Cookson, a Wisconsin anti-fascist of the 15th International Brigade who died during the closing stages of the war during the Ebro offensive. (Photo: J.W)

Republic, the Republican Government, the Civil War, the repression that occurred during the dictatorship, the exiles and deportations. The new law is intended to address the self-imposed amnesia of the past and to recover the collective memory from as many viewpoints as possible. The bunker-like Memorial at Camposines is typical of this new millennium of remembrance. The memorial is built beside the old chapel of St. Bartholomew and is the first monument erected in memory of all combatants of the Battle of the Ebro. Its function is twofold. It is in part a monument to all those who participated in the battle, regardless of ideology. The ten individual biographical memorial plaques lining the walls are representative of combatants from both sides of the war. David Guest stands for the Brigaders. Its other role is that of ossuary. The newly reclaimed areas around the former battlefield are slowly returning the fallen. Three hundred and ninety four skeletal remains were found scattered over an area of about 27 hectares in various parts of the mountains west of Mas de la Pila, in Corbera d'Ebre. Femurs and skulls unprotected under a bush or among the stones were brought to the Memorial de Camposines and found to correspond to thirty-five adult men aged 21 to 45 years. The thirty-five men now lie in dignified rest.

The Memorial de les Camposines is just one of over fifty *Memorial Democratic* designated sites in Catalonia. There is El Merengue on the River Segre near Lleida, a hill fortification that has been restored to illustrate the defences of this near impregnable bastion. It is essentially a small hill surrounded by relatively flat land and with a clear view of the larger mounts of the Montsec. In 1938, a force of Republican troops (The "Biberons" or Baby Bottle Soldiers as they were known due to their age. They were not meant to commence their military service until 1941) were ordered to take the hill. Their officer ordered them to attack with the words "Come on boys let's take this hill like we were eating a meringue." The reality turned out to be far from this as the attacks over seven days in May were a disaster and both sides suffered horrendous casualties. In one day, for example, 300 were killed. One can feel their ghosts even under the heat of the Catalan sun. A simple stone tor on the summit is inscribed *Recordem-ho sempre perque mai mes no torni a succeir*; "Always remember so it will never happen again."

It is becoming increasingly more difficult for Catalonia to ignore its past. The orange and white signs of the *Memorial Democratic* mounted onto rusted columns serve as constant *aide memoires* of the Civil War. From the Segre to the Ebro, memorials and former battlefields are being restored and resurrected in the collective consciousness. There is an openness and enthusiasm which pervades many of the indigenous populace, a sign of a recently established democracy gaining confidence and reaching maturity. Both public and private museums and collections of civil war memorabilia abound with each curator keen to share their trove. Slowly the shroud of silence is being removed. Catalonia is yielding her secrets.

One such secret is the XV Brigade memorial high in the Sierra Pandols. Unlike the majority of Republican memorials which were destroyed or desecrated under Franco's regime, this shrine lay forgotten and hidden for many years. Constructed during the battle of the Ebro by a company from the XVth International Brigade in August 1938, the three-stepped cement pyramid is inscribed with the names of many fallen Brigaders. Weathered by time and the elements and despite its hasty construction, the inscribed names are still visible. Harry Dobson of the Rhondda Valley and Robert Hale Merriman (misspelt 'Merryman') Commander of the Lincolns are remembered alongside many of their comrades including Spanish Brigaders.

Our last day in Catalonia dawned and a heavy morning fog smothered the mountains and valleys. We drove along the Corbera to Gandesa road until we came to the site of the last stand of the British Battalion in late September 1938. Again as on the rocky peaks surrounding Hill 481, the signifiers of past violence were immediately apparent; bullets and shrapnel carpeted the ground; large heavy fragments of artillery shells; lethal razor-like shards of unidentifiable rusted metal; wafer thin punctured carcasses of Laffite grenades; deformed bullets and cartridge casings; a hideous potpourri of devastation. It was the site I'd been looking forward to visiting however, a certain degree of unease sat in the pit of my stomach. Here the British Battalion fought its final desperate action only to be decimated under the unforgiving Nationalist onslaught. Somewhere near to the ridge where I stood, within sight of Corbera, Ivor Hickman had been fatally wounded and died on that dreadful final day. The chill of the morning fog slowly lifted as we walked among the trench lines and dugouts. A probable *puesto de mando* (command post) had been dug into the side of the ridge. I crawled into the claustrophobic burrow. In the candle-light I traced the cutaways into the rock where the previous occupants had placed their candles and oil-lights. The tunnel narrowed towards the rear and was accessible only by lying down and crawling commando-style through the pitch black. The entrance betrayed signs of modern times, empty bottles and discarded waste, but the deeper in I went, the fewer the signs of contemporary man. The only sign of life in this nocturne place were the sand-mottled lizards illuminated under my candle flame. I squeezed as far into the depth as my claustrophobia would allow before emerging back into the damp air. *How did these men stand being buried under here while artillery shells shook the very ground they sought shelter in?* More caves and observation points overlooked the terraces and olive trees across to Corbera and the surrounding hills. I pictured Ivor studying the ongoing battle through binoculars from one of these points, marking and reporting the flashes of artillery fire across the panoramic vista. Once again the whole area was covered with rosemary, pungent and coarse to the touch.

Nearby is the recently rediscovered XVth Brigade *Estado Mayor* described so vividly by both Billy Griffith in his memoirs and by Alvah Bessie in *Men in Battle* and *Volunteer for Liberty*. Vol II, no 33, October 6th 1938 – after extensive research the *Estado Mayor* was located by Alan Warren and colleagues in November 2009. Despite the passing of over seventy years some of the features such as the walls survive. The large boulders which litter the area are possible testament to the bombardment suffered by the cave's occupants. On the horizon the infamous "Hills of widows and orphans", Hill 356 is clearly visible from the cave's entrance. This cave was from where John Cookson was called out to repair the lines on September 9th and was mortally wounded before being evacuated to Mas d'en Magrinya hospital near Marca and subsequently buried where his tombstone still stands. On September 10th, 1938, a shell landed at the entrance wounding six to eight members of staff including Malcolm Dunbar, Brigade Chief of Staff. The *Estado Mayor* was subsequently evacuated as it was obviously under direct observation and artillery fire from Hills 362, 368 and 356 to the West and

North West. A small plaque placed in the cave on August 3rd, 2008 on the seventieth anniversary of the Battle of the Ebro tells of its later use as a shelter for the civilian population.

The morning passed, time ticked by and it was time to leave and catch the flight from Reus to Birmingham. Before we left I had one final self-imposed obligation to fulfil. Under a small rock on the edge of the ridge where Ivor and his comrades had fought and died, I dug a shallow hole. I took a black and white photograph out of my pocket of the stranger whom I had grown to know so well. I wrote a few private words on the back of the photograph of Ivor Rae Hickman and placed it in the hole, covering it with the rock. I paused, reflecting on both Ivor's brief life and upon the odyssey on which he had led me. From a bench in Sixth Form College in Hampshire to a ridge in Catalonia, it had been an incredible journey and one which had changed my life.

It was time to go home.

Ivor and Juliet Hickman

An Afterword

Fiction has an end; the tying up of loose ends and what people these days often call 'closure'. Within his publication *Morphology of the Folk Tale*, the Russian critic Vladimir Propp carefully analyses the fictional narrative. Each character serves a purpose within the fictional construct and every event propels the protagonist towards their eventual prize (usually a beautiful "princess"). There is always an ever-present villain attempting to block this quest while the "hero" is aided by a less able but humorous helper. A multitude of books, films and plays can be analysed and stripped down to these bare bones. That is fiction for you.

The story I have told here is not a work of fiction however. It does not dovetail neatly into Propp's theory of storytelling. Each piece of research can, often when you least expect, branch out tangentially along a new or long-forgotten path. Links within links, connections and bonds joined in an inexorable chain of humanity. Juliet and others like her are surely worthy of more than just an Epilogue or Afterword. Ivor's struggle was her struggle too, after all, as it was the struggle of hundreds, thousands, and eventually tens of thousands like them who, each in their own way, contributed to the fight against the ongoing march of fascism across the European theatre of repression, persecution, and war of the 1930s and 40s.

During the final stages of preparing the manuscript of this book for publication, new details – fragments – of the Hickman family's devotion to democracy in Spain came to light. I already knew from Ivor's letters that he was eager that his wife should join him in Spain (albeit fully aware that they would find it hard to meet in the midst of war). Indeed Juliet tried but, for whatever reason, due to still unknown obstacles that may have lain in her path was unable to bring her desire to fruition.

What the forgoing pages do not outline (because we cannot know) is just how hard she tried and exactly *why* it was that she did not succeed, but the fact that she did *intend* to make that journey across the Pyrenées like Ivor must say something of their shared conviction that he was fighting a just war. Hers was no mere sentimentalism, surely. Yet, just as there is no known photograph of Ivor and Juliet together (was a wedding photograph lost perhaps, or destroyed when Juliet remarried? maybe there simply were none? we cannot know) we can only glimpse small parts of their relationship – fragments again – and as has been clear throughout, we see it largely through Ivor's eyes.

Juliet's part in this story took place back in England where, as we have glimpsed, she worked with the child refugees of the Spanish Civil War. We know this not just because there are brief references in Ivor's letters, but also because his sister (or somebody close to her) had the foresight to deposit some personal effects of the Hickman family in an archive and by whatever means they eventually found their way into the Modern Records Centre of the University of Warwick. Indeed, among the items and personal effects that eventually became deposited at Warwick, was an obituary clipped from a Southampton newspaper of September 1938. As far as can be ascertained, apart from a couple of letters from Ivor's comrades, reproduced in this book – no doubt treasured possessions in themselves – the obituary from a now unknown Southampton newspaper was probably the last 'official' news that Juliet received of Ivor's death. Again we can never know for sure. As the headline reads however: *Former Winchester Scholar – Killed While Fighting in Spain.*

Reading the obituary (seen right) we come full circle then, to where we started out, at Peter Symonds' School and Christ's Church, Cambridge, both of which are mentioned. Referenced too is Ivor's time as an apprentice at Metropolitan-Vickers in Manchester and the fact that, "not long after his marriage [...] Mr. Hickman gave up his career to offer his services to the Spanish Government." Meanwhile, says the obituary,

> ...his wife became a volunteer at the Ipswich home for Basque refugee children. She had wanted to accompany her husband in order to offer her services as a nurse on the battlefield, but had been refused permission.

By whom, and why? As the obituary painfully concludes, "On the day on which British members of the International Brigade returned to England, Mr. Hickman was severely wounded. He died the following day." Was Ivor Hickman really *the last to fall* in Spain? If not, he was certainly one of them.

MSS. 393/4/2

FORMER WINCHESTER SCHOLAR

Killed While Fighting in Spain

Southampton-born Ivor Rae Hickman, the 24-years-old son of Mrs. R. J. Adams, of the Foresters' Arms Hotel, Dunster, was killed recently while fighting with the Government forces in Spain.

He was educated at Peter Symonds' School, Winchester, where he obtained a scholarship to Christ's College, Cambridge.

About two years ago he left the University with a B.A. degree, and subsequently he took up an appointment on the research staff of Metropolitan-Vickers.

Not long after his marriage, which took place just over a year ago, Mr. Hickman gave up his career to offer his services to the Spanish Government. Crossing to France, he reached the Spanish frontier on foot, and, presenting himself for service, was commissioned as a topographical officer.

Meanwhile his wife became a volunteer at the Ipswich home for Basque refugee children. She had wanted to accompany her husband in order to offer her services as a nurse on the battlefield, but had been refused permission.

On the day on which British members of the International Brigade returned to England, Mr. Hickman was severely wounded. He died the following day.

Photocopy of Ivor's obituary that appeared in an unidentified Southampton newspaper, September 1938. The obituary was kept by his sister, and held among papers pertaining to both Ivor and Juliet.
(Courtesy: University of Warwick, Modern Records Centre).

What we do know is that Ivor Rae Hickman was one of thirty-five men and women with links to Hampshire who, brimming with idealism travelled to Spain to serve the Republican cause. Some shared Ivor's tragic fate whilst others returned home to continue the fight, by whatever means they could and with whatever opportunity they found available to them. Thirty-four more stories which surely deserve more than just a name inscribed on a memorial or a bench now tucked away among the many buildings of a much expanded Hampshire sixth-form college.

Those who have become accustomed to the melding of fact and fiction to produce mere entertainments out of war, may wonder at the relevance of my recounting here the story of a small-town Hampshire boy and his part in an obscure twentieth-century civil war. But think on for a moment. From the Balkans to the North African Arab states, from the Middle-East to the sub-Asian continent, debates concerning the ethics and the ramifications of any interference in another nation's affairs continue to this day. Whether through overt and aggressive acts that are manifest in the "boots on the ground" approach of recent wars, to more 'subtle' measures deployed under the guise of what is often conveniently termed "collective foreign policy" (sanctions, embargoes and the like) the rights and wrongs of intervention are never easy to discern, though in a world of rolling news and social media, the polarisation of debate would seem to dissuade such a view. In truth each and every situation requires a different approach and there are never any easy answers.

What is easy (all *too* easy in fact) is to see such events in the black and white of the epic scale and to ignore the *intimacies of the individuals who are directly affected*. It is the individual who bleeds and suffers as a result of the machinations of governments and it is the individual who is so easily buried and forgotten. Ivor Hickman, like his wife Juliet, are just two such people. One of them, who made the ultimate sacrifice, we are fortunate enough to know just a little about and for the reason that the letters he sent home were to become the treasured possessions of a wife who had enjoyed just a few short months with him. *Her* story is more obscure though, and so it will remain, for the letters Juliet sent Ivor, as far as it is safe to assume, never found their way back from Spain and are, much as we might like things to have turned out differently, simply lost to history. That is the stuff not of fiction. There can be no convenient tying up of loose ends here. Much as we would like it to be otherwise, some things we can simply never know.

John L. Wainwright
2012

Photographic Appendix to Third Edition

Monument to the men of the British Battalion who were killed during the Ebro campaign on Hill 705. (JW)

The author (right) and Alan Warren studying the battle lines for the assaults on Hill 481. (CJW)

Artifacts of the Ebro excavated from farm land at La Fatarella in Catalonia. Reminders of the war litter the ground to this day. (JW)

The author with the photograph of Ivor Hickman at the last stand of the British Battalion. Catalonia 2009. The town of Corbera is visible on the horizon. (CJW)

Notes

A Very Brief Background Concerning the Spanish Civil War
1) Spain had 31,000 priests, 20,000 monks, 60,000 nuns and 5,000 convents while the army consisted of 15,000 officers, including 800 generals.
2) The Popular Front won 268 seats to the right-wing National Front's 157. The centre parties held 48 seats.
3) Some of the early volunteers were athletes and others who had come to Barcelona for the Workers' Olympiad, due to have taken place 19-26 July in opposition to the Berlin Olympics.
4) Ironically Cornford would die in a manner fit for Lord Byron. He was killed by a sniper while reconnoitring at Lopera in December 1936. The poet's head was still wrapped in a white bandage from a wound he'd received weeks before during the defence of Madrid. His Byronesque figure offered a perfect target for the expert Nationalist snipers.

Chapter 1: A Local Boy in a Photograph
1) In a letter dated November 11, 1937, Ivor was later to recall the date as October 12, 1919, though remarking that he found it odd that he could not remember the detail relating to his father's death.
2) Ivor's legacy at Peter Symonds was such that a subsequent pupil, Lawrence Levy, lobbied successive Headmasters to put up a memorial plaque to Ivor in the school's library. A memorial was finally erected in the 1960s, in the form of the plaque on the oak bench outside the Northbrook building.

Chapter 2: Cambridge, Politics & Love
1) As stated on the Glasgow Digital Library web site Red Clydeside: A history of the labour movement in Glasgow 1910-1932, James Maxton was one of the leading figures of the Independent Labour Party (ILP) in Glasgow and a key political figure during the Red Clydeside period. Like many of his colleagues in the ILP, Maxton was a pacifist and campaigned against Britain's involvement in the First World War and against conscription. Maxton was imprisoned in 1916 for delivering pro-strike speeches at a demonstration to oppose the Munitions Act. He was elected MP for Bridgeton in 1922 and devoted much of his political life to alleviating poverty within the city of Glasgow.
2) It is reasonable to speculate that here Ivor refers to the rodeo star John Van "Tex" Austin (1886-1938). Austin, who was born Clarence Van Nostrand, was the self-styled "King of the Rodeo" renowned for his efforts to popularize the spectacle beyond the American West. He was in London during 1934-1935 performing with his Rodeo at Wembley Stadium.

Chapter 3: A Northern Industrial Town
1) Ivor matriculated on 3 November 1933, having been admitted to Christ's College. He was placed in Class 1 in Part 1 of the Mathematical Tripos in 1934 and in Class 3 (i.e. Among the Junior Optimes – actually a II.2 not a III) in Part II of the same Tripos in 1936. He graduated BA by proxy on 23 June 1936. (Note: Research pertaining to Ivor's academic career at Cambridge, as well as his subsequent post-Cambridge letters to Wittgenstein, also referred to, has been courteously provided by Cambridge University Archivist Jacky Cox).

Chapter 5: A Noble Cause
1) Raymond Arthur Cox was one of the seven British volunteers killed. He is remembered along side Ivor on the memorial plaque in Southampton City Centre. Raymond Cox was working as a clerk with a building contractor in Southampton at the time the Nationalists launched their rebellion in Spain. He immediately gave up his job and at his own expense travelled to Spain to offer his services to the Republican Government. Before leaving he told his widowed mother and his elder brother that he had felt the call to go and assist the Spanish people in their fight for liberty. He wrote "I believe that by fighting for the Spanish Government against the forces of Fascism I shall be helping to preserve peace throughout Europe, because if the Spanish Government wins the war it will mean that a European conflict will be further off." Raymond Cox was among the first to volunteer in September 1936 and was one of the first to die on December 15, 1936 when he was mortally wounded during the defence of Madrid. He was aged just 22 years old.
2) McCartney, who had been imprisoned for spying for the U.S.S.R, was assisted by David Springhall as political commissar. In early February 1937, McCartney was injured while cleaning his pistol with Peter Kerrigan, the political commissar at the base in Albacete. Rumours of foul play persist despite the lack of evidence. (Anon. International Brigade Memorial Trust: "Spain July 1936")

Chapter 7: "Poverty Make Better Soldiers than Poetry" [This chapter is titled after an expression used by David Marshall in interview with the author, 2009].
1) The following volunteers are recorded as having served in the British Anti-Tank Battery. Bill Alexander, Otto Estenson, Jimmy Arthur, Ianto Evans, George Baker, Jack Black, Jim Brewer, Eddie Brown, Tommy Chilvers, Jim Coombs, Bill Cranston, Fraser Crombie, Malcolm Dunbar, John Dunlop, Alan Gilchrist, Ben Glaser, Tom Jones, John Longdragon, Jeff Mildwater, George Murray, Arthur Nicol, Hugh O'Hanlon, Paul Pavlovski, Frank Proctor, Hugh Slater, Chris Smith, Hughie Smith, Jimmy Sullivan, Fred Thomas, Miles Tomalin, Andy Winter, "Moses", Bates and Croft. (Thomas, 1996)
2) The Principality of Asturias played its part in the events that led up to the Spanish Civil War. The Marxist workers' movement had fought the right-wing government of the Second Spanish Republic in the 1934 Revolution of Asturias. A socialist republic was temporarily formed with a Marxist administration, but troops under Franco's command were deployed to put down the rebellion, followed by years of oppression. The Asturias remained loyal to the democratic republican government during the Spanish Civil War however. Following the war, the Asturias was known as the "Province of Oviedo", from 1936 until Franco's death in 1975. The province's name was only fully restored after the return of democracy in 1977.

Chapter 8: The Calm
1) Volunteer for Liberty 1938: The following men graduated at the same time as Ivor. Rubin Ryant (Lincoln Battalion) Killed in action at Belchite 10th March 1938, Robert Turner (Mackenzie Papineau Battalion) Repatriated December 1938, James Adrian Gunning (Lincoln Battalion) Killed in action at Gandesa April 3, 1938, Joe Latus (British Battalion) Repatriated December 1938, John Coward (British Battalion) Prisoner of War then repatriated June 1939, Herbert Conner (Lincoln Battalion) Killed in action at Belchite 10th March 1938, Samuel Wren (Lincoln Battalion) Repatriated December 1938, Marion Massey (Lincoln Battalion) Killed in action at Caspe 17th March 1938, William Boyak (Mackenzie Papineau Battalion) Repatriated December 1938, Maurice Bloom (Lincoln Battalion) Deserted and left Spain on a ship bound for Marseille, John Rody (Lincoln Battalion) Repatriated December 1938, Douglas/Robert Hitchcock/Colver (Mackenzie Papineau Battalion) Killed in Action at Gandesa 1st April 1938, George Buck (British Battalion) Repatriated December 1938, Andrew Mitchell (Lincoln Battalion) Killed in action at Gandesa between March 30 - April 2, 1938. In addition to the aforementioned volunteers, the following men also graduated on the January 16, 1938, Jack Roberts, Ramon Castel, Archibald Cook, J. Lyons, Thane Summers, Louis Carter, Milton Weiner, Henry Buska, Faise Surin, Mack Coal, Morris Davies, Leo Kaufman, Joseph Hecht, Murray Nemeroff, George Watt, Albert Fanchil, William Bell, Bill McChrystal, T. W. Gregory, Jack Corrigan, John McGrandle, Jack Reid, Joseph Vaughan, J. W. Croll, Harry Dobson and Bert Ramero. (Volunteer for Liberty. February 5, 1938.)
2) For a full investigation into Herrick's claims see: Barnfield, Ramsey & Cohen (Eds.) (2008)

Chapter 9: Baptism & Retreat
1) Ivor's Wittgenstein classmate was Donald Hutchinson. He was about 20 when he arrived in Spain, around the 20th August 1936. According to Jim Carmody, he served as an aerial Gunner on the Potez Bombers of Andre Malraux's 'Esuaadra España'. A holder of a pilot's licence, though listed on the Squadron Roll in September 1936 he was thought to lack enough experience to fly military aircraft. He fought for a short while in the Thaelmann Batt., but then joined the Spanish 5th Rgt., becoming a Sergeant and was subsequently wounded in the hand and/or wrist in the Casa de Campo, November 1936. With the help of journalist Geoffrey Cox, he was evacuated by the Scottish Ambulance Unit onto an Air France aircraft from Alicante and was treated for a septic wound in Paris (from November 1936 to January 1937). Cox interviewed him for The Daily Mail (December 15, 1936. p3) He returned to Spain summer 1937 and was with the British Battalion as an Interpreter, Clerk and Runner, and with the Q/M at Tarazona. He was repatriated in May, 1938.

Chapter 11: Ebro
1) The French border was re-opened on March 17, 1938, which allowed weapons and supplies into the Republic. Prime Minister Negrin produced his 13-point agenda which was intended to draw similarities with policies then in existence in other European countries. These failed to change the political stance of Britain, France and the USA.

Chapter 12: Hill 481
1) Harry Dobson actually survived the trip to the cave hospital at Bisbal de Falset only to die there

and to be buried along with sixty nine other soldiers in a mass grave. In her book, Beyond the Battlefield. Testimony, Memory and Remembrance of a Cave Hospital in the Spanish Civil War, (Warren & Pell, 2005) Angela Jackson movingly describes the final hours of Harry Dobson's life.

2) Information on Ivor's "very good men" provided by Jim Carmody and the IBMT. Claudio Orte Cerrillo, according to the Battalion Pay Rolls, is listed as being in the Battalion in December 1937, February 1938 and was still present at the time of Ivor's letter. Unfortunately there are very few records concerning the Spanish members of the British Battalion.

Chapter 13: The Last Post

1) The reference referred to may be located at the Marx Memorial Library. IB Archive Box 21/B/7g.

Chapter 14: One of Eighty-Nine

1) Although quoted in numerous accounts of the British Battalion, the village of Sandesco did not and does not actually exist. Possibly in a way similar to 'Chinese whispers', a location ("d'Ascó") was mispronounced in pigeon-Spanish and has simply been taken at face value in subsequent accounts.

2) The letter referred to may be located in IBA Box C, File 25/5. (Cited Baxell p112)

3) There were two locations in Ipswich where the Basque refugee children were placed. One was at Wherstead Park; the other was at Plomesgate House in Wickham Market. It is not known at which location Juliet worked.

Chapter 15: Survivors & Premature Anti-Fascists

1) La Pasionaria (Dolores Ibarurri). Barcelona, 28th October 1938. – In June 2009, the Spanish government finally kept its promise and granted the seven surviving volunteers Spanish citizenship. Although sadly too late for Jack Jones and Bob Doyle who had died earlier in the year, the seven veterans, Sam Lesser, Thomas Watters, Lou Kenton, Joseph Kahn, Penny Feiwel, Jack Edwards and Paddy Cochrane received the honour from Spanish ambassador Carles Casajuana. Les Gibson declined to attend the ceremony due to ill health. Of the occasion Casajuana said: "It should have been done earlier, but better late than never."

2) After a rebellious life of activism, Bob Doyle died in January 2009. He was a few weeks short of his 93rd birthday. He was the last surviving Irish volunteer.

3) Originally published in Overtures to Death Anthology, 1938.

Chapter 16: Remembrances & Resurrection

1) The sculpture shows a figure being lifted up by four other smaller figures. The main figure is larger and has a blindfold or bandage across its eyes and around its head. The left hand is missing, severed at the wrist; the right hand trails on the ground palm up. The arms of the four smaller figures, two on each side, combine together to cradle the dying figure, raising it up. On the left side the arms of the smaller figures are raised, palm open, in an upward defensive gesture; on the right side a hand is raised in the defiant, clenched fist salute of the Republican cause. From a distance the arms and hands look like wings stretching upwards to the sky to lift the fallen figure. A third inscription taken from Lord Byron's 'Childe Harold's Pilgrimage' is cut into the left-hand side of the plinth. It reads "Yet Freedom! Yet thy banner, torn, but flying. Streams like the thunder-storm against the wind." The inscription on the reverse of the plinth reads, "This memorial, unveiled by Michael Foot, October 5, 1985, was made possible by the support of many democratic organizations, individuals and the Greater London Council." For further information, see: Anon. (IBMT) "Shapes of Time." (2011).

Bibliography

Alexander, B. (1982). *British Volunteers for Liberty*. London: Lawrence & Wishart.
Arthur, M. (2009). *The Real Band of Brothers*. London: Harper Collins.
Baxell, R. (2007). *British Volunteers in the Spanish Civil War: The British Battalion in the International Brigade, 1936-1939*. Torfaen: Warren and Pell.
Beevor. A. (2003) *The Spanish Civil War*. London: Cassell.
Berman, P. (1996a, July 22). 'Interview with Paul Berman'. *Village Voice*.
Bessie, D. (Ed.). (2002). *Alvah Bessie's Spanish Civil War Notebooks*.
   Lexington KY: University of Kentucky Press.
Bradley. K. *International Brigade in Spain 1936-39*. London: Osprey Publishing. 2002.
Brenan. G. (1974) *The Spanish Labyrinth*. Cambridge: Cambridge University Press.
Christ's College Magazine (CCM). No. 144, 1939. Cambridge: Christ's College.
Clark, B. (1984). *No Boots to my Feet*. Stoke on Trent: Student Bookshop.
Day-Lewis, C. (1946). *Overtures to Death and Other Poems*. London: Jonathan Cape.
Deegan, F. (1980). *There's no Other Way*. Liverpool: Toulouse Press.
Graham F. (1999) *The Spanish Civil War- Battles of Brunete and
   the Aragon*. Privately Published: Frank Graham.
Griffith, W. J. (1997). *Spain: Memoirs of the Spanish Civil
   War*. Swansea: South Wales Miners' Library.
Gurney, J. (1976). *Crusade in Spain*. Newton Abbot: Readers Union.
Heath, E. (1988). *The Course of My Life*. London: Hodder and Stoughton.
Henry. C. (199) *The Ebro 1938*. London: Osprey Publishing.
Hopkins, J. K. (1998). *Into the Heart of Fire*. Palo
   Alto, CA: Stanford University Press.
Jackson, A. (2008). *At the Margins of Mayhem: Prologue and Epilogue to the
   Last Great Battle of the Spanish Civil War*. Pontypool: Warren and Pell.
―――― . (2005) *Beyond the Battlefield. Testimony, Memory and Remembrance
   of a Cave Hospital in the Spanish Civil War*. Warren & Pell.
Jackson, M. W. (1994). *Fallen Sparrows: The International Brigades
   in the Spanish Civil War*. Darby, PA: Diane Publishing.
Linklater, E. (1929). *Poet's Pub*. London: Penguin.
MacDougall, I. (Ed.). (1986). *Voices from the Spanish Civil War*. Edinburgh: Lothian.
McCallum, R. B. (1944). *Public Opinion and the Last
   Peace*. Oxford: Oxford University Press.
Miller. M. (1938) *The Volunteer for Liberty*. No 32. September b). 17, p.8
Mitchell D. (1982) *The Spanish Civil War*. London: Granada Publishing.
Orwell. G. (2011) *Orwell in Spain*. London: Penguin.
Hickman, I. R. – *Peter Symonds' School Magazine*. (1932,
   1933) Lent and Summer Term Issues.
Preston P. (1990) *The Spanish Civil War*. London: Weidenfield & Nicolson.

Romilly, E. (1937). *Boadilla*. London: Hamish Hamilton.
Rust, B. (2003). *Britons in Spain: A History of the British Battalion of the XVth International Brigade*. Pontypool: Warren & Pell.
Snow, C. P. (1939) *Christ's College Magazine*, No. 144. Cambridge: Christ's College.
Snow, P. (1997). *The Years of Hope: Cambridge, Colonial Administration in the South Seas and Cricket*. London: The Radcliffe Press.
Thomas, F. (1996). *To Tilt at Windmills*. East Lansing, MI: Michigan State University Press.
Thomas H. (2001) *The Spanish Civil War*. London: Penguin Books.
Wheeler, G. (2003). *To Make the People Smile Again*. Newcastle upon Tyne: Zymurgy Publishing.

Manuscripts, Archives & Online Sources

Anon. *African Americans in the Spanish Civil War: The War in Spain*. Retrieved December, 2011, from http://www.alba-valb.org. Abraham Lincoln Brigade Archives New York, NY.
Anon. (International Brigade Memorial Trust). *Shapes of Time: International Brigades national memorial*. Retrieved December, 2011, from http://www.shapesoftime.net/.
Anon. (International Brigade Memorial Trust). "Spain, July 1936: from uprising to civil war", In. *Volunteers in the British Battalion in the Spanish Civil War, 1936-1939*. Retrieved December, 2011, from http://www.international-brigades.org.uk/.
Aitken, G. "*Letter from George Aitken to the Political Bureau*", IBA Box C, File 17/7.: International Brigade Memorial Trust.
Berman, P. (1996b). Interview with Paul Berman [*Village Voice*]. In G. Barnfield, J. Ramsey & V. Cohen (Eds.), *Reconstruction* Vol. 8, No. 1, 'Class, Culture and Public Intellectuals' 2008 "*Anatomy of an Anticommunist Fabrication: The Death of Oliver Law, An Historiographical Investigation / Grover Furr*": Retrieved December 2011, from http://reconstruction.eserver.org/081/furr.shtml.
Cambridge University Archives. *Restricted Access Data* supplied by University Archivist of Jacky Cox (courtesy Cambridge University).
Cooney, B. (1994). "*Proud Journey*": Marx Memorial Library, Box A-15/3, 109.
Downing, E. (2010). *Interview*. (website) Retrieved February 2010, [December 2011, Server returns 404 Page Not Found].
Fisher. (1937). *Letter dated July 29*, p.187. In G. Barnfield, J. Ramsey & V. Cohen (Eds.), *Reconstruction* Vol. 8, No. 1, 'Class, Culture and Public Intellectuals' 2008 "*Anatomy of an Anticommunist Fabrication: The Death of Oliver Law, An Historiographical Investigation / Grover Furr*": Retrieved December 2011, from http://reconstruction.eserver.org/081/furr.shtml.
Imperial War Museum Sound Archives (IWM a): 9963/10 Reel 6.
——— . (IWM b): 000804/06.
Kerrigan, P. (1938). "*Letter from Peter Kerrigan to Harry Pollitt, 27th September 1938.*"

IBA Box C, File 25/5.: International Brigade Memorial Trust.
Knox, B. (1998). *Premature Anti-Fascist, The Abraham Lincoln Brigade Archives* - Bill Susman Lecture Series. King Juan Carlos I of Spain Center - New York University, 1998. Retrieved December, 2011, from http://www.english.illinois.edu/.
Longstaff, J. (1994). Unpublished memoirs. *Runner and Rifleman*: Imperial War Museum.
Marx Memorial Library. IB Archive Box 21/B/7g.
Miller, M. *Volunteer for Liberty*. Abraham Lincoln Brigade Archives New York, NY. [Multiple issues held, cited in text].
Multiple Authors (n.d.) *Voices from the Spanish Civil War*. Unpublished.
Stevenson, G. *Communist Biographies: David Guest*. Retrieved December, 2011, from http://www.grahamstevenson.me.uk/.
University of Strathclyde: Research Support Libraries Programme. *The Glasgow Digital Library: The Maxton Papers – Red Clydeside: A history of the labour movement in Glasgow 1910-1932*. Retrieved December, 2011, from http://gdl.cdlr.strath.ac.uk/.

Interviews & Correspondence

Lesser, S. (2005). Interview with the Author [March 11].
Marshall, D.. (2005). Interview with the Author [March 30].
Moya, J. (2009). Personal Correspondence with the Author [August 6].

Picture Credits

The Author would like to express his gratitude to the Tamiment Library, New York University, New York, for permission to reproduce photographs held in collections there. Photographs appearing on the front cover, and pages 113, 136 and 138: Harry Randall: Fifteenth International Brigade Photographic Unit Photographs Collection (Courtesy: Tamiment Library, New York University); Photographs appearing on pages 95, 156 and 161: International Brigades Archive, Moscow Selected Images (Courtesy: Tamiment Library, New York University); Gratitude also to Juliet's daughters, Sarah Rhodes and Janie Shepherd for their kind permission to reproduce the photographs of Ivor Hickman and their mother that appear on pages 12, 14, 20, 37, 38; Photograph appearing on page 47: International Brigade Memorial Trust; Reproduction of Document appearing on page 192: Courtesy Modern Records Centre, University of Warwick; All remaining photography © John Wainwright, 2012, all rights reserved. Reasonable effort has been made to identify photographers unknown. Information leading to the identification of uncredited photographers will be gratefully received by the author and due credit/correction will be made in future editions of this publication.

Acknowledgements

This book would have been impossible without the help of so many. In fact I had the easy task, linking the strands of research together. Firstly I would like to thank Alan Lloyd for his unending sources and contacts without which this project would never have been completed, and his partner Beth whose transcription skills were of invaluable. Jim Carmody is 'the man' for all things related to the British Battalion and without his encyclopedic knowledge this project would still remain unfinished. To Alan Warren, I would like to extend my gratitude for his time, advice and extensive body of research which he allowed me to pool. His enthusiasm for the subject has been a great motivator throughout. I also appreciate the time he took in reading correcting any factual errors. I am also hugely grateful to Brian McGuinness for allowing me to publish extracts from the Wittgenstein correspondence, and Chris Brooks for supplying information and research on the men of the Lincoln Battalion. Thank you to Richard Baxell, not only for writing the definitive book on the British Battalion, but for introducing me to Alan Lloyd directly after our prolonged acquaintance via email. Marlene Sidaway of the IBMT has been of great help, particularly in introducing me to David Marshall and Sam Lesser; to both of these men I extend my eternal and unwavering thanks. Thank you also to the many archivists who have assisted me, including Erika Gottfried of the Tamiment Library's Abraham Lincoln Brigade Archives, Julie Came of Swansea University Library, Jacky Cox of Cambridge University Archives, and Carole Jones of University of Warwick Library. The family of Ivor's wife Juliet; Jean Moya, Sarah Rhodes and Janie Shepherd were invaluable in their support and I cannot thank them enough for sharing their family history with me with such generosity and openness. To Peter Symonds College I would also like to extend my thanks to bursar, Paul Warren, and the staff who have been of help and support during my writing and research. My sister Pat and brother-in-law Bob have, as always, been of massive support and help throughout this project, ever keen to be updated on the book's progress. Finally my unending gratitude and thanks go to my wife Claire whose patience, encouragement, belief and support while listening to my regular 'rants' and 'rambles', and being able to (mostly) sleep through my restless dreams of the dry rock strewn slopes of the Sierra del Pandols. All of the facts within this book have been corroborated by leading experts on the history of the British Battalion, yet any mistakes are mine and mine alone, and I offer my sincere apologies if any are encountered.

Salud one and all.
John Wainwright
2012

www.ingramcontent.com/pod-product-compliance
Lightning Source LLC
Chambersburg PA
CBHW032251150426
43195CB00008BA/403